Wineries of the
Eastern States

Sandra,
I hope that you enjoy
this, you oenophile!
Good times are a comin'!
Yes they are!
— Nora

Suzi Forbes Chase

The Gazebo at Pellegrini Vineyards, Cutchogue, Long Island.

WINERIES OF THE EASTERN STATES

THIRD EDITION

Marguerite Thomas

Berkshire House Publishers
Lee, Massachusetts

On the cover and frontispiece:
Front Cover: *Winery in the Finger Lakes region,* photo © Peter Finger.
Frontispiece: *The gazebo at Pellegrini Vineyards, Cutchogue, Long Island,* photo by Suzi Forbes Chase.
Back cover: Photo of Marguerite Thomas by Jerri Banks.

Wineries of the Eastern States, Third Edition
Copyright © 1996, 1997, 1999 by Berkshire House Publishers
Cover and interior photographs © 1996, 1997, 1999 by Marguerite Thomas and other credited sources.

Library of Congress Cataloging-in-Publication Data

Thomas, Marguerite.
     Wineries of the eastern states / Marguerite Thomas. — 3rd ed.
         p.   cm. — (The great destinations series)
     Includes bibliographical references (p.) and index.
     ISBN 1-58157-007-4
     1. Wine and winemaking—East (U.S.) II. Series.
  TP557.T474   1999
  641.2'2'0974—dc21   98-52927
                              CIP

ISBN 1-58157-007-4
ISSN: 1056-7968 (series)

Editor: Marcia Stamell. Managing Editor: Philip Rich. Design and page layout: Dianne Pinkowitz. Cover design: Jane McWhorter. Maps: Ron Toelke Associates.

Berkshire House books are available at substantial discounts for bulk purchases by cor-porations and other organizations for promotions and premiums. Special personalized editions can also be produced in large quantities. For more information, contact:

Berkshire House Publishers
480 Pleasant St., Lee, MA 01238
800-321-8526

Manufactured in the United States of America
First printing 1999
10 9 8 7 6 5 4 3 2 1

Berkshire House Publishers'
Great Destinations™ travel guidebook series

Right on the money.

— THE NEW YORK TIMES

Smart, literate, well-reported, and incredibly comprehensive.

— MID-ATLANTIC COUNTRY

. . . a crisp and critical approach, for travelers who want to live like locals.

— USA TODAY

Great Destinations™ guidebooks are known for their comprehensive, critical coverage of regions of extraordinary cultural interest and natural beauty. The authors in this series are professional travel writers who have lived for many years in the regions they describe. Each title in this series is continuously updated with each printing, in order to insure accurate and timely information. All of the books contain over 100 photographs and maps.

Neither the publisher, the authors, the reviewers, nor other contributors accept complimentary lodgings, meals, or any other consideration (such as advertising) while gathering information for any book in this series.

Current titles available:
The Adirondack Book
The Berkshire Book
The Charleston, Savannah & Coastal Islands Book
The Chesapeake Bay Book
The Coast of Maine Book
The Hamptons Book
The Monterey Bay, Big Sur & Gold Coast Wine Country Book
The Nantucket Book
The Newport & Narragansett Bay Book
The Napa & Sonoma Book
The Santa Fe & Taos Book
The Sarasota, Sanibel Island & Naples Book
The Texas Hill Country Book
Wineries of the Eastern States

If you are traveling to, moving to, residing in, or just interested in any (or all!) of these enchanting regions, a **Great Destinations**™ guidebook is a superior companion. Honest and painstakingly critical, full of information only a local can provide, **Great Destinations**™ guidebooks give you all the practical knowledge you need to enjoy the best of each region. Why not own them all?

In memory of

Frank S. Jewett

Contents

INTRODUCTION
HISTORY, GRAPES, AND MARKETING
1

PART ONE
THE BENCHLANDS
9
Southeastern New England 12
Long Island 27
Southeastern New Jersey and Coastal Virginia 47
Lake Erie Region 62

PART TWO
THE ATLANTIC UPLANDS
77
Northern New Jersey and the Delaware River Region 80
Southern Pennsylvania and Maryland 95
Northern and Central Virginia 109
Western Connecticut 127
The Hudson River Valley 132
The Finger Lakes 145

PART THREE
THE MOUNTAINS
179
The Virginia Highlands 181
Central Pennsylvania 196

Contents

Acknowledgments

With deepest thanks to the many people who encouraged, advised, and shared their knowledge and time with me. First, to the vintners whose expertise and enthusiasms for this project helped to steer me in the right directions. To Marsha Palanci, Lila Gault, Lynn O'Hare Berkson, and the many others who guided and inspired me with their common sense and creative ideas. To my family, friends, and colleagues who helped me taste and evaluate the wines. And special thanks to Jean Rousseau, publisher of Berkshire House, to managing editor Philip Rich for his unfailing patience and thoroughness, to my editor Marcia Stamell for all her good work, and to sales and marketing director Carol Bosco Baumann for her thoughtful and energetic promotion of the book.

Preface

The happy news that marks the third completely revised edition of this book is that the wine industry in the East continues to grow faster than the wine media generally recognizes. The quality of the wines has improved dramatically. Local enthusiasm has increased in response to this change. More vineyards have been planted, and there continues to be more demand than supply for grapes grown in the Eastern United States. Twenty-two *new* wineries will be given full coverage in this edition of the book — a truly amazing number that doesn't even take into account the handful of start-up wineries that were too new to be evaluated this time around.

The realization of a competitive wine industry in the East has taken 350 years to achieve. When Peter Stuyvesant was governor of New Netherland more than three centuries ago, he planted grapes on Manhattan Island in an attempt to develop a wine industry. In 1662, Lord Baltimore called his land grant in Maryland "The Vineyard" and, in his enthusiasm for wine, planted his own 300-acre plot of vines. Connecticut's official seal depicts three grapevines bearing fruit, a symbol of that state's early viticultural aspirations. George Washington grew grapes at Mount Vernon, but it was Thomas Jefferson who proved to be the most zealous early proponent of wine. He yearned to see serious wine produced in America. "It is desirable that it should be made here," he wrote, "and we have every soil, aspect, and climate of the best wine countries." For thirty years Jefferson tried unsuccessfully to grow European grapes at Monticello.

What went wrong? Until recently, wine produced in the Eastern United States failed to attract the praise West Coast wines have garnered for decades. It's not just that California is better at promoting its product. The reason Eastern wineries failed to receive unconditional thumbs up from critics and consumers is, to put it bluntly, because their wine simply wasn't as good. To be sure, a few isolated examples of superior wine were made in the East, but on the whole, wines from East Coast states had not, until now, exhibited the dry character and clean, fruity flavors that consumers want today. The reasons are fascinating and complex.

I have been as prejudiced against East Coast wines as anyone. Because I spent my childhood in France and much of my adult life in California's wine country; I may even have been more biased than others. When I first moved to New York, then to Connecticut and eventually back to New York, I *wanted* to like New England wines — after all, the notion of drinking wine from one's own locale was a tradition I believed in. In addition, I strongly believe in supporting local grape farmers, partly because wineries help to keep agricultural land from being overrun by housing developments and shopping malls, and also because I believe it's important for children to witness the practice of local farming. Furthermore, I think children should be part of an environment where sensible wine consumption keeps family and friends gathered around the dinner table fostering relaxed and extended conversation.

Nevertheless, after a few attempts to find an Eastern wine I liked, I gave up and went back to the California and European wines I love. Despite a couple of Long Island vintages which, I admit, showed promise, I thought the odds were against the East Coast ever developing into a region of world-class winemaking.

And then, several years ago, a funny thing happened. Through a mutual friend, my husband and I were introduced to Susan and Earl Samson, who own Sakonnet Vineyards in Rhode Island. We hit it off, and so, when Susan and Earl invited us to spend the weekend at their home in Little Compton, my only concern was that I wouldn't be able to come up with anything nice to say about their wine.

Sitting in the Samsons' cozy kitchen, I swirled my first glass of Sakonnet Chardonnay nervously. I took a sniff, thankful that at least the wine smelled pretty good. With the first sip, I was amazed. I sipped again. Why, this stuff tasted just like *real* wine! By the end of the weekend, I knew something interesting was going on in winemaking, at least in Rhode Island.

After more research, I called several of the editors at the wine magazines I write for and told them I wanted to write about New England wines. Since then, I have turned out several articles about wines from the Eastern states, and I have been a judge in national competitions where East Coast wineries have beaten out competitors from the West Coast. Although only a small percentage of the wine made in the East can be considered premium, the picture has changed so rapidly over the past few years. Instead of counting the number of quality Eastern wineries on the fingers of one hand, there were suddenly enough to actually fill a book, with many more emerging every year. The wines get better and better as the vines become more mature, the winemakers more knowledgeable, and the public more discerning.

A couple of decades ago much of the wine in the East was still being made from the hardy native American grape varieties that serious wine drinkers consider inferior. Then French-American hybrids began squeezing out native grapes. Now the best European grapes are becoming the norm. Furthermore, although most Eastern wine has traditionally been white, Cabernet Franc, Cabernet Sauvignon, Merlot, Pinot Noir, and other red wines favored by serious wine drinkers are in the ascendancy.

California, with its temperate climate and hospitable environment, has been turning out rivers of premium wine for several decades, while the rest of the country — where temperatures regularly range from root-splitting sub-zero to wilting stretches of high humidity in the upper nineties — lagged behind. Now, thanks to a host of factors coming together at the same time, including technological advances, agricultural improvements, and more progressive winery licensing regulations, we are at the dawn of a new era in American winemaking, particularly in the Eastern states.

It is an exciting time for writers such as myself, who specialize in wine. It is also an exciting time for winemakers, who suddenly have a whole new universe of possibilities open to them. Above all, it is an exciting time for consumers, who love good wine and who love discovering new wineries and new varieties of wine.

For those of us with a passion for travel, the birth of scores of new wineries gives us new reasons to visit the American countryside. The Eastern segment of the nation, where the concentration of wineries is greater than anywhere except California, is a particularly rewarding travel destination. Vines seem to grow best in places where the landscape is spectacular. From the comely beauty of New York's Finger Lakes, to the maritime attraction of New England's coast, to the lush and fertile plateau of the Shenandoah Valley, there's plenty of dramatic scenery to explore. A sojourn in the Eastern wine regions is also an opportunity to become reacquainted with the history of our country.

In addition, as wine is meant to accompany food, visits to the wine country should also include samplings of the best regional foods. As the public's palate has become more refined, gastronomic entrepreneurs and small-scale farmers, like the wine producers, are responding by growing, producing, and preparing more sophisticated ingredients and dishes.

The unpredictable climate and weather, and the variety of plant pests and diseases, will always make winemaking in the Eastern states a challenge. It is now undeniable, however, that the supreme effort will pay off for both the winemaker and the wine drinker, especially in the best viticultural regions. With a greater number of wineries producing better and better wines, today's wine enthusiast can visit more cellars and sample the product in more tasting rooms than ever before. In fact, as most wineries in the East are small, producing anywhere from a few hundred to several thousand cases a year, the only way most of us will ever have a chance to taste some wines is by visiting the wineries themselves. If we come home with an extra case of wine in the trunk, it will be a vacation to remember every time we pour a glass for ourselves and our friends.

Happy travels, and *Santé!*

THE WAY THIS BOOK WORKS

THE WINE REGIONS

When we contemplate travel in this country, we tend to think in terms of various states. But where wine is concerned, this doesn't make much sense, particularly in the East where state lines have not been drawn according to the climactic and geologic criteria that influence grape production. Wine from the Connecticut coast, for example, has more in common with Long

Island wine than with anything made in the far western section of Connecticut, where the climate is not moderated by the Atlantic. Grapes grown in the fertile farmland of eastern Pennsylvania will taste more like those in neighboring New Jersey than like anything from the rugged northeastern part of the state. Think of the differences between Sonoma and Santa Barbara, or Burgundy and Bordeaux to understand how important the image, as well as the different flavors, of separate wine regions can be. And so, the problem remains as to how to delineate the Eastern region into separate viticultural areas.

One useful method of defining Eastern wine regions is based on the ideas of Eric Miller, winemaker-owner of Chaddsford Winery in southeastern Pennsylvania. Under Miller's system, the East is divided into three distinct geologic regions: the Benchlands, the Atlantic Uplands, and the Mountains. Each of these regions has its own characteristic climate and soil type. In each, vines perform in a relatively similar fashion and the wines reflect the individuality of the land.

I have organized this book around these three separate divisions, which have been further broken up into smaller sub-sections based on American Viticultural Appellations (AVA's). Like the *appéllations contrôlées* that designate and control France's geographically based names, the labels on wines from official AVA's specify quality according to geographical regions, such as: Napa Valley, southeastern New England, Hudson River.

THE WINE AND WINERIES

The intent of this book is to identify the best wine made from grapes in the Eastern states rather than to provide a definitive guide to every single winery in the East. A few of the places that are included produce wine that is as good as any in the world. Others make wine that may not win first place in wine tasting contests, but is still a pleasant enough beverage. Those few wineries that make truly mediocre wine or even bad wine, or wine that would appeal to a very limited audience, have not been included. Similarly, I have tried to avoid wineries that concentrate more on tour attendance than on making wine.

In addition, although I have included some wineries that produce wine made from fruit in addition to grape wine, I don't mention places that make *only* fruit wine (I have nothing against fruit wine — it simply isn't the focus of this book).

THE *TERROIR* OF EASTERN WINE REGIONS

One of the characteristics of wine that attracts discerning consumers is the element the French call *"terroir"* — the individual characteristics imparted to wine by specific types of climate, soil, and other geologic factors. For example, the crisp, mineral-scented wines from the cool Burgundy region of Chablis are typically very different from the richer, flowery white wines from the Côte de Nuits section of Burgundy, although both are made from the same Chardonnay grape. A robust, intensely colored Cabernet from Long Island is unlike the light, delicate Cabernet produced in the Finger Lakes. Some of these differences are a result of the deliberate stylistic imprint and philosophy of individual winemakers, but much of the character of wine is a consequence of the locale where the vines grow.

In the Eastern United States, as in much of Europe, *terroir* is more important than in California, where variations in climate are less pronounced. Here, individual microclimates have a profound effect on the grapes, which means that wine made from fruit grown in a specific region is more apt to possess a personality of *place*. The reflection of locale in wine contributes some of the subtle charm and mystery, as well as the individual character that we look for in the best wines. And so — while some vintners purchase grapes or juice from California or even, in some cases, France — the wineries included in this book grow at least a portion of their grapes on their own property or purchase them from vineyards in the same viticultural region.

Although much of the wine evaluated for this book was sampled by various tasting panels whose judgment I took into account, when all else is said and done, the final decision about which wineries to include was based entirely on my own subjective reactions. If I liked the wine, if I thought it would in some way enhance one's dining experience, and if I believed that a majority of wine drinkers would also have a favorable impression of it, then that winery was included in this book. In all cases, I have given my own brief subjective description of the wines and the wineries.

WINERIES AND LOCAL RESTAURANTS

When the first edition of this book came out in 1996, it included suggestions for dining in restaurants where local wines were served. At that time such restaurants were few and far between (as one of the subjects I interviewed put it, a few years ago it would have taken an Act of Congress to make a restaurant serve local wines.) In a very short time, that picture has changed dramatically as wineries improved both their product and their marketing skills. Although there is still plenty of room for improvement in restaurant support, today it is the rule, rather than the exception that local wines will be featured on the wine list. Since there are now so many eateries pouring the local stuff, I decided to drop this category altogether rather than attempt to evaluate such a great number of restaurants. So the bad news is that readers who found this guidance helpful in past editions of the book will no longer be able to rely on it for dining out. The good news is that Eastern wines are now fine enough to demand a place on restaurant wine lists side by side with wines from Europe and California.

A developing trend in wine country is the number of wineries that feature their own dining opportunities, ranging from small snack bars to full-blown gourmet restaurants. Many wineries also own B&Bs, providing cozy and sometimes very elegant accommodations right in the heart of the vineyards.

THE LISTINGS

We have included (in small type alongside each winery's entry) such practical information as we believe is helpful. While we have made every effort to ensure that these facts are true as of publication, they are of course subject to change. It's a good idea to call ahead if you're planning a trip to a winery.

New in this edition are the web and e-mail addresses for wineries that have them. These, too, are subject to change, as wineries take advantage of the Internet to reach an ever-wider audience. Many wineries that do not now have web addresses will very likely have them in the future.

ABOUT THE RATINGS

Earlier editions of this book rated the overall quality of individual wineries as an attempt to help those visitors sort out the great from the mediocre wines in what was then a veritable minefield of uneven quality. Today, the quality of Eastern wine has progressed to the point where truly inferior wines are rare. Oh yes —you can still find them. But most of the wineries listed in this book now turn out wines that may not all be inspiring, but will seldom disappoint. A few wineries have the magic touch with everything they make, while others may excell particularly with one or two wines. As a general consumers' guide, at the head of each entry I've singled out the wine (or wines) which I think are particularly outstanding at that particular winery, followed, in the text, by a brief description of those wines. Again, I had occasional help from other wine professionals, but the ultimate calls are a reflection of my own judgement and tastes. But because the quality of wine in any given winery is constantly influenced by factors such as changes in personnel, equipment, individual vintages, and so forth, I urge readers to use all of this as a very general guide rather than an unimpeachable assessment of the wines. Your own taste buds will always be the best guide to what you like.

Wineries of the
Eastern States

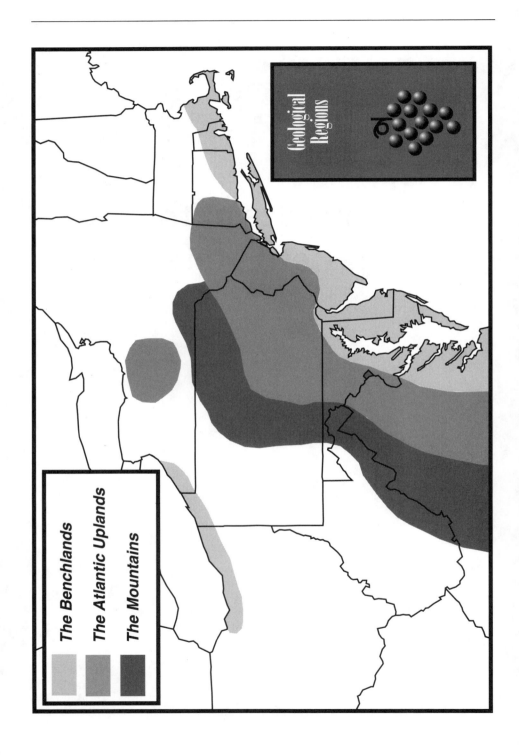

Geological Regions

The Benchlands

The Atlantic Uplands

The Mountains

INTRODUCTION
History, Grapes, and Marketing

From Peach Wine to Pinot Noir, from Scuppernong to Sauvignon Blanc, every state in the union produces wine of one sort or another. Our wine-making origins date back to the beginning of our history as a nation. The Jamestown colonists started vinifying local grapes as soon as they got here, and we've been trying to make decent table wine ever since.

The colonists had no lack of native fruit to work with. In A.D. 1000, the Norse explorer Leif Eriksson was so impressed by the riot of grape vines he saw cascading from the trees in North America that he dubbed the place "Vinland." In fact, more grape varieties grow naturally between the Atlantic coast and the Rocky Mountains than in any other place on earth.

The problem, from the early settlers' thirsty point of view, was that the fermented juice of native grapes had a powerful, musky smell and a stronger, more aggressive flavor than the more refined wines they were used to. Had the European settlers simply acquired a taste for wine made from grapes in their adopted land, they wouldn't have spent the next 350 years trying to coax European vines into growing in the harsh conditions of the New World.

The English monarchy, and eventually the individual states, worked to establish a viticultural industry in the New World. Both invested heavily, with the hope of reaping substantial economic returns. European vine cuttings were first imported to Virginia about 1619. From then on, determined viticulturists all along the Atlantic seaboard imported vines from every major wine-producing region in Europe.

For reasons that were not understood at the time, these vines always died. But since hope is part of the job description of a winemaker, the trials continued. French vignerons were imported to Virginia as consultants, French Huguenot exiles came to the Carolinas, and German winemakers immigrated to Pennsylvania. None of these experts, however, could get Vitis vinifera to grow in the New World.

THE RAVAGES OF DISEASE

While they never gave up trying, European vineyard specialists were forced to acknowledge that European vines would not do well in the new country. The vines that didn't die in the freezing winters would inevitably be killed off by American diseases, against which they had no inherent immunity. Native American grapes, by contrast, were resistant to Pierce's disease, black rot, phylloxera, and a variety of mildews and other fungal problems.

Of all the problems besetting the American vinifera wine industry, phylloxera was its ruin. This minuscule, yellow louse attacks vines by sucking the life out of the plant through its roots. California's vinifera-based wine industry, which had been thriving in the 19th century, was decimated by phylloxera. To make matters worse, the disease was inadvertently imported into France on the roots of American vines around 1860. There, phylloxera spread like the plague it was, almost wiping out most of the major wine-producing regions of France. In fact, few winemaking regions in the world escaped. The insect invaded the vineyards of Russia, South Africa, Australia, and New Zealand, as well as those of other European countries.

Finally, in the late 1800s, it was discovered that native American vines were resistant to phylloxera. Eventually, grafting of vinifera vines onto native American rootstock became the established method of combating phylloxera. Today, most of the world's grapevines grow on native American roots.

Even after the threat of phylloxera diminished, raising vinifera vines remained an extraordinary challenge in the Eastern states, although they flourished in California's mild climate. In the search for hardy grapes that would also produce palatable wines, viticulturists in the East turned to French-American hybrids. These new strains, developed in France after the phylloxera devastation, are American vine species crossed with European vinifera vines. They are more disease resistant than traditional vinifera, while their fruit is less pungently flavored than native American grapes. Thanks to these hybrids, the Eastern wine industry finally began to grow. Leading production centers developed around Lake Erie, in Missouri and Ohio, and in New York's Finger Lakes region.

By 1900 the future looked good. As Leon D. Adams wrote in The Wines of America, "Wine growing was a full-grown, proud American industry. The brands of leading California, New York, Ohio, Missouri, and New Jersey wineries were competing with European vintages on many of the best restaurant wine lists."

PROHIBITION

Just when the wine industry was reaching maturity, however, a disaster far more deadly than disease or climatic catastrophe struck, as America headed into Prohibition. In 1919, 55 million gallons of wine were produced in the United States; by 1925 the figure had dropped to barely 3.5 million gallons.

It is hard to imagine how rapidly this new calamity advanced, but the seeds of destruction had been gathering for almost a hundred years. Temperance societies and religious organizations lobbied Congress and terrorized the American public into accepting Prohibition. At first, local communities and cities went "dry"; then, in 1851, Maine became the first state to declare itself alcohol free. In 1920, the 18th Amendment to the Constitution of the United States, prohibiting the manufacture, sale, transportation, or importation of alcoholic beverages, was passed. Intoxicating liquor, as defined by Congress, was any beverage that contained 0.5 percent alcohol, and included all wine and beer. Some uses of wine were still permitted: for religious ceremonies, for medicinal purposes, for food flavoring, and for other non-beverage purposes.

Abuse of the law was rampant, however, and enforcement virtually impossible. In 1933, the 21st Amendment, repealing the 18th, was ratified. But, as The Oxford Companion to Wine, edited by Jancis Robinson, observes, "Unfortunately, the [21st] Amendment left to the separate states the entire regulation of the liquor traffic within their borders, with the result that the US liquor laws, including local and state prohibitions, remain a crazy quilt of inconsistent and arbitrary rules, another lastingly destructive effect of national prohibition. . . . Liquor — wine very much included — continues to be an object of punitive taxation, of moral disapproval, and of obstructive legislation in the United States today."

During the 13 years of Prohibition, thousands of wineries across the nation went out of business. No one in the wine industry received any compensation for losses. In addition to personal and financial tragedies, the economic loss to local communities and to entire states was disastrous.

California ventured forward on the road to recovery immediately after Repeal, thanks in part to a more enlightened government than in most states. But in the East, the wine industry lay in a coma for nearly half a century, until the 1960s and 1970s, when it finally began to emerge from its long slumber and reinvent itself. While hardly the "Vinland" that dazzled Leif Eriksson, the wine-growing regions of the Eastern United States today are beginning to prosper again. Most of us would even consider much of the wine produced in the East to be above average in quality. And, more and more frequently, a truly great wine emerges.

FROM VINEYARD TO TABLE

Numerous factors affect the production of wines and our enjoyment of them. But no factor is as influential as the quality of the wine grapes themselves. The history of Eastern winemaking is very much a story of shifting preferences in fruit. Today, European strains prevail, but a few vintners still argue for the superiority of French-American hybrids. In part the debate is one over marketing, as Eastern winemaking evolves from a fledgling industry into a mature one.

GRAPE TYPES

Vinifera: The world's most common wine grape comes from the vine species called Vitis vinifera, a native of Europe and West Asia. There are approximately 10,000 varieties of vinifera. These include Chardonnay, Sauvignon Blanc, Riesling, Pinot Noir, Cabernet Sauvignon, Merlot, and all the other grapes that are used to make traditional European wines.

Labrusca and rotundifolia: Of the many grape varieties that are native to America, only two are still used for winemaking in any quantity:

- *Vitis labrusca,* found in the Northeastern United States, produces intensely aromatic grapes with a pronounced flavor that is often described as "foxy." Grape juice and raw Concord grapes have a typical foxy smell, which scientists attribute either to a component called methyl anthranilate, or to o-amino acetophenone. Whatever its cause, "foxiness" is seldom a complimentary term when applied to wine.

  The Concord, from which grape juice and many sweet, kosher wines are made, is the most widely planted labrusca grape, and the most common grape in the United States after the Thompson seedless table grape. Catawba, another well-known labrusca, was for many years the leading wine grape in America. It is still used today, especially to make sparkling wines that have a pronounced grapey flavor. Longfellow described this wine as "dulcet, delicious, and dreamy." Today's wine buff might be more inclined to characterize it as foxy, funky, and forgettable. And yet, well-made sweet Catawba and Concord wines can be uniquely delicious.

- *Vitis rotundifolia,* a native of the Southern states, produces the Scuppernong grape, which yields a sweet, musky wine that is still popular in some parts of the South.

Hybrids: French-American hybrid grapes are crosses between two grape varieties, usually vinifera and labrusca. The earliest vinifera vine cuttings imported from Europe sometimes survived here for a few years. During that time a natural hybridization took place by exchange pollination between the imported vines and local American species. The earliest offspring of these crosses, first noticed in the mid-18th century in Pennsylvania, became known as the Alexander. It was the basis for the first commercially successful winery in North America.

In the early 1800s, many more of these accidental crossings were discovered, and by the middle of the century, controlled hybridization began in America. By the late-19th and early-20th century, after the devastation of the French vineyards by phylloxera, French hybridizers developed a host of hardy, flavorful grapes — Seyval and Vidal Blanc, Chambourcin, Baco, and Rayon d'Or among others. For many years these vines were planted all over France; but since 1955, French planting regulations have discouraged vine varieties that are associated with inferior wines, including many of the hybrids. While hybrid plantings have been phased out throughout most of France, they remain popular in regions of the United States where vinifera can't grow.

In the 1930s a hobbyist winemaker named Philip Wagner began experimenting with French-American hybrids in his vineyard in Maryland. At the time, it seemed unlikely that vinifera grapes could ever survive anywhere in the Eastern states, while the flavor of labrusca grapes would never be accepted. The better hybrids that Wagner helped develop and popularize seemed an exciting alternative.

When the Eastern wine industry began its revival in the 1960s, hybrids were the principal grapes planted. Today, however, more and more wine producers are ripping out hybrid vines and replacing them with vinifera. Most new vineyards are planted exclusively with vinifera grapes. The switch resulted from a number of factors, among them the evolution of hardier vinifera vines, and the use of more advanced technology in combating disease. New understanding about vineyard management — including new forms of trellising and pruning — also helps to keep the vines healthy. Generally milder winters for the past few years have been another factor in increased vinifera plantings. Furthermore, most contemporary American vintners, like their French cousins, believe vinifera grapes make the best wines. Why work with mediocre grapes, they argue, when vinifera grapes have proven to be the best for winemaking?

On the other hand, not all wineries have rushed to raise Chardonnay, Pinot Noir, Sauvignon Blanc, Merlot, and other European grapes. Some vintners believe that the best wines made from superior hybridized grapes, such as Seyval and Vidal Blanc, can hold their own. They further insist that wine made from hybrid grapes has a unique American flavor, with as much varietal appeal as any other wine. Finally, they worry that the European vines will not survive here over the long haul. History, they point out, is not on the side of vinifera in the East.

From an economic standpoint, however, vinifera has the edge. No matter how good the wine from hybridized grapes might be, marketing them is an uphill challenge. Skeptics wonder how, in a world awash in wine, the consumer can be persuaded to buy a bottle of unknown Baco over a similarly priced Merlot, or an obscure Aurora over a reliable Chardonnay. In addition, producers are influenced by the fact that wines from vinifera grapes command higher prices.

Many viticulturists in the Eastern states hedge their bets, planting both vinifera and hybrids. In many ways this diversity is fortunate for consumers, who can taste and test their way through a wide range of wines: from simple country hybrids — many of which, in spirit and sometimes in palate, resemble some of France's regional *vins de pays* — to midrange, moderately priced wines, all the way up to beautifully crafted examples of premium wines made from both hybrids and the world's noblest grapes.

MARKETING WINE

It's a challenge of Sisyphean proportions to market wine made in the East. The first obvious difficulty is promoting an unknown product. The relatively small production of Eastern wineries, ranging from a few hundred cases to a couple of thousand, is another. Add to this a complex web of licensing, distribution, taxation, and retail regulations, and one begins to understand why growing grapes is considered the easy part of winemaking! Distribution problems are compounded when a winery sells and transports its wines from one state to another. As one New England winemaker described the convoluted logistics of interstate wine distribution, "If your hat blows off in Rhode Island and lands in Connecticut, you have to apply for a license to go get it."

For all these reasons, and because Eastern wineries still produce relatively small quantities, most Eastern wine is sold in the state where it's produced. All Eastern wineries sell their own wine, and for many, the wine is only available through the winery. Increasingly, regional wines are available in local restaurants, while a handful of the most successful wineries such as Bedell, Chaddsford, and Sakonnet, for example, may be featured on wine lists throughout their own state. The biggest producers, such as Rhode Island's Sakonnet Vineyards or Virginia's Williamsburg, are served in a few fine restaurants across the country. Several audacious wineries, such as Long Island's Palmer, have even begun to crack the European market.

Direct Shipping
Why you can't get home delivery — and what you can do about it

Have you ever tried to send a case of wine home from a winery you were visiting, or called an out-of-state winery to have wine shipped? It is a lot of fun to do, *if you can*. But if you have tried, the chances are you have been told either that it's illegal to ship to your state, or that the common carriers won't deliver wine to individuals because state regulations are too complicated.

More than half our states either forbid or partially restrict direct shipment of wine to consumers. These laws are not just obsolete relics of the Prohibition era. Many have been retained on the books despite reasonable efforts to remove them, and several states have enacted them in recent times. Sad to say, some liquor distributors and retailers, fearful of losing their market share of wine sales, have played upon public fears of underage access and the potential loss of state tax revenue to persuade state legislatures to forbid direct home shipment of wines. Both concerns are provably unfounded, but in the absence of any organized voice on behalf of the consumer, the law sustains an antiquated distribution oligopoly.

As the number of wineries all over the country increases (from 377 in 1963 to more than 2,000 today) and the number of distributors decreases (from 10,900 in

1979 to fewer than 2,750 today), the possibility of buying a favorite wine at your friendly local wine emporium is decreasing drastically. Direct purchase and shipment from winery to consumer is clearly the answer. It works very well, meets an obvious need, and creates no illegal access or tax-evasion problems in the states where it is permitted. Indeed, as wineries collect and forward state alcoholic beverage taxes (easily done in this electronic era), the states benefit from expanded commerce in wine. And it doesn't really hurt distributors. In those states where direct shipment is permitted, the distributor/retailer network still accounts for 95 percent of wine sales.

Winemakers and wine lovers are beginning to speak up for fair treatment. This is especially important for winemakers and consumers in the Eastern states. Winemaking is flourishing in more and more locales, and wine lovers are awakening to the pleasures of wines of the Eastern states, but are unable to purchase any but a small fraction of them. There are so many wineries, most of them with an output too small to attract the attention of distributors, especially out-of-state ones. There are so many states, and thus so many potential bars to direct delivery. Direct sale from winery to consumer is the logical answer. If you care about it — do something!

The Wine Institute and winemakers associations have organized *Free the Grapes* as a body to lobby for unfettered direct shipment of wine throughout the country. Contact *Free the Grapes* on web at www.freethegrapes.org or by phone at 707-254-9292. Add your voice to those of other wine lovers all over the U.S.A. who are reshaping the debate on this issue.

PART ONE

The Benchlands

Southeastern New England

Connecticut
Massachusetts
Rhode Island

Long Island

North Fork
South Fork

Southeastern New Jersey and Coastal Virginia

Southeastern New Jersey
Coastal Virginia

Lake Erie Region

New York
Pennsylvania
Ohio
Island Wineries

PART ONE

The Benchlands

Winemaker John Sotelo (left) and owner Earl Samson at Sakonnet Vineyards, Little Compton, Rhode Island.

Marguerite Thomas

The viticultural region of the eastern Benchlands includes southeastern Massachusetts and the coastal sections of Rhode Island, Connecticut, Long Island, New Jersey, and Virginia. The bench of sand, sediment, and stone characterizing this region was formed by the debris left behind by a massive melting glacier that drifted across the land tens of thousands of years ago. Benchland soils are typically low in most trace minerals except silica. The soil in some areas, such as parts of Long Island, may be gravelly.

The Benchlands tend to have moderate weather because of the influence of the Atlantic Ocean and Long Island Sound. The effect of this relatively mild climate was dramatically demonstrated in 1994, when a particularly severe winter cut a wide swath inland, killing vines from the Finger Lakes down through Pennsylvania and northern Virginia, but leaving most of the coastal area unscathed.

Because a warmer climate leads to riper grapes than in colder interior sections of the Northeast, wine from the Benchlands is frequently characterized by a more pronounced color and flavor, and a softer texture. It is often slightly lower in acidity than wine from cooler regions. At its best, this wine will be full-bodied and luscious. With some exceptions, it is best consumed young.

SOUTHEASTERN NEW ENGLAND

Tempered by the jet stream and situated just above Latitude 40 (making it slightly more southerly than France), New England ought to have reliable, moderate weather — but it doesn't. Mark Twain wrote about New England's weather: "In the spring, I have counted 136 different kinds of weather inside of 24 hours." Most vintners in this part of the world know exactly what he meant.

And yet, despite winter freezes, schizophrenic springs, steamy summer heat, and vine-flattening hurricanes, people have been making wine here since 1632, when the first vineyard was planted on Governor's Island in Boston Harbor. For those blessed with enough cash and a determined Yankee spirit, the odds in favor of producing wine sometimes outweigh the risks. An obsessive desire to succeed certainly helps. As Bob Russell, owner of Massachusetts's Westport Rivers winery puts it: "Anyone going into the wine business has to do it because they love it — because they have a dream, a passion."

The land beside the coast, protected as it is by the Atlantic, has proven to be the most suitable place for growing vinifera grapes in New England. The Chardonnay grape that is harder to grow further inland does well here because of a relatively long growing season — about 190 days, compared to the average of 145 days in other parts of New England. Other white wine grapes, especially Seyval and Vidal Blanc, also thrive along the coast.

While white wine predominates, New England is beginning to prove that it can produce some above-average red wines too, with Cabernet Franc and, in some instances, Merlot, showing particularly well. A handful of very promising new wineries has entered the market in the past couple of years (notably on Cape Cod, upper Connecticut, and Newport, Rhode Island) while virtually all of the original vintners have made stunning progress in the quality of their wines. This promising viticultural region will surely continue to attract wineries in the future.

In addition to its wines, Coastal New England offers a memorable travel destination, filled with charming villages and historic houses, antique stores and art galleries, picturesque farmland undulating down to the sea, colorful harbors and ports, wildlife refuges, woodlands, and beaches. With all this and wine too, New England is truly a blessed place.

CONNECTICUT

CHAMARD VINEYARDS
860-664-0299;
 fax 860-664-0297.

Classic New England stone walls that undulate picturesquely across the land edge Chamard's 20 acres of vines. An agrarian pond sparkles out-

The view from Chamard's tasting room: a lovely pond with vineyards beyond.

Marguerite Thomas

115 Cow Hill Rd., Clinton, CT 06413.
Directions: From I-95 take exit 63 to Rte. 81 north. Just past the Clinton Crossing Outlet Complex turn left onto Walnut Hill Rd., which merges into Cow Hill Rd. after 0.8 mile. Continue to winery on the left.
Owner: William Chaney.
Open: Year-round, Wed.–Sat. 11am–4pm.
Price Range of Wines: $9.99 for Chardonnay; $12.99 for Merlot; $14.99 for Cabernet Sauvignon and Estate Reserve Chardonnay.

• Chardonnay
• Cabernet Sauvignon
• Merlot
• Cabernet Franc

side the tasting room. It's a charming country setting, but there certainly is no rural clumsiness in these sophisticated wines.

The winery's owner, William Chaney, is also chairman of the board and C.E.O. of Tiffany & Co. In the mid-1980s Chaney began searching New England for a place to plant a vineyard when, by a stroke of luck, he found a 40-acre farm for sale in Clinton, Connecticut, the same coastal community where he owned a weekend house. Now the Kansas-born Chaney spends weekends and vacations in the vineyards or in the winery working alongside winemaker and general manager Larry McCulloch. McCulloch, after training as a horticulturist, learned winemaking at Benmarl, a Hudson River winery. Both men share the strong belief that great wines come from great vineyards. "We've proven that if you pick the right site and put your mind and money into it, you can make nice wine. It may not be easy, but it can be done," McCulloch insists.

Chamard's exceptional recent Chardonnays have a concentration of fruiti-ness balanced by high levels of acidity and a pronounced mineral aftertaste. Very fine Estate Cabernet Sauvignon and Merlot are also produced here in limited amounts. The outstanding Cabernet Franc, says winemaker Larry McCulloch, is great with spicy ribs and Cajun shrimp or chicken. Chamard Vineyard's total production is 6,000 cases. The wines continue to evolve with Chamard's characteristic good flavor-balance of fruit, oak, acid, and alcohol, plus the mystery and intangibles that make good wines so alluring.

HERITAGE TRAIL VINEYARDS

860-376-0659; fax 860-376-6478.
E-mail: vineyard@snet.net.
291 North Burnham Hwy., Lisbon, CT 06351.
Directions: From I-395 take exit 83A; turn left on Rte. 169 and proceed to winery.
Owner: Diane Powell.
Open: May–Dec: Fri.–Sun. 11am–5pm; Jan–Apr.: by appointment.
Price Range of Wines: $9.95 for Quinebaug White and Shetucket Red to $18.95 for Chardonnay and Cabernet.
Special Feature: Light fare such as cheese boards with fresh fruit available in the tasting room.

Housed in a Colonial-style building attached to the owner's own 18th-century house, the cozy tasting room overlooks an informal garden backed by woods, with the six-acre vineyard just visible below the garden. Among the wines are Quine-baug White, an "off-dry" — which is to say slightly sweet — blend of Vignoles and Cayuga, and Shetucket Red, a blend of Baco Noir and Buffalo, another American hybrid; both wines are named after local rivers. There's also Chardonnay and Cabernet Franc. A small gift shop, a fireplace, and a sundeck are among the other attractions here.

SHARPE HILL VINEYARD

860-974-3549;
fax 860-974-1503.
108 Wade Rd., P.O. Box 1, Pomfret, CT 06285.
Directions: From I-395 take exit 93. Go west on Rte. 101 (which becomes Rte. 44) for 7 miles to Rte. 97 (in Abington district of Pomfret). Go south on 97 exactly 4 miles to Kimball Hill Rd. Turn left and go 1.8 miles to winery. From I-84 take exit 69; go east on Rte. 74

This exciting newcomer has burst on the scene with some astonishingly good wines. Owner Steven Vollweiler, whose first career is in the metal-recycling business, has realized a 20-year-old dream with this winery. Current production is about 4,000 cases, which will increase as the seven-acre vineyard is gradually expanded.

It's a long drive to get to Sharpe Hill (but, trust me, well worth it) along a curving rural road, past woods and farms and a great number of authentic Colonial houses. You might want to stop off in Pomfret for some antiquing, if that's your kind of thing. In Sharpe Hill's tasting room, fashioned after an 18th-century taproom complete with antique furnishings and decorations, sample the Ballet of Angels, a white wine that manages to be both crisp

Marguerite Thomas

Lunch is served in the Wine Garden at Sharpe Hill Vineyard.

to the end. Make a left onto Rte. 44 east and go to Abington district of Pomfret. Turn right onto Rte. 97 south and proceed as above.

Owners: Steven and Catherine Vollweiler.

Open: Fri.–Sun. 11am–5pm.

Price Range of Wines: $8.99 for Ballet of Angels to $17.99 for Select Late Harvest.

Special Features: Lunch served in the wine garden.

- Ballet of Angels
- Chardonnay
- Cabernet Franc
- Red Seraph
- Select Late Harvest

and slightly sweet, with heavenly aromas. Made from Seyval and Cayuga grapes, this award-winning wine makes a nifty aperitif and is also a good accompaniment to spicy foods. The elegant barrel-fermented Chardonnay and the earthy, peppery Cabernet Franc are outstanding. Red Seraph, a pleasing light red wine made from a cold-hardy hybrid named St. Croix plus a dash of white wine and a whisper of Cabernet Franc is, like the Beaujolais it resembles, best served slightly chilled. The Select Late Harvest wine, made only in the best years (I tasted both the 1996 and 1997), is sublime, one of the best dessert wines in the East — or anywhere else, for that matter. Too many dessert wines are syrupy and cloying — this one is endlessly lively and bright in the mouth.

Don't even *think* of going anywhere else for lunch. Sharpe Hill's wine garden is nicely situated at the base of the eponymous slope of vines. Work up an appetite before lunch with a stroll up the hill through the vineyard for a fabulous view over Connecticut, Massachusetts, and Rhode Island. Catherine Vollweiler's light but flavorful fare will tickle any wine taster's fancy. Okay, the service can be slow — but how many other places do you know where the butter is flown in on the Concorde from France, the Stilton from England?

Howard Burson

"I've been working in the wine industry for over a quarter of a century," says Howard Burson. "I've been involved in it everywhere, from China, to South Africa to the Finger Lakes."

Like many people, Howard stumbled into his profession more by accident than by design. As a graduate student polishing up his doctoral dissertation in philosophy at Cornell University, he found a part-time job swabbing out tanks at Bully Hill Vineyards. "It was fun and it was a good place to learn about wine. I got to do everything there." Although he ended up as Bully Hill's cellar manager, Howard hadn't quite severed his ties with academia. After two years of teaching at Wells College, however, he finally decided to dive into the wine business full-time. Travels, especially to France and Spain, played an important role in his career, giving him critical familiarity with the world's best wines. "It has been my good fortune to pick up a few tricks along the way," he adds modestly.

Howard and his wife spent time in India adopting first one daughter and later a second baby. In 1980 the family moved to Pomfret, Connecticut, where Howard started up, designed, and ran Hamlet Hill Winery. There he sharpened his skills and was awarded many prizes for his wines, but the venture simply wasn't profitable enough; in 1990, Hamlet Hill went out of business. Howard, at the age of 43, went back to school to study grape-tissue culture, with the ultimate goal of opening a biotech-based grapevine nursery. As it turned out, he couldn't quite pull off the start-up financing for the project, but at about that time Steven Vollweiler came on the scene looking for a winemaker for Sharpe Hill Vineyards. "I jumped back into winemaking with a vengeance. It really is what I love to do," says Howard.

Howard is characteristically humble when it comes to explaining the success of his wines. Noting that a good winemaking facility is important, Howard mentions almost as an aside that he designed Sharpe Hill's winery himself. Good equipment, he adds, especially the right choice of barrels, counts. Good vineyard management is essential, as is the right choice of grapes. Some grapes, such as Cabernet Sauvignon, are impossible to grow in this particular climate; therefore Howard says Sharpe Hill concentrates on grapes that adapt to the region. Among the grape varieties that appear to be successful here are Cabernet Franc and the white wine varieties Chardonnay, Pinot Blanc and Gris, Gewürztraminer, Riesling, and Melon de Bourgogne. "If you can coax these grapes to grow here, their fruit is absolutely incredible," says Howard. At Sharpe Hill, it seems that Howard Burson has been doing an excellent job of coaxing.

STONINGTON VINEYARDS
800-421-WINE;
    fax 860-535-2182.
E-mail: stonington@
    aol.com.
523 Taugwonk Rd., P.O.
    Box 463, Stonington, CT
    06378.

Stonington Vineyards, set in the hills a few miles inland from the borough of Stonington, provides an informal rural setting in which to picnic or simply sample wines. Nick Smith, who arrived in the wine world via international banking, believes strongly in maintaining the individual character of regional wines. While 50 percent of his grapes are grown on the Stonington property (12 acres of vine-

Directions: Heading east on I-95, take exit 91. Turn left on Taugwonk Rd. and follow signs 2.5 miles to winery on the left.
Owners: Happy and Nick Smith.
Open: Daily 11am–5pm.
Price Range of Wines: $7.99 for Seaport White and Seaport Blush; $8.99 for 375-ml bottle Riesling; $13.99 for Chardonnay.
Special Feature: Art gallery.
Special Events: Annual food and wine festival, May sale and barrel tasting.

- Seaport White
- Rosé

yards), the rest are purchased from local vineyards, including Long Island, which is visible just across Long Island Sound.

Under the supervision of winemaker Mike McAndrew, the wines at Stonington Vineyards continue to improve year after year. The Chardonnay sometimes has a beguiling aroma of jasmine. Seaport White is a user-friendly blend of Chardonnay, Vidal, and Seyval, which Smith describes as "a real New England wine, great with scallops and lobster." Fumé Vidal is Stonington's newest wine.

Stonington's production is currently at about 7,000 cases. Stonington Borough is a lovely seaport village, with many fine historic houses and an outstanding collection of antique shops, art and craft galleries, and restaurants. Mystic Seaport Aquarium, one of the best in the East, and Mystic Seaport are a 15-minute drive from Stonington.

MASSACHUSETTS

Cape Cod Winery's welcoming sign in East Falmouth, Massachusetts.

Marguerite Thomas

CAPE COD WINERY
508-457-5592;
   fax 781-235-4946.
681 Sandwich Rd., East Falmouth, MA 02536.

Boston physician Antonio Lazzari and his microbiologist wife, Kristina, commute out to their winery and six-acre vineyard where they make Nobska White (Seyval and Vidal) and Nobska Red

Directions: From Bourne
Bridge take Rte. 28. At
the first intersection after
the 2nd rotary, take Rte.
151 East right onto
Sandwich Rd. The
winery is about 2.5 miles
on the left.
Owners: Dr. Kristina
Lazzari and Dr. Antonio
Lazzari.
Open: Jun.–Aug.:
Thurs.–Sun. 12noon–5pm,
tours Sat. & Sun. 2 p.m.;
May & Oct.: Sat. & Sun.
12noon–5pm.
Price Range of Wines: $10
for Nobska White; $18
for Merlot.

• Nobska Red

MELLEA WINERY
508-943-5166
or 508-949-2539.
E-mail: mellea@aol.com.
108 Old Southbridge Rd.,
P.O. Box 1328, Dudley,
MA 01571.
Directions: From I-90 take
exit 9 (Rte. 131) onto Old
Southbridge Rd. Follow
signs to winery. From I-
395 take exit 2 (Webster/
Douglas) onto Rte. 16;
turn left onto
Southbridge Rd.
Owners: Joe and Allie
Compagnone.
Open: Apr.–Labor Day: Sat.
& Sun. 12noon–5pm;
Labor Day–Dec.:
Fri.–Sun. 12noon–5pm.

**TRURO VINEYARDS
OF CAPE COD**
508-487-6200.
11 Shore Rd., P.O. Box 165,
North Truro, MA 02652.
Directions: Follow I-95 to
Rte. 6. Continue past

(a blend of Cabernet Sauvignon and Cabernet Franc). Nobska, the name of their local lighthouse, was selected to retain a local feeling for their wines. This young winery released its first Pinot Grigio and Merlot in 1998 (the Merlot sold out two weeks after it was released). Though born in Brazil, Antonio has childhood memories of his family's enthusiasm for the wines from their original homeland, the Veneto, the Italian wine region near Venice. Determined to re-create Italian Pinot Grigio and other European-style wines in America, the Lazzaris are off to a good start. They produce about 2,000 cases annually.

Kristina draws on her biochemical background when she's making wines. The Lazzaris never use insecticides on their vineyard and try to keep all other chemicals to a minimum. "People come back here for more wine because they find they don't get a headache from it," says Antonio.

Mellea's three-acre vineyard is too unprotected for vinifera grapes to survive cold Massachusetts winters, but Seyval and Vidal grow here with relative ease. Chardonnay and other grapes are purchased from Long Island. Mellea is an easy 15-minute drive from historic Old Sturbridge Village.

The first vines were planted in this scenic spot at the tip of Cape Cod in 1992, and the winery opened in 1994. Owners Kathleen Gregrow and Judy Wimer, who share the work in the cellar and in the vineyards, are still experimenting with both jobs. One thing they've learned so far is that

Marguerite Thomas

Judy Wimer and Kathleen Gregrow, owners of Truro Vineyards of Cape Cod.

signs to Wellfleet to North Truro. Turn left on Rte 6A. Winery is on the right.

Open: Mid-May–Oct.: daily 12noon–5pm; Nov.–Dec.: Fri.– Sun. 12noon–4pm; closed midwinter.

Owners: Kathleen Gregrow and Judy Wimer.

Price Range of Wines: $9.99 for Cape Blush to $14.99 for Cabernet Franc.

Special Features: A five-room inn at the winery, antique wine-making display.

Special Event: Annual autumnal grape stomp.

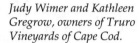

• Cabernet Franc

Cabernet Franc appears to be the best grape for Cape Cod's climate and sandy, low-vigor soils. "It's less disease-prone than other varieties," explains Kathleen. It also gets a chance to ripen thoroughly, adds Judy. "We're 30 miles out in the ocean, which gives us a unique situation. Our grapes ripen about a week after Long Island's vineyards." Indeed, the taste of thoroughly ripe grapes shines through in Truro Vineyards' deliciously fruity Cabernet Franc. The Chardonnay reflects the big, buttery style of Palmer Vineyards (Long Island) winemaker Dan Kleck. Dan was a consultant here during Truro Vineyard's start-up, along with Howard Burson (now at Sharpe Hill). The surprisingly good quality coming from this new winery proves once again the critical importance of skillful, experienced winemakers. Truro's Merlot vines still needed a couple of years to mature before they could be harvested (Merlot's a slower grower than Cabernet), but the wonderfully fragrant Cape Blush — a blend of Cabernet Franc and Cayuga — is already a runaway success. "People love it. It flies out of the tasting room," says Kathleen. The Vignoles, a semi-dry dessert wine, is another success story, selling out within six weeks of its release. Kathleen and Judy produce about 1,600 cases of wine from their own four acres of vines plus fruit purchased from Long Island and the Finger Lakes. "We want to get a little larger," says Judy, "but we don't want to get out of control since we do all the work." These two energetic women also have started collecting antique barrels and other winery equipment for what will eventually become a museum. The winery's five guest rooms (each with king- or queen-sized bed and private bath) are furnished with antiques echoing the period of this handsome early-1800s farmstead. Sumptuous country breakfasts are included.

**WESTPORT RIVERS
   VINEYARD & WINERY**
508-636-3423;
   fax 508-636-4133.
www.westportrivers.com.
417 Hixbridge Rd.,
   Westport, MA 02790.
Directions: From I-95 take
   Rte. 88 south to
   Hixbridge Rd. Turn left
   to winery.
Owners: Bob and Carol
   Russell.
Open: Daily 11am–5pm.
Price Range of Wines: $7.95
   to $35 for Sparkling
   Wine.
Special Features: Art
   gallery, wine and food
   education center,
   Buzzard Bay Brewery.
Special Events: Annual
   Chardonnay festival
   (Aug.), Annual Sparkling
   Wine Independence Day
   Gala, Thanksgiving
   weekend open house,
   other seasonal events.

• Riesling
• Chardonnay
• Sparkling Wines

Set on an old Massachusetts farm, on a spit of land facing Rhode Island, Westport Rivers is a family-run winery. Bob Russell decided to leave the security of his job as a metallurgical engineer for the uncertainty of operating a winery almost 25 years ago. The decision was based partly on the Russells' desire to find an interest and occupation where "we could grow old together." The Russells also were influenced by long discussions with Carol's father, who had owned Germania Wine Cellars in Hammondsport, New York. "With my father's memories, our love of food and wine, our common concern for environmental issues, and a long-standing desire to preserve working agricultural land, a vineyard and winery was an obvious choice," explains Carol.

The Russells could have gone anywhere — California, Oregon, Australia — but they opted for this corner of the world for one simple reason: they loved the New England landscape. By 1982 the Russells had purchased a farm and were planting Chardonnay vines. Their son Bill apprenticed with Eric Fry at Long Island's Lenz Winery before joining the business as winemaker. Another son, Rob, manages the vineyard.

Ninety percent of Westport Rivers' wine is made from grapes that are raised on the property. With 165 acres of vineyards, Westport Rivers has the largest number of vinifera grapevines planted in New England. The remaining 10 percent of fruit is imported from Long Island. All of the estate wine is made from vinifera grapes. Chardonnays and Rieslings exhibit the classy character of cool-climate wines, but can also be lush and ripe in warmer years. The Blanc de Blancs is pure and fresh. The Brut Cuvée RJR is a classic that is sure to please all true Champagne lovers, and the Blanc de Noirs is creamy and delicious. About 8,500 cases of wine are produced each year at Westport Vineyards.

Buzzard Bay Brewery, which opened in 1998, is turning out American versions of British Pale Ales. Westport Rivers will be growing its own hops and burleys for the beers.

Westport Rivers is the only New England winery to produce a sparkling

wine made from vinifera grapes that uses traditional French Champagne vinification techniques. This is a charming wine, with fruity flavors, a bracing acidity, and tiny, persistent bubbles. Westport Chardonnay tastes ripe and lush in
warm years, restrained but still flavorful when it's cooler. I recently enjoyed a
bottle of 1995 Chardonnay that — although it was almost four years old — had
lost none of its bright fruit flavors.

Westport's setting, deep in the picturesque farmland, is lovely. The Russells'
commitment to the environment remains strong: From 1993 on, a portion of
the profits from every bottle of wine has been donated to an organization dedicated to the preservation of farmland in Massachusetts.

RHODE ISLAND

Coastal Rhode Island is emerging as an exciting new wine region, with
Sakonnet having paved the way. The wines themselves are a good reason
to visit, but so is the beautiful coastline. Newport alone draws people from all
over the world, who peer back through history for a glimpse of the place
Henry James described thus: "They danced and they drove and they rode,
they dined and wined and dressed and flirted and yachted and polo'd and
Casino'd . . . past the low headlands I saw their white sails verily flash, and
through the dusky old shrubberies came the light and sound of their feasts."
All that was missing from those feasts was a decent local wine. Today's feasts
won't have that problem.

GREENVALE VINEYARDS
401-847-3777.
E-mail: operations@
  greenvale.com.
582 Wapping Rd.,
  Portsmouth, RI 02871.
Directions: From Fall River:
  Take Rte. 24 south. Cross
  the Sakonnet River, take
  exit 1. Go under the
  highway and merge with
  Rte 138 south. Pass State
  Police barracks and take
  a left onto Sandy Point
  Ave. Take first right onto
  Wapping Rd. Winery
  driveway is 0.9 mile on
  left. From Newport: Take
  Rte. 138 north. Just past
  the "Entering
  Portsmouth" sign, take a
  right onto Braman's

Picture a tranquil river winding through fields,
marshes, and vineyards. Picture a charming
Victorian house and stable-cum-tasting-room designed by famed Boston architect John Sturgis in
the 1860s (the buildings are listed on the State and
National Registers of Historic Places). Now picture
yourself sipping delicious wines such as a zesty,
spicy Cabernet Franc and a flavorful, golden Chardonnay. The place is Greenvale Vineyards, which
has been in the same family since the farm first
started in the 19th century. Nancy and Cortlandt
Parker and their daughter, Nancy Parker Wilson,
first planted grapes in 1982 as a means to develop a
productive use of their family farm. At first they
sold grapes to Sakonnet Vineyards, but by the
1990s they started making their own wine. Winemaker Larry Perrine, now at Channing Daughters
on Long Island, got them off to a good start.

Lane. At the end, take a
right into Wapping Rd.,
then a left onto the
winery driveway,
Greenvale Lane.
Owners: Cortlandt and
Nancy Parker.
Open: Sat. & Sun.
12noon–4pm.
Price Range of Wines: $8
for Skipping Stone
White; $17 for Cabernet
Franc.

Currently Richard Carmichael, formerly at Williamsburg Winery, is making the wines. This winery hopscotch is indicative of an industry that has reached maturity, when a skilled, experienced winemaker is indispensable for a winery to be competitive. Greenvale Vineyards' wines are the proof that this is so.

NEWPORT VINEYARDS
401-848-5161;
  fax 401-848-5162.
www.newportvineyards.
  com.
909 East Main Rd. (Rte.
  138), Middletown, RI
  02842.
Directions: From Newport:
  Drive east on Memorial
  Blvd. past Easton's
  Beach, then north on
  Aquidneck Ave. (Rte.
  138A) to East Main Rd.
  (Rte. 138). Turn right and
  go 0.75 mile to the winery. From Providence:
  Drive east on Rte. 195 to
  Rte. 24 south; take exit 1,
  bear right and follow Rte.
  138 south for 10 minutes.
  Winery is on the left.
Owner: John F. Nunes Jr.
Open: May–Oct.: Mon.–Sat.
  10am–5pm, Sun.
  12noon–5pm, tours Sat.
  & Sun. 1 and 3pm;
  Nov.–Apr.: by appoint-
  ment.
Price Range of Wines: $8.95
  for Seyval Blanc to $17.95
  for Port.

The Nunes family bought the former Vinland Cellars vineyards and winemaking facility in 1988. The recent purchase of a local potato farm has expanded the vineyard by 20 acres. With the possible exception of some Cayuga and Vidal, all the new plantings will be vinifera grapes, including Merlot, Cabernet Franc, Cabernet Sauvignon, and Pinot Blanc (all the vines and rootstocks come from Ontario). The purchase of the Perry potato farm, incidentally, was made possible through a public-private partnership that took advantage of a state program to buy development rights and keep agricultural land green. The winery is off to an excellent start — I've particularly enjoyed an off-dry blend of various white grapes, and Gemini, a smoky red wine made from Merlot and Maréchal Foch grapes. With 30 acres under cultivation, the winery produces 7,000 to 10,000 cases annually.

SAKONNET
VINEYARDS
401-635-8486, 800-998-8486;
  fax 401-635-2101.
www.sakonnetwines.com.
Email:sakonnetri@aol.com.

Sakonnet Vineyards is ideally situated on one of the handful of Rhode Island peninsulas poking out into Narragansett Bay. Established in 1975, Sakonnet is New England's largest winery, with an annual production of 50,000 cases. Owners Susan

162 West Main Rd. (Rte.
77), P.O. Box 197, Little
Compton, RI 02837.

Directions: From I-195 take
Rte. 24 south and
continue to the Tiverton-
Little Compton/ Rte. 77
exit. Go south on Rte. 77
through a traffic light at
Tiverton Four Corners.
Sakonnet is 3 miles from
this junction on the left.

Owners: Susan and Earl
Samson.

Open: June–Oct.: daily
10am–6pm; Nov.–May:
daily 11am–5pm.

Price Range of Wines: $6.75
for blended wines; $9.75
for Estate Fumé Vidal;
$20 for Estate Cabernet
Franc.

Special Events: Cooking
classes, food and wine
events throughout the
year.

Special Feature: The Roost,
a B&B.

- Chardonnay
- Gewürztraminer
- Vidal Blanc
- Fumé Blanc
- Sparkling Wine

and Earl Samson came to the wine business from backgrounds far removed from anything resembling agriculture — she from the Broadway theater, he from the world of investments and capital venture — but they have embraced Sakonnet Vineyards as a way of life as much as a commercial undertaking. Winemaker John Sotelo came to Sakonnet from Iron Horse Vineyards in Sonoma in 1994, while vineyard manager Joetta Kirk has been here since 1983. Most of the grapes for the winery's premium wines are from Sakonnet's own 45-acre vineyard, although some additional grapes are purchased, mostly from local vineyards.

Particularly noteworthy among Sakonnet's overall excellent wines is the Gewürztraminer, with a powerful, floral aroma, rich flavor, and good body; it's a good sipping wine and an excellent accompaniment to a variety of foods, from smoked salmon to spicy Chinese menus. The Vidal Blanc has flavors reminiscent of ripe peaches and melons, plus enough acidity to make it a fine accompaniment to shrimp, oysters, and other seafood. The barrel-fermented Fumé Blanc is another classy food-friendly wine, with flavor that lingers like the glow after a perfect sunset. The Chardonnay is round and rich. The sparkling wine — not yet released when I tasted it — promises a combination of power and finesse as impressive as any non-Champagne sparkling wine I've ever tasted. Sakonnet also produces a few inexpensive, agreeable, lightweight wines for its Newport Series, including America's Cup Red and White, and Eye of the Storm, a fruity blush named after the hurricane that devastated much of the surrounding area while sparing the Sakonnet vineyards a few years ago. Sakonnet's Seaborne series is a blend of domestic wine plus wines brought in from France. As many Eastern winemakers struggle to find an adequate supply of grapes, this type of venture may become more common in the future.

Sakonnet is set in a particularly attractive location, and Little Compton is a charming and attractive New England village. Swimming beaches, fishing, and historic attractions are nearby. The Roost, a Bed & Breakfast located in the original farmhouse on the property of Sakonnet Vineyards, has three nicely furnished bedrooms, each with its own bath.

Joetta Kirk

Joetta Kirk never set out to become a vineyard manager. On the contrary, her career path began evolving in a perfectly ordinary, conventional way. First she was a hairdresser, then a salesperson in a shop, followed by a stint in an advertising agency. Along the way she fell in love, got married . . . and got divorced.

At the time of the divorce, she was living in a cottage on an estate in rural Massachusetts, where she agreed to do groundswork in exchange for rent. Her fate was sealed as she embarked on her lifelong love affair with agriculture.

Characteristically, Joetta first learned everything she could about managing an agricultural property, from property management to equipment maintenance. Then, on a whim, she contacted Jim and Lolly Mitchell, the original owners of Rhode Island's Sakonnet Vineyards, after reading an article about their winery. The Mitchells, who happened to be looking for someone who knew how to operate a tractor, invited her to lunch, and the rest, as they say, is history.

Joetta Kirk became not just Sakonnet's vineyard manager, but also one of the most respected authorities on cool-climate vineyards, especially those in the Atlantic coastal states. For almost two decades she literally spent her life in the vineyards, habitually putting in seven-day weeks. "It was stupid and crazy," she sighs, "but I needed to learn a lot. And I *did* learn a lot, and I also witnessed many extraordinary changes during that time." What are some of these changes?

"One is that the technology of growing grapes in marginal regions has advanced significantly in the last ten years," Joetta explains. "The difference between the early 1980s and the 1990s is dramatic. Take the advancement of clonal selection: we've found that the most popular Chardonnay clone in California isn't that good here. The clone that's right for us is called Colmar, from France.

"Then there is the issue of canopy management that I first heard about at an international symposium in New Zealand in 1988. [Canopy management refers to pruning and trellising techniques that allow sunlight to reach all parts of the vine.] If some parts of the vine are shaded, it's defeating itself. You want the plant to photosynthesize properly, and we now know you have to supply sunlight to the leaves, the shoots, and the fruit. You should not allow the vines to droop to the ground."

Although Joetta talks about building more of a personal life after all these years of devotion to the vine, it is clear that the vineyard still enthralls her. "I can't imagine another crop that would be as fascinating as vines," she confesses. "A vineyard is a controlled environment that wants to run amok. There's an emotional bond there. It's a contest between grower and vine and you wonder who's going to win; who's going to be happy. Of course, I want both to win."

Joetta mentioned another worker at Sakonnet who trims the hedges around the vineyard. "He comes in sometimes to tell me the vines look happy. So we go out and stand there admiring them. And you know, they *do* look happy."

OTHER SOUTHERN NEW ENGLAND WINERIES

DIAMOND HILL VINEYARDS (800-752-2505; fax 401-333-8520; www.favor-label.com; e-mail: berntson@efortress.com; 3145 Diamond Hill Rd., Cumberland, RI 02864) This winery specializes in fruit wines, but it does have a four-and-a-half acre vineyard from which an exceptionally good Pinot Noir wine is produced in limited amounts (about 300 cases annually). When the weather is too cool to make red wine, owners Clara and Peter Berntson turn out a dry, crisp Pinot Noir Blanc — a white that would be a fine match for local seafood. The vineyard's total annual production of all wines is about 3,000 cases.

NANTUCKET VINEYARD (508-228-9235; fax 508-325-5145; e-mail: ack-wine@nantucket.net; Bartlett Farm Rd., Nantucket, MA 02554; Mail: P.O. Box 2700, Nantucket, MA 02584) Nantucket is a particularly difficult location for a vineyard, as the island is unprotected from the elements by a landmass. Nantucket Vineyards cultivated vines on their site for a number of years, but the grapes had a hard time ripening fully in this microclimate. The vines are now gone, and all grapes are imported from the mainland for the wines made here. Tastings occur in the spring, summer, and fall.

Oysters

New England's commercial fishing fleet is still productive, and so is a new breed of farmer: The aquaculturist, or farmer of the sea, raises fish and shellfish in inlets and salt ponds near the shore. While most of the local seafood is well suited to Eastern wines, there is nothing quite so delicious as the taste of sweet and briny oysters fresh from the sea accompanied by one of the lively white wines from the Atlantic coastal regions.

Like grapes, the flavor of oysters varies tremendously, depending on where they are raised. No one yet understands all the factors that contribute to this variation in flavor, but it is safe to assume that the degree of salinity, as well as the fluctuations in water temperature, may affect both the oysters and the microscopic algae, called phytoplankton, upon which they feed.

While oysters from different locales have individual flavors, they all — except for the French Belon oyster that one East Coast farmer is beginning to experiment with — originate from the same oyster family. Whether they are called Bluepoint, Peconic Bay, Wellfleet, Fishers Island, or Cotuit, virtually all oysters raised on the East Coast are grown from the seed of the American oyster.

CUTTYHUNK SHELLFISH FARMS (508-990-1317 in summer, 508-636-2072 in winter; Bayview Drive, P.O. Box 51, Cuttyhunk Island, MA 02713. Raw bar open: May–Oct.)

One of the most notable oyster farms is located just off the coast of Massachusetts, not far from Westport Rivers winery. Oyster farms, like vineyards, are vulnerable to weather patterns, explains owner Seth Garfield. In addition to oysters, Cuttyhunk also harvests wild quahog clams. The plan is to gradually begin cultivating these clams as they become less available in the wild. Cuttyhunk oysters may be enjoyed in many East Coast restaurants, from Boston to New York. Visitors are welcome at the farm. A ferry travels to the island from New Bedford.

MOONSTONE OYSTERS (401-783-3360; e-mail: oyster@ids.net; 264 Foddering Farm Rd., Narragansett, RI 02882. Open by appointment only).

Moonstone supplies its trademarked oysters to some of the best restaurants in the East, including Manahattan's acclaimed Le Bernardin and the Oyster Bar in New York's Grand Central Station. Both native species and Belon oysters are raised in coastal salt ponds at Moonstone; scallops are grown as well.

FISHERS ISLAND (516-788-7899)

Fishers Island oysters are raised in nets off the harbor bottom on Fishers Island, NY, a private island nestled between Connecticut and Long Island in Long Island Sound. Ninety percent of the oysters go to restaurants in Manhattan, while the rest are reserved for other East Coast restaurants. Not open to the public.

LONG ISLAND

The dramatic main building at Pellegrini Vineyards, Cutchogue.

Marguerite Thomas

Long Island is a 120-mile-long bed of gravel and silt left behind by a glacier sliding in slow motion over the land some 10,000 years ago. Looking at the flat and almost treeless land now, it is hard to believe that when the first Europeans arrived they found a thickly forested place inhabited mostly by bears and snakes. A small population of Native Americans planted corn and tilled the fields lying beyond the sandy beaches.

Like their predecessors, the European newcomers found that because of well-drained soil and temperate climate, Long Island was a good place to grow a variety of crops. Many of the early settlers raised table grapes on arbors near their houses. In the 1950s, John Wickham planted the first experimental vinifera grapes on his farm in Cutchogue, on Long Island's North Fork. Rather than attempt to make wine, he sold the grapes at his farm stand.

Today, 14 of Long Island's 18 wineries are on the North Fork, a 159-square-mile band of well-drained soil. Surrounded on three sides by water, with the moderating Gulf Stream paralleling the island some 50 miles offshore, this region has the longest, coolest growing season of any viticultural region in the Northeast. Because the water cools down slowly in the winter, reflecting heat back onto the land, the severe freezes that threaten other regions are mostly unknown here. In the summer, the water warms up gradually, keeping temperatures from soaring disastrously.

The North Fork is the sunniest part of New York State, with at least 210 growing days per season (compared to 150 days in the Finger Lakes) This long and sunny season allows vinifera grapes, whose ripeness is often unpredictable from year to year in other areas in the Northeast, to ripen consistently here. Furthermore, the constant sea breezes that blow across the vineyards discourage the formation of molds and mildew on the grapes.

This is not to say that the area is trouble-free. In addition to the usual vagaries of weather and pests that threaten viticulture everywhere, Long Island's vineyards are particularly susceptible to damage from wind and hurricanes, as well as from great flocks of birds, who love nothing better than to dine on grapes.

Alex and Louisa Hargrave planted Long Island's first commercial vineyard in 1972. There were four more by 1980, when the first big flush of vineyard planting on Long Island began in earnest. During the economic slump of the late '80s things slowed down, but today, with 2,000 acres of vines and 18 wineries operating on Long Island — and more on the way — the boom may be back.

Virtually all of the grapes grown on Long Island are vinifera. In addition to white grapes such as Chardonnay and Gewürztraminer, Merlot, Cabernet Franc, Cabernet Sauvignon, and other red wine grapes also perform consistently better than they do farther north.

The remarkable improvement in Long Island wines over the past few years can be explained by the increased age of the vines, as well as by better vineyard management that allows the grapes to ripen more completely on the vine. It seems likely that Long Island wines will continue to improve. Based on the quality of the harvest, local vintners already feel that 1998 may be one of the best vintages ever.

Long Island wines are generally more intense in color and flavor than those from New York's Finger Lakes, but they are more delicate and restrained than wines from California. Critics agree that some of the Long Island Chardonnays are as good as any in the world, and interest in the reds also is increasing. "I think we'll be known first for our Merlot," said winemaker Kip Bedell. "The grape ripens just after Chardonnay, and it is our most consistent producer. Eventually, I think we'll be known for our Cabernet Sauvignon and Cabernet Franc too. In good years we already make world-class red wines."

Long Island wines, with an average price of $12 per bottle, are the most expensive in the East, rivaling California's premium wines. Long Island produces 2 percent of New York State's total wine output, but 90 percent of its high-end wine. With the added bonus of its proximity to New York City, the most sophisticated and largest per-capita wine consumption center in the East, Long Island has a unique marketing advantage. Long Island sells about 10 percent of its crop each year to other wineries, mostly in New York State, New Jersey, and New England. Despite the ever-present threat of development, farmland remains agricultural as potato fields continue to metamorphose into vineyards. Two significant vineyards were planted in 1997, and at least two more are in the works — harbingers of new wineries.

Long Island's wine country is approximately a two-hour drive from Manhattan, and an hour and a half by ferry from Connecticut. Most of Long Island's wineries are located on the North Fork, along a 35-mile-long strip of land that is scarcely five miles wide. The drive to the South Fork wineries will take approximately three hours from Manhattan. They can be reached from the North Fork by driving through Riverhead or by taking the ferries that connect to Shelter Island.

NORTH FORK

BEDELL CELLARS
516-734-7537;
  fax 516-734-5788.
www.bedellcellars.com.
E-mail: wines@bedell
  cellars.com.
Main Rd. (Rte. 25),
  Cutchogue, NY 11935.
Directions: From I-495 take
  exit 73 in Riverhead,
  continue east on Old
  Country Rd. (Rte. 58) to
  Rte. 25 east. Continue
  east to winery.
Owners: Kip and Susan
  Bedell.
Open: Daily 11am–5pm.
Price Range of Wines: $7.49
  for Cygnet to $27.50 for
  Eis.

• Cygnet
• Chardonnay
• Merlot
• Cabernet
• Cupola
• Eis

Bedell is housed in a turn-of-the-century potato barn that has been embellished in an understated fashion with stained glass windows and a small tasting bar. There are 30 acres of fields planted with grapes, and the winery bottles 6,200 cases annually. Bedell wine labels are easily recognized by the stylized pair of swans on a black-and-white background. "We wanted to represent some of Long Island's marine bird life on the label," explains owner-winemaker Kip Bedell.

The most popular Bedell wine, called Cygnet, is an alluring blend dominated by Riesling and Gewürztraminer grapes. "It's as close to a blush wine as we'll ever get here," says Kip. But this luscious and somewhat sweet wine is far more complex and classy than any blush could hope to be. The Reserve Chardonnay is soft and elegant with discreet, rather than overbearing, vanilla flavors picked up from oak barrels and malolactic fermentation. This is a particularly good wine to serve with chili, says Kip. Cabernet and Merlot are both exceptional, as is Cupola, a blend of Cabernet Sauvignon and Cabernet Franc. Main Road Red, a blend of 80 percent Cabernet Sauvignon/20 percent Merlot, is an easy-drinking wine that's just the thing to have with informal foods. The label on this wine depicts the old red '51 Ford pickup that has been put out to pasture next to the winery. Bedell's Merlot and Cabernet Sauvignon are excellent, as is Eis, a Riesling dessert wine.

BIDWELL VINEYARDS
800-698-9463;
  fax 516-734-6763.

In the attractive, new, sun-filled tasting room overlooking the vineyards, visitors can sample Chardonnay, Sauvignon Blanc, Merlot, Cabernet

Kip Bedell

It was a slow journey from running a fuel oil business to opening a winery, but John (Kip) Bedell inched along his chosen path patiently. After buying a potato farm in Cutchogue in 1980, Kip and his wife, Susan, spent the next ten years commuting from their home in Garden City to Long Island's North Fork. Gradually they began planting grapes and tending the vineyard. When he arrived on the North Fork, there were only four other pioneering wineries — Hargrave, Lenz, Pindar, and Peconic Bay. Barely aware of what the others were doing, each invented his own rules for growing grapes and turning out wine, learning by trial and error what would work in this environment.

Kip Bedell made his first wines in 1989. He had, as it turned out, selected the perfect site for a vineyard. He also seemed to be gifted with an unusually fine palate and a talent for creating superior wine. "Nobody — nobody — is more gifted," said *The New York Times* writer Howard G. Goldberg in *Fine Wine Folio*.

In 1990, after ten years of juggling winemaking and marketing with the family fuel-oil business, he sold the oil company. He and Susan moved to Cutchogue and he became a full-time winemaker. "I'm still in a business that depends on the weather. And I'm still just pumping liquid from one container to another," he jokes, "but at least now I can drink the product."

Kip Bedell is a winemaker's winemaker, a widely respected technician and experienced vintner to whom others turn for inspiration and advice. He also makes some of the best wines in the region. "There's no doubt that some of our earlier wines weren't great," he acknowledges. "Our vines were young and we made some mistakes. We're still fine-tuning some of our viticultural practices, but there's been a great improvement over the past five years."

Marguerite Thomas

The future looks rosy from Kip Bedell's perspective. "We're sitting next to the biggest market in the world, which we've only just begun to tap," he explains, cocking his head in the direction of New York City. In fact, the market is already beginning to respond. Bedell wines are sold in several Manhattan stores and in many of the city's finest restaurants. "The Long Island style is just beginning to evolve. We'll be able to define it better when our region gets a little more time under its belt. We're poised right on the edge of a very exciting time."

North Rd. (Rte. 48),
Cutchogue, NY 11935.
Directions: From I-495 take
exit 73 in Riverhead,
continue east on Old
Country Rd. (Rte. 58) to
Rte. 25. Continuing east,
turn left on Rte. 105 and
go to end, Sound Ave.
Turn right, go east 6-7
miles on Sound Ave. to
Rte. 48, continue 2-3
miles to winery on the
right.
Owners: Bob, Jim, and
Kerry Bidwell.
Open: Daily 11am–5pm.
Price Range of Wines: $9.99
for White Riesling to $27
for Cabernet Sauvignon.

COREY CREEK VINEYARDS
516-765-4168;
fax 516-765-1468.
www.liwines.com/corey
creek.
Main Rd. (Rte. 25), P.O. Box
921, Southold, NY 11971.
Directions: From I-495 take
exit 73 in Riverhead,
continue east on Old
Country Rd. (Rte. 58) to
Rte. 25 east. Continue
east to Southold.
Owners: Joel and Peggy
Lauber.
Open: Daily 11am–5pm.
Price Range of Wines:
$10.49 for Corey Creek
Rosé to $17.99 for Merlot.

GRISTINA VINEYARDS
516-734-7089;
fax 516-734-7114.
www.mcadam.buyrite.
com/gristina.
Main Rd. (Rte. 25), P.O.
Box 1269, Cutchogue, NY
11935.
Directions: From I-495 take
exit 73 in Riverhead,
continue east on Old

Sauvignon, and Riesling. Bidwell produces 8,000 cases of wine from 30 acres of vines.

Joel and Peggy Lauber bought an established vineyard in 1993 with the intention of selling grapes to local wineries. The temptation to have their own label proved overwhelming, and Corey Creek now has 30 acres of vines, a tasting room, and handsome labels, but no winery. Various North Fork winemakers make the wines (including Chardonnay and Merlot); about 3,500 cases are produced annually.

Before the Gristinas purchased their property, it was a potato farm. Now it is a modern vineyard and state-of-the-art winery, owned by Jerry Gristina, M.D., a physical medicine specialist, and his family.

Gristina's son, Peter, manages the business and vineyards. Coming from a family who respects and understands wine (his parents owned a 5,000-bottle cellar), Peter grew up with a keen interest in the

Peter Gristina, manager,
Gristina Vineyards.

Marguerite Thomas

Country Rd. (Rte. 58) to Rte. 25. Continue east to winery.

Owners: The Gristina family.

Open: Daily 11am–5pm.

Price Range of Wines: $8.49 for Avalon (sweet white Riesling-Muscat) to $27.99 for Andy's Field Cabernet Sauvignon.

Special Events: Gristina hosts seminars and other popular events all year.

• Chardonnay
• Cabernet Sauvignon
• Merlot
• Avalon

subject. When the Gristinas purchased the Long Island property in 1983, it seemed natural that Peter would come to work here, especially after apprenticing with North Fork's guru-growers Dave and Steve Mudd, who taught him how to plant, grow, and prune vines.

Among the best of Gristina's very fine wines are the Andy's Field Chardonnay, Cabernet Sauvignon, and Merlot. These wines are made only in the best years, ". . . when Mother Nature gives you a true Indian Summer," says Peter Gristina, who determines when to harvest by going down the rows of vines tasting grapes. "I test the tannins on my teeth without paying much attention to anything else. I just go by the taste." Named after Peter's grandfather, Andy Criscolo, who helped Peter plant the vineyard in 1984, the Andy's Field wines demonstrate the importance of mature vineyards, fully ripe grapes, and just the right amount of flavor from barrel fermentation.

Gristina also makes a very pleasing barrel-fermented, oak-aged Chardonnay, a Merlot with a touch of Cabernet Sauvignon added for backbone, a well-rounded Cabernet Sauvignon with complex aromas, and a fine, perky Rosé of Cabernet Sauvignon. Avalon is an appealing semi-sweet white wine. Gristina has 30 acres under cultivation, and annual production is around 5,500 cases. At the back of the tasting room, huge windows look down into the cellar, giving visitors a good view of the tanks and other winery apparatus.

HARGRAVE VINEYARD

516-734-5111, 800-734-5158;
fax 516-734-5485.
North Rd. (Rte. 48), P.O.
Box 927, Cutchogue, NY
11935.
Directions: From I-495 take
exit 73 in Riverhead,
continue east on Old
Country Rd. (Rte. 58) to
Rte. 25. Continue east to
Cutchogue. Rte. 48 is just
north of Rte. 25 and
parallel to it.
Owners: Louisa and Alex
Hargrave.
Open: May–Dec.: daily 11
am–5pm.
Price Range of Wines: $6.99
for Chardonette to $35
for the 1995 Pinot Noir
(while it lasts).
Special Feature: Tiffany
stained-glass window in
winery.
Special Events: Art shows,
concerts, and wine
seminars.

• Chardonnay
• Pinot Noir

Hargrave was the first commercial vineyard and winery on Long Island. Like many American vintners, Louisa and Alex Hargrave did not set out to be winemakers. Louisa had graduated from Smith College and Alex was getting his degree in Chinese from Harvard. They lived in Boston and drank great French wines while contemplating a scholarly life. But then Alex was sidelined by back surgery. After a period of recuperation in New York's Finger Lakes region and California, the couple gradually became more interested in winemaking than in academia. After searching up and down both coasts for an appropriate spot to make the French-style wines they loved, they heard about John Wickham, a farmer who was raising a small, experimental plot of vinifera grapes in Cutchogue. If he could do it on a modest scale, they reasoned, why shouldn't they succeed on a larger one?

They planted their first vines in 1973. "We were here eight years before anyone else came," said Louisa. "At that time we weren't thinking in terms of this becoming a viticultural region someday. One reason we came here is that it was a farm community, so we knew we could get tractor parts."

Today the Hargraves own 84 acres, of which about 40 are planted. They produce 8,000 to 10,000 cases a year, depending on the vintage. Their wines include a mellifluous Chardonnay and a good Pinot Noir. The handsome winery which, like so many others in the region began its life as a potato and hay barn, looks now as if it's on the way to becoming a wine museum. Among the objects on display are a Greek amphora from 209 B.C. and a spectacular Tiffany stained-glass window.

For months, the buzz on Long Island was that the Hargraves, exhausted after so many years in the wine business, were ready to move on to another life. By the summer of 1998 the rumors became official: Hargrave Vineyard is on the market. "It might take years to sell," Louisa says. "Our main concern is that whoever takes over be well equipped to do it." Those of us who have admired the Hargraves' contributions and dedication to fine winemaking also have our fingers crossed that this will be so.

JAMESPORT VINEYARDS

Phone & fax: 516-722-5256.
842 Main Rd., P.O. Box 842,
Jamesport, NY 11947.

Jamesport produces about 5,000 cases of wine mostly from its own 42-acre vineyard (which includes one of the highest elevations in the region at 40-plus feet.) Fourteen different wines, from

Directions: From I-495 take exit 73 in Riverhead, continue east on Old Country Rd. (Rte. 58) to Rte. 25. Continue east to winery.
Owner: Ron Goerler Sr.
Open: Daily 10am–6pm.
Price Range of Wines: $9.95 for the semi-dry Island Blanc to $18.95 for the sparkling Grande Cuvée.

LAUREL LAKE VINEYARDS

516-298-1420;
fax 516-298-1405.
E-mail: laurellake@email. msm.com.
3165 Main Rd. (Rte. 25), Laurel, NY 11948.
Directions: From I-495 take exit 73 in Riverhead, continue east on Old Country Rd. (Rte. 58) to Rte. 25 east. Continue east to winery.
Owner: Michael McGoldrick.
Open: Daily 11am–6pm.
Price Range of Wines: $7.99 for Windsong; $13.99 for Merlot; $23.99 for Cabernet Sauvignon (while it lasts).

LENZ WINERY

516-734-6010,
800-974-9899 (NY only); fax 516-734-6069.
www.lenzwine.com.
Main Rd. (Rte. 25),
P.O. Box 28, Peconic, NY 11958.
Directions: From I-495 take exit 73 in Riverhead, continue east on Old Country Rd. (Rte. 58) to Rte. 25. Continue east to winery.
Owners: Peter and Deborah Carroll.

Sauvignon Blanc through Cabernet Franc, may be sampled in the very popular tasting room.

In 1994, Michael McGoldrick bought 13 acres of Chardonnay vines that had been planted in 1980. Another 30 acres of Merlot, Cabernet Franc, and Cabernet Sauvignon vines have recently been planted. In the winery, which opened in 1997, visitors can taste Chardonnay, Rosé, and the slightly sweet Windsong; Cabernet Sauvignon is available only as long as present supplies last. Annual production of all wines is 6,000 cases.

Winemaker Eric Fry got his start in California at the Robert Mondavi and Jordan wineries under the tutelage of the legendary André Tchelistcheff. Following a stint in Australia, he made his way to the Vinifera Wine Cellars in New York's Finger Lakes region and then to Westport Rivers in Massachusetts, settling finally at Lenz in 1989.

The lower sugar content of the Eastern wines, and their lower alcohol content (12 percent versus 14 percent) distinguish them from wines from the warmer regions of California and Australia, says the peripatetic winemaker. Their flavors and the acid structure of the grapes are also different. But the biggest surprise, he says, is the amount of acidity in Eastern wines. "What's the drug of choice for

Open: Daily 10 am–6pm;
winter months: daily
10am–5pm.
Price Range of Wines: $7.99
for Blanc de Noir; $30.00
for Merlot.
Special Events: Wine
tasting parties at various
times throughout year.

- Chardonnay "Vineyard
Selection"
- Pinot Noir
- Cabernet Sauvignon
- Merlot

Eastern winemakers?" he asks. "Acid. First it shocked me. Then I began to get used to it. Now, I want more and more of it all the time, like any true junkie. One advantage of acidity is that it adds to wine's compatibility with food."

With a Viking-like beard and a mane of russet curls, Fry is not the type of winemaker to coddle his grapes. His approach is to let them ripen in the vineyard to a maximum degree and then "mash the hell out of them to extract every bit of color and flavor." The results are red wines that do indeed have good color and flavor intensity, including a wonderfully aromatic Pinot Noir and a rich old-world style Cabernet Sauvignon characterized by cherry flavors and a pleasant, long finish. Lenz Chardonnays tend to be well-rounded, with layers of peach and pear flavors along with a hint of spiciness on the palate. Fry has been experimenting with Pinot Blanc, striving for the kind of fragrant, high-acid wine found in Alsace. Sparkling wines, a passion for Fry, are crisp and elegant. With 60 acres of vines, Lenz is aiming for an annual production of 10,000 cases; current production is about 9,000. The tasting room is in a typical converted Long Island potato barn.

MACARI VINEYARDS
516-298-0100;
fax 516-298-8373.
www.macariwines.com.
E-mail: macari@peconic.
net.
150 Bergen Ave., P.O. Box
2, Mattituck, NY 11952.
Directions: From I-495 take
exit 73 in Riverhead,
continue east on Old
Country Rd. (Rte. 58) to
Rte. 25 east. Turn left
(north) on Rte. 105 and
continue to Rte. 48. Turn
right on Rte. 48 and
continue east. From Rte.
48 turn onto Bergen Ave.
and continue straight to
winery.
Owners: The Macari family.
Open: Daily 11am–5pm.

It's still too early to evaluate the wines at Macari, one of Long Island's youngest wineries (the tasting room opened 1998), but there is clearly enormous potential here for producing top-notch wines. Joe Macari Sr. and his son, Joe Jr., come to the North Fork from a lifetime in the real estate business. The Macaris seem to be giving new meaning to the old cliché that the best way to make a small fortune is to take a large one and start a winery. With money seemingly no object, they've built an immensely attractive tasting room designed by architect Carol Vinci (who has produced some of Manhattan's hot-chic restaurants such as Patria and Citrus). They've purchased one of the largest vineyard sites in the region: a 330-acre former potato farm. The first 145 acres of vineyards they've planted have been scrupulously prepared. "We've used 150,000 tons of fish so far, plus other organic materials for compost," says Joe Jr., emphasizing that no chemical fertilizers will be applied. They've installed $40,000 worth of birdnetting, and invested in state-of-the art planters, harvesters, and computers. They've hired Gilles Martin, a French winemaker who's had stints at sparkling wine shrines such as Roederer and Gloria Ferrer. I tasted the Macari '97 barrel-fermented Chardonnay drawn from stainless steel tanks just before it was bottled, and the Rosé made from Cabernet Sauvignon and Cabernet Franc. Both wines showed tremendous promise. All signs point to a great future for this exciting new winery.

OSPREY'S DOMINION
516-765-6188;
  fax 516-765-1903.
www.opsreysdominion.
  com.
E-mail:winemakr@
  ospreysdominion.com.
44075 Main Rd. (Rte. 25),
  P.O. Box 275, Peconic,
  NY 11958.
Directions: From I-495 take
  exit 73 in Riverhead,
  continue east on Old
  Country Rd. (Rte. 58) to

Owned by two pilots, the winery is named after the majestic fish hawk that soars over Long Island skies. Osprey's Dominion has been producing its own wines since 1993, although the oldest of its 72 acres of vines was planted in 1986. Annual production is now 20,000 cases annually. The quality of the wines is still somewhat uneven, but the '95 Cabernet Sauvignon and the Regina Maris Chardonnay are both appealing, well-made wines. The Regina Maris, a particularly good value at $9.99, is named for a resident tall ship;

Rte. 25 east. Continue
east to winery.
Owners: Bud Koehler and
Bill Tyree.
Open: Jun.–Sept.: Mon.–Sat.
10am–6pm, Sun.
12noon–6pm; Oct.–May:
Mon.–Sat. 10am–5pm,
Sun. 12noon–5pm.
Price Range of Wines: $9.99
for Regina Maris
Chardonnay and Non-
Vintage Cabernet to $25
for Reserve Chardonnay.

PALMER VINEYARDS
516-722-9463, 516-722-4080;
fax 516-722-5364.
www.palmervineyards.
com.
Sound Ave. (Rte. 48), P.O.
Box 2125, Aquebogue,
NY 11931.
Directions: From I-495 take
exit 73 in Riverhead,
continue east on Old
Country Rd. (Rte. 58) to 4th
traffic light, Osbourne
Ave. Turn left on
Osbourne and continue to
end. Turn right onto
Sound Ave. and go 6 miles
to winery on the left.
Owner: Robert Palmer.
Open: Apr.–Oct.: daily
11am–6pm; Nov.–Mar.:
daily 11am–5pm.
Price Range of Wines: $8.99
for Blush Wine; $24.99
for Bordeaux-style Select
Reserve Red.
Special Events: Annual
Yard Sale (wine
bargains), Memorial Day
Celebration, Fourth of
July Hot Dog Event,
Harvest Festival, all with
music on the deck.

• Pinot Blanc
• Barrel-fermented
Chardonnay
• Gewürztraminer
• Merlot

part of the sales proceeds go towards the ship's
restoration.

Palmer is owned by Robert Palmer, a former
advertising exec and marketing genius who has
parlayed Palmer into what is arguably the most
recognized winery in the East. (Palmer wines are
poured in 23 states and five foreign countries.) One
of the reasons for Palmer's success is its former
winemaker, Dan Kleck, who was recently wooed
away from Long Island by California giant Kendall
Jackson Winery. With any luck, Palmer wines will
continue to dazzle even without the talented Kleck.
Palmer's production, at 20,000 cases, is sizable
compared to other wineries in the region, and the
100-acre vineyard is bigger than most. Even the
wines are fuller-bodied and bolder-flavored than
the average Eastern libation.

Palmer's barrel-fermented Chardonnay exhibits
complex fruit and vanilla aromas. The Pinot Blanc
and Gewürztraminer both have the lush characteristics of classic Alsatian varieties. Dan Kleck once
remarked that the wines are also distinguished by
a whiff of citrus, a lemony flavor that is imparted
by Long Island soils. There is also a hint of salt air
in the wines, he said; the ocean not only affects flavor but also moderates temperatures and humidity
levels.

An ideal spot for a vineyard, right? Not quite.
The land is in the path of a North-South flyway for
migratory birds, so every acre must be covered by
birdnetting. There is the added danger of hurricanes from late August until October.

When there's no hurricane afoot, visitors can
take advantage of Palmer's outdoor picnic area. In

inclement weather, they can move into the English pub-style tasting room and sit in one of the Victorian booths that really were once part of an English pub.

PAUMANOK VINEYARDS

516-722-8800; fax 516-722-5110.
Main Rd. (Rte. 25), P.O. Box 741, Aquebogue, NY 11931.
Directions: From I-495 take exit 73 in Riverhead, continue east on Old Country Rd. (Rte. 58) to Rte. 25. Continue east to winery.
Owners: Charles and Ursula Massoud.
Open: Daily 11am–6pm; Sun. 12noon–6pm.
Price Range of Wines: $12.99 for Cabernet Sauvignon to $39 for a half bottle of the rare Late Harvest Sauvignon Blanc.
Special Events: Sunset at the Vineyard (music, gourmet dishes from local restaurants, wine tastings), classical music, jazz concerts, Harvest Festival, Christmas music and wine tasting.

• Chenin Blanc
• Merlot
• Assemblage
• Late Harvest Sauvignon Blanc

"Paumanok" was Long Island's native name. Lebanese-born Charles Massoud, Paumanok's owner, says that he woke up one day and realized that he would never become the president of IBM, where he was an executive. He was determined to start looking for something else that would provide an interesting and creative outlet for his interests and skills. The Massouds elected to settle on Long Island's North Fork, where they began planting vines in 1983. (Ursula Massoud's family has been in the wine business in Germany for several generations.) Finally, in 1992, Charles left IBM.

Charles has long claimed that once the vines were mature enough, his wines would be exceptional. Time — and good winemaking skills — has proven him right. Initially, Paumonok's strength was in its white wines. The Chardonnay, Riesling, and Chenin Blanc are all impeccable. The Late Harvest Riesling and Sauvignon Blanc ought to convert more Americans to dessert wines. They might be served by themselves at the end of a special meal or with a simple dessert such as biscotti. "Don't swallow sweet wines too quickly," advises Charles. "Let them sit in your mouth for a moment while you look for the dried-fruit flavors."

Within the last couple of years, the reds have caught up and may now be counted among the very top labels on Long Island. Most of the reds are unfiltered and aged in both French and American oak. The Grand Vintage Merlot is big and bold. The Cabernet Sauvignon is lively and long-lasting in the mouth. And the Assemblage (a Bordeaux-style blend of Cabernet Sauvignon, Cabernet Franc, and Merlot) is, quite simply, a knockout — too bad only a few hundred cases of it are made, and at that, only in good years.

The winery has 50 acres under cultivation, producing 7,000 cases a year.

PECONIC BAY VINEYARDS
516-734-7361;
  fax 516-734-5876.
www.liwines.peconicbay. com.
Main Rd. (Rte. 25), P.O. Box 709, Cutchogue, NY 11935.
Directions: From I-495 take exit 73 in Riverhead, continue east on Old Country Rd. (Rte. 58) to Rte. 25 east. Continue east to winery.
Owner: Ray Blum.
Open: Mon.–Fri. 10:30am–5pm; Sat–Sun. 10:30am–6pm.
Price Range of Wines: $8.99 for Blush; $10.99 for Vin de l'Ile Blanc; $25 for Merlot Epic Acre.

PELLEGRINI VINEYARDS
516-734-4111;
  fax 516-734-4159.
www.pellegrinivineyards. com.
23005 Main Rd. (Rte 25), Cutchogue, NY 11935.
Directions: From I-495 take exit 73 in Riverhead, continue east on Old Country Rd. (Rte. 58) to Rte. 25. Continue east to winery.
Owners: Joyce and Bob Pellegrini.
Open: Daily 11am–5pm.
Price Range of Wines: $8.99 for East End Select Chardonnay; $23.99 for "Vintner's Pride Encore" (Cabernet blend); $25 for a half bottle of "Finale" (dessert wine).

- Chardonnay
- Merlot
- Cabernet Sauvignon
- Cabernet Franc
- Finale

Retired air-traffic controller Ray Blum is owner, vineyard manager, and winemaker at Peconic Bay Vineyards. The vineyard, which has grown from 30 acres to 76 in recent years, is planted in Chardonnay, Riesling, Cabernet Sauvignon, and Merlot. Twelve different wines may be sampled in the tasting room. Total production is 6,000–7,000 cases per year.

Pellegrini is across the street from the site of Fort Cutchogue, where some of Long Island's first European settlers lived in the 17th century. The communal farmland surrounding the fort was known as "Commonage," which is the name Pellegrini uses for a line of very good, easy-sipping, everyday wines. Pellegrini also produces some of Long Island's finest, most serious wines. The Vintner's Pride Chardonnay is lush, with a big burst of fresh pear flavor and enough acidity to make it a good food wine. The Cabernet Sauvignon is full bodied, with hints of mint, cedar, and chocolate flavors, while the Merlot is chockablock full of fresh plum and berry tones. "If Bordeaux-style Cabernet is the king of red wines," says Australian-born winemaker Russell Hearn, "Merlot is the queen. It's supple and soft, not as hard and closed as Cabernet." Pellegrini's superb Cabernet Franc proves that this may be Long Island's best grape variety. Another of Russ Hearn's winners is Finale, a lush dessert wine made from late-harvested Gewürztraminer and Sauvignon Blanc grapes that are frozen before pressing.

Pellegrini is owned by Joyce and Bob Pellegrini

— she's a retired teacher, he's the owner of a successful New York graphic design business. Everything about this winery reflects the good taste of a superior designer, from the handsome, stylized wine labels to the modern, cathedral-like tasting room, where a few café tables and chairs provide a nice spot to relax and sip. The building itself, which opened in 1992, is the North Fork's most spectacular winery, designed by local architects Samuels and Steelman. It is built around a grassy courtyard flanked by white columns. The cellars lie beneath. Outdoor balconies allow visitors to look down into the tank room, where 10,000 cases of wine are processed each year. Thirty acres are being added to the 32 acres already under cultivation.

PINDAR VINEYARDS

516-734-6200;
    fax 516-734-6205.
Main Rd. (Rte. 25), P.O. Box
    332, Peconic, NY 11958.
Directions: From I-495 take
    exit 73 in Riverhead,
    continue east on Old
    Country Rd. (Rte. 58) to
    Rte. 25. Continue east to
    winery.
Owner: Dr. Herodotus
    Damianos.
Open: Daily 11am–6pm.
Price Range of Wines: $7.99
    for simple blended wines,
    such as Long Island
    Winter White, to

As one might expect from a place named after a Greek poet, Pindar is of heroic proportions. It has a larger production, with about 80,000 cases, and more land, 300 acres planted in vines, than any other winery on Long Island. Even the number of people its picnic pavilion can accommodate, three hundred, is larger than other wineries.

Pindar was founded in 1979 by Dr. Herodotus Damianos, a physician who is affiliated with several Long Island hospitals. And it outdoes its neighbors in other ways as well. The variety of grapes planted is greater: fourteen in all, including the standard Chardonnay, Cabernet, and Merlot, as well as unusual varieties such as Malbec, Viognier, and Pinot Meunier.

$27 for the Cuvée Rare sparkling wine.

Special Events: Food and wine pairings, such as red wine and chocolate desserts in February, Riesling and Irish soda bread in March.

- Cuvée Rare Sparkling Wine
- Merlot

PUGLIESE VINEYARDS
516-734-4057;
fax 516-734-5668.
Main Rd. (Rte. 25), P.O. Box 467, Cutchogue, NY 11935.
Directions: From I-495 take exit 73 in Riverhead, continue east on Old Country Rd. (Rte. 58) to Rte. 25 east. Continue east to winery.
Owners: Patricia and Ralph Pugliese.
Open: Daily, 10am–5pm.
Price Range of Wines: $7.99 for White Table Wine and Blush to $26.99 for Port Bello, a fortified dessert wine.

- Sparkling Wine
- Port Bello

TERNHAVEN CELLARS
516-477-8737.
E-mail: hwesleyw@aol.com.
331 Front St., P.O. Box 758, Greenport, NY 11944.
Directions: From I-495 take exit 73 in Riverhead, continue east on Old Country Rd. (Rte. 58) to Rte. 25. From beginning of Rte. 25 drive 20 miles to Greenport. The winery is on the right after you enter the village.

Pindar produces 18 different wines, including Mythology, Long Island's first blended red wine. Among the winery's fine sparkling wines, Cuvée Rare is particularly outstanding — dry, yet full of rich, pleasing, yeasty flavors. This elegant sparkler is made from 100 percent Pinot Meunier grapes, one of the traditional varietals used in France as a Champagne blending grape.

Winemaker Mark Friszolowski, a Long Island native, has been at Pindar since 1994.

It would be hard not to like this straightforward winery and the Pugliese family who run it. Ralph Sr. declares proudly, "I've been making wine since I was a kid." Ralph Jr.'s photographs of local landscapes hang on the walls. Ralph's wife, Pat, hand-paints special bottles with nail polish (I don't usually like gussied-up bottles, but these are surprisingly pretty). The sparkling wines are particularly good, especially the Blanc de Noirs (100 percent Pinot Noir) and Blanc de Blancs Brut. Port Bello is a delicious Port-style dessert wine made from Merlot and Cabernet. The winery has 37 acres under cultivation and produces 27,000 cases annually.

Ternhaven, which opened in the summer of 1998, is another newcomer with promise. Carole Donlin, a partner in a Manhattan firm providing services for companies reorganizing under bankruptcy laws, is co-owner of Ternhaven along with Harold Watts, an economics professor at Columbia University. Harold, who began making wine in his Manhattan apartment, says that their goals are modest — he's aiming to produce 800–1,000 cases of red wines only (present production is about 600 cases). It's too early to tell, but with five

Owners: Carole Donlin and Harold Watts.
Open: May–Oct.:
Tues.–Sun. 11am–6pm;
Nov.–Dec.: Sat. & Sun. 11am–5pm.
Price Range of Wines: $15.99 for Cabernet Sauvignon to $19.99 for Merlot.

prime acres of 14-year old vines, and with first releases of rich, well-structured Cabernet, Merlot, and Claret (a Bordeaux-style blend), there's good reason to be hopeful about Ternhaven.

OTHER NORTH FORK WINERIES

SCHNEIDER VINEYARDS (P.O. Box 1152, Cutchogue, NY 11935) Despite its name, Schneider owns no vineyards, nor does it have a winery or a tasting room. For the moment, Bruce and Christiane Baker Schneider content themselves with hand-harvesting grapes from the best North Fork vineyards and having Bedell Cellars' Kip Bedell oversee the winemaking. Schneider wines, available in some local restaurants and wine shops or by mail, are absolutely top notch, and the Schneiders do plan to have their own winery in the near future. Keep your eye on this young couple — they have a definite flair for wine. Meanwhile, they can be contacted at their Web site: www.schneider vineyards.com.

SOUTH FORK

CHANNING DAUGHTERS
516-537-7224;
fax 516-537-7243.
E-mail: channingdaughters @peconic.net
1927 Scuttlehole Rd., P.O. Box 2202, Bridge-hampton, NY 11932.
Directions: From I-495 take exit 70. Follow County Rd. south to Montauk Hwy. (Rte. 27) through Southampton commercial district to Water Mill. After about 0.5 mile, watch for sign for Sag Harbor at Scuttle-hole Rd. Vineyard is

This is a brand-new winery — the tasting room opened late July 1998 — whose first efforts are impressive indeed. Channing Daughters (named after the owners' four girls) is proof that if certain rules are followed, you aren't guaranteed fabulous wines, but your chances of producing them are certainly greater. Rule Number One: Be prepared to invest money — lots and lots of money. Walter Channing, for example, is a venture capitalist involved in health care and medical technology whose financial resources could withstand the tremendous expense of starting a vineyard and winery. Second Rule: Every credible winemaker in the world will tell you that good wine begins in the vineyard, so make sure you have great grapes, preferably

about 3 miles from Rte. 27. Owners: Walter and Molly Channing. Open: Daily 11am–5pm. Price Range of Wines: $12 for Scuttlehole Chardonnay to $16.99 for Brick Kiln Chardonnay and Merlot.

- Sauvignon Blanc
- Chardonnay
- Merlot

from older vines. Walter Channing, who began planting vines in 1982, now owns some of the oldest vineyards on the South Fork. Additional grapes from older vines are purchased from North Fork growers. Rule Three: Hire an experienced winemaker who knows what good wine is supposed to taste like (this may seem obvious, but it's amazing how many winemakers lack first-hand knowledge of great wines). Channing Daughters' winemaker, Larry Perrine, formerly winemaker at Gristina, fills both requirements. The rest of the rules are pretty much the same as for any venture: Have high standards, be creative, market your product well, and have a clear vision of your goals. "In sculpting our project into the future we're trying to focus on bright, fresh lighter wines," says Larry. "We're not trying to imitate Pomerol. We want wines in tune with summer dining." All the Channing Daughter wines and Channing Perrine wines (made from small lots of fruit from vines 18 years and older) I've tasted are charming and endlessly interesting. The Sauvignon Blanc is particularly notable as this grape is a relative rarity on Long Island. Made from vines planted in 1975, it's a classic example of my kind of Sauvingon Blanc — not soft and fruity, but lively, fresh, and lightly herbaceous, a wine that demands food.

One more good rule: Set realistic goals. With 21 acres under cultivation, Channing Daughters now produces about 1,500 cases of wine, with an ultimate goal of 7,500.

APHRODITE

**DUCK WALK
  VINEYARDS**
516-726-7555;
  fax 516-726-4395.
231 Montauk Hwy., P.O.
  Box 962, Water Mill NY
  11976.
Owner: Dr. Herodotus
  Damianos.
Directions: Take Rte. 27
  (Montauk Hwy.) all
  the way through
  Southampton to the
  winery, on the left .
Open: Daily 11am–6pm.
Price Range of Wines: $9
  for Pinot Gris,
  Chardonnay, and Pinot
  Blanc to $26.99 for
  Special Reserve Merlot.
Special Events: May–Oct,
  Sat. & Sun., live music
  on the patio.

• Merlot

**SAGPOND VINEYARDS/
  WOLFFER ESTATE**
516-537-5106;
  fax 516-537-5107.
www.sagpondvineyards.
  com.

If it's true that the third time is the charm, Duck Walk Vineyards is in for a good run, and indeed, all signs thus far point to success. Formerly Le Rêve, then Southampton Winery, Duck Walk was launched in 1994 by Pindar's proprietor, Dr. Herodotus Damianos. Duck Walk owns about 38 acres of vines in Southampton plus 50 in Mattituck, and produces about 27,000 cases of wine a year. The good Pinot Noir is a particular surprise since, in general, this grape doesn't grow well on Long Island. Perhaps Duck Walk's Pinot comes from a particularly successful clone. Or possibly the particular four or five acres on which it's grown provide a microclimate well suited to Pinot Noir. Or maybe consultant Dimitri Tchelistcheff dispensed just the right words of advice about winemaking. These are the sort of issues that determine the success of a wine. In any event, Duck Walk's first couple of vintages of Pinot Noir are impressive. Southampton White is an agreeable dry wine, and Aphrodite is a very popular dessert wine that can be stunning in good years. The Merlot Reserve is among Long Island's best.

I applaud this winery's approach to making fewer types of wine, but making them *well*. More wineries in the East would benefit from scaling back their overly long list of different wines, concentrating instead on a few wines beautifully made.

139 Sagg Rd., P.O. Box 9002, Sagaponack, NY 11962.
Owner: Christian Wolffer.
Directions: From I-495 take exit 70 in Manorville. Travel south to Rte. 27. Take Rte. 27 east to Bridgehampton. At the first traffic light after leaving Bridgehampton, turn left onto Sagg Rd.. The winery is 0.25 mile on the right.
Open: May–Oct.: daily 11am–6pm; Nov.–Apr.: daily 11am–5pm. Tours.
Price Range of Wines: $9.99 for a sophisticated, European-style Rosé; $24.99 for Reserve Chardonnay; $34.99 for Pinot Noir.

- Chardonnay
- Merlot

Conditions for growing grapes on the South Fork are sometimes more challenging than on the North Fork: it's a flatter and siltier place, with somewhat cooler temperatures. Grapes that require lighter soils, such as Cabernet Sauvignon, do better on the North Fork, says winemaker Roman Roth. "But in the hot and dry years," he explains, "the South Fork has the advantage with its heavier, loamier soils that hold moisture. The grapes retain more acidity, so we can let them hang longer on the vine with less danger of disease."

Raising grapes wasn't what owner Christian Wolffer had in mind when he first moved out here in 1977. When he purchased his 14-acre potato farm, his goal was to create a horse farm. Today his property — 173 acres in all — includes 13 acres of jumping rings. This enterprise has helped make equestrian pursuits one of the Hamptons' hottest hobbies. Christian also built a nursery, but when Hurricane Gloria blew down all the trees in 1988, he decided to plant a vineyard instead. The first wines were released in 1992, and today the production from 50 acres of vines is about 9,000 cases a year.

Christian Wolffer, a native of Hamburg, Germany, made his fortune in real estate and venture capital investments in South America and Canada. He still travels constantly, racking up a million Frequent Flyer miles a year, while remaining deeply involved in his Long Island projects. When a writer once asked him how he managed to keep up the pace, Christian answered, "I drink a lot of wine and ride a lot."

That wine is getting better every year. The vines have aged enough to yield wines of greater complexity, and Roman's skills, like those of the other first generation of top Long Island vintners, have grown along with their under-standing of the *terroir*. A new vineyard manager has brought improvements, and a new sales force and public-relations team will help broaden the market (Sagpond's wines are already served at Jean-Georges, Montrachet, and other top Manhattan restaurants).

Roman's goal has always been to make wine for food. "The whole structure of wine is meant to accompany food," he says. The palate-cleansing acidity that tempers the fruit-rich flavors of Sagpond's Chardonnays and Merlots does, indeed, make them ideal food wines. The Reserve Chardonnay typically presents a resonant chorus of flavors evoking both fruit and the kind of min-eral quality often found in fine Burgundy whites. The Reserve Chardonnay has concentrated flavors and a rich, almost oily texture, but finishes up with crisp apple nuances at the end. The Merlots have lip-smacking cherry flavors backed up by complex innuendoes derived from long maceration on the skins (up to 28 days, compared to the 15 averaged by many of Roman's Long Island colleagues). Sagpond produces almost 12,000 cases of wine; it owns 45 acres of vineyard and leases 10 more. The Sagpond label, incidentally, has been changed to "Wolffer."

One other project close to Roman's heart is the cheese business he entered into with Ryan Leeman, assistant winemaker at Paumonock Vineyards. Milk is supplied by two cows from a neighboring farm, while Ryan — whose family owns a cheese business in Ohio — provides the expertise. The result is a Swiss Emmenthaler-style cheese that's appropriately well suited to pairing with wine.

SOUTHEASTERN NEW JERSEY AND COASTAL VIRGINIA

Dr. Frank Salek inspects his vines at Sylvin Farms, Germania, New Jersey.

Marguerite Thomas

The Benchlands continue southward along the New Jersey coast and down into coastal Virginia, including the Northern Neck of Virginia (a large peninsula bordered by the Chesapeake Bay and the Potomac and Rappahannock Rivers). Vine-friendly clay/loam and sandy soils, as well as a moderate maritime climate, provide an excellent home for both large and tiny wineries.

SOUTHEASTERN NEW JERSEY

New Jersey has always been known as the Garden State, and today much of its commercial agriculture is in the form of vineyards — just as it was in the mid-1700s, when wine-producing grapes were cultivated in New Jersey for the British Empire. Those early efforts were so successful that in 1767 two New Jersey vintners were praised by London's Royal Society of Arts for producing the first bottles of quality wine from the Colonies. After early triumphs, however, things went downhill. First American vine diseases and then Prohibition brought the state's wine industry to a virtual standstill.

Today, with 15 wineries in the state, wine is once again becoming a viable New Jersey product. With tourism in mind, the state has designated four separate wine trails: The Delaware Valley Wine Trail (including Lafollette and Cream Ridge); the Atlantic Wine Trail (Amalthea, Balic, Cape May, Renault,

Sylvin Farms, and Tomasello); Skyland Wine Trail (Amwell Valley, King's Road, Poor Richard's, and Unionville); and Warren Hills Wine Trail (Alba, Four Sisters, and Tamuzza).

The state has two separate viticultural regions, one in the north, in Warren and Hunterdon counties, the other south and west of Atlantic City. The northern section is in the Uplands country of rolling hills, with limestone, clay, and shale soils. Southern Atlantic County, a Benchlands region, is largely flat, with sandy soils and a maritime climate. Set in the Pine Barrens, the strange landscape features mile after mile of short, stiff pine trees carpeting the countryside like bristles on a giant hairbrush. There isn't a whole lot to distract one in terms of sightseeing or shopping along Routes 30 and 40, where most of the wineries are located, and there are few places to eat or sleep. That this region is so undeveloped is surprising, considering how close it is to major urban centers.

New Jersey wine is almost all made from vinifera grapes these days. While the wine industry is not as advanced as on Long Island, this is a promising region that will undoubtedly develop further in the near future. Cape May, with climate and growing conditions similar to Long Island's, may prove to be one of New Jersey's best viticultural areas, but for now there is only one winery there.

AMALTHEA CELLARS
609-768-8585;
  fax 609-753-1099.
209 Vineyard Rd., Atco, NJ
  08004.
Owners: Louis and Gini
  Caracciolo.
Directions: From NJ
  Turnpike take exit 4.
  Take Rte. 73 south to
  Atco RR station; stay in
  the right lane and take
  the exit for Rte. 30 east.
  Go 2 miles to the first
  right after Atco Lake.
  Travel 1 mile to the
  winery on the right.
Open: Sat. &
  Sun.11am–5pm, or by
  appointment.
Price Range of Wines:
  $6–$20.

• Chardonnay
• "Elara Blanc"

Amalthea is named for one of the moons of Jupiter. So is Metis, Amalthea's blush wine. The winery's logo features a mandala, the concentric geometric image adopted by the Woodstock generation. Does this take you back to the days of patchouli oil, love-ins, Joplin, and Hendrix? The *esprit* here may be from the 1960s, but the wine is a reflection of contemporary tastes. Some 25,000 cases are produced annually from Amalthea's 10-acre vineyard, where both vinifera and hybrid grapes are grown. The Chardonnay is an appealing, well-balanced wine. Elara is a simple sipping wine made of Seyval, Riesling, and Chardonnay. The Chancellor is an unassuming country wine: "our peasant wine" is the way Amalthea describes it.

BALIC WINERY
609-625-2166.
Rte. 40, Box 6623, Mays
    Landing, NJ 08330.
Directions: From Garden
    State Pkwy. take exit 37
    to Rte. 40.
Owner: Salvo Balic.
Open: Mon.–Sat.
    9:30am–5pm., Sun.
    11am–4pm; closed
    Nov. & Dec.
Price Range of Wines:
    $6.95–$11.95

Salvo Balic, a native of the former Yugoslavia, became one of New Jersey's vinous pioneers when he established this winery in 1974. It's a modest place that produces 16 different kinds of wine (40 acres under cultivation), most of them inexpensive. Included in the selection are several wines made from Chancellor and other hybrid grapes. This winery is a good stopover on the way to Atlantic City.

**CAPE MAY WINERY &
    VINEYARD**
609-884-1169;
    fax 609-884-5131.
709 Townbank Rd., Cape
    May, NJ 08204.
Directions: At the south
    end of Garden State
    Pkwy. follow Rte. 9
    south. At 4th traffic light,
    turn right onto Rte. 644.
    At the next light turn
    right onto Rte. 648; go
    one half block to the
    winery, on the left.

The newest and smallest New Jersey winery (and the only one in the state with drip irrigation), Cape May opened July 1, 1984, and now produces from 500 to 800 cases of very attractive Chardonnay, Cabernet, Merlot, and an understandably popular blush wine. Almost all of the wine is now allocated to the best restaurants in Cape May, but owners Joan and Bill Hayes (he's an engineer recently retired from the Coast Guard) plan to expand both vineyard and winery. Let's hope that the high quality of these wines and the

From Cape May Ferry:
Take Rte. 9 north to 2nd
traffic light. Turn left
onto Rte. 644 and
proceed as above.
Owners: Joan and Bill
Hayes.
Price Range of Wines: $10
for Chardonnay; $16 for
Merlot.
Open: by appointment.

- Chardonnay
- Cabernet
- Merlot

attractive Cape May region itself encourages other potential vintners to plant vines in this area.

Gardens of the historic Renault Winery, Egg Harbor, New Jersey

Marguerite Thomas

RENAULT WINERY
609-965-2111;
    fax 609-965-1847.
www.renaultwinery.com.
72 N. Bremen Ave., Egg
    Harbor City, Galloway
    Township, NJ 08213.

Not only is this New Jersey's oldest winery, it's also the longest continuously operating winery with its own vineyard in America. It's worth a visit for its historical importance alone.

Renault Winery was founded by Louis Nicholas Renault, a French Champagne maker, who came to

Directions: From Garden State Pkwy. take the parkway service exit at mile marker #41. Go to the north end of service area and follow the signs to Jimmy Leeds Rd. At the traffic light turn left, then bear right at the fork and continue on Rte. 561 to Bremen Ave. Turn right onto Breman and go 1.5 miles to the winery.

Owner: Joseph P. Milza.

Open: Mon.–Sat. 10am–5pm, Sun. 12noon–5pm.

Price Range of Wines: $6.99 for Pink Lady to $13 for Chardonnay; the popular Blueberry Champagne is $11.99.

Special Features: Lunch cafeteria open Mon.–Sat. 11:30am–3pm; restaurant open Fri., Sat, Sun. until 10pm; Sunday brunch served.

the United States in 1855 to establish a vineyard that would be free of the phylloxera organism that was destroying European vineyards. First he went to California, but he found the vines there were also ravaged by phylloxera. When Renault learned about phylloxera-resistant native American labrusca grapes, he traveled to New Jersey, where labrusca was thriving. Finding a climate and soil that reminded him of France, he settled outside of Egg Harbor and established his own vineyard. By 1870 he was producing Concord grape "Champagne." Before long he had become the largest distributor of sparkling wine in the nation. Egg Harbor (so named because of a profusion of nesting sea birds) also became known as "the wine city."

Louis Renault died in 1913 at the age of 91. The next owner, John D'Agostino, continued to operate the winery even during Prohibition by obtaining a government permit that allowed him to make Renault Wine Tonic, a product that contained 22 percent alcohol and was sold in drugstores throughout the nation. After Repeal, Renault began blending its New Jersey fruit with grapes imported from California to create an immensely popular sparkling wine. In 1948, Maria D'Agostino took over the winery following her brother's death. It was Maria who built the chateau-like structure, and it is her collection of wine glasses that today's visitors admire in the winery museum.

Under the direction of current owner Joseph P. Milza, who was formerly a newspaper owner and publisher, Renault is New Jersey's winery giant. Fifty of its 1,400 acres are planted in grapes, and it produces 80,000 cases of wine annually.

Renault makes what writer John Baxavanis has described as "a bewildering assortment of wines." The most popular selections include Chardonnay, Pink Lady (a sweet rosé), and Blueberry Champagne.

Renault has dining facilities and an enormous gift shop. A popular stop on the tour-bus circuit, Renault receives 100,000 visitors a year.

SYLVIN FARMS
609-965-1548, 973-778-1494; fax 973-778-9165.
24 N. Vienna Ave., Germania, NJ 08215.

This is the most remarkable winery in New Jersey. Frank Salek is a civil engineer who retired as a college professor in upstate New Jersey. After 20 years of commuting to his modest winery and vineyard on weekends, Frank will now

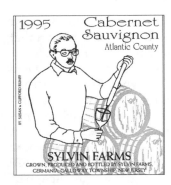

Directions: From Garden
State Pkwy. take exit 44.
Bear right onto Moss Mill
Rd. (Alt. 561) and travel
4.2 miles to Vienna Ave.
Turn right in 800 ft. at
winery entrance.
Owners: Franklin and
Sylvia Salek.
Open: By appointment.
Price Range of Wines: $9.50
for Riesling to $18 for
Blanc de Noirs.

• Chardonnay
• Sauvignon Blanc
• Merlot
• Cabernet Sauvignon
• Cabernet Franc
• Sparkling Wines

spend most of his time in the vineyard and the wine cellar. Year after year, Frank continues to turn out some of the best wines in the East. What's his secret? Maybe it's the vineyard's location. "Could be," Frank nods. "After all, we're on the highest point around."

Standing with him in his fields, I stare incredulously across the flat vista of the Chardonnay section of vineyard. Well, okay, maybe the land does sort of swell up into a little mound toward the center.

"Even the slightest rise makes a difference," Frank assures me. "And in this location the steady southwest winds permit the vines to dry off in summer, so we have less of a problem with fungal diseases." Both the Atlantic Ocean and the Mullica River moderate the temperature, Frank explains, and he has learned, usually by hard experience, which grape varieties and clones will do well here.

The wine cellar at Sylvin Farms is not one of those quaint cellars full of neatly stacked oak barrels and high-tech, computerized gizmos. It's an unprepossessing basement crammed full of stainless steel containers and a few wooden barrels. Nevertheless, the Chardonnay made here is distinguished and golden; the Pinot Noir is redolent of fresh berries; the Cabernets Sauvignon and Franc have great flavor intensity; the Merlot is juicy and ripe. Frank Salek makes some of this country's classiest sparkling Blanc de Noirs, and his sparkling Muscat draws consistent rave reviews. "Wine is made in the vineyard," Frank says modestly. "I decided a long time ago that you had to have good grapes to make good wine. When I couldn't find ones I liked, I decided to grow my own. Everyone thought I was really crazy."

Nobody thinks he's crazy now. Frank Salek is the guru for most New Jersey commercial winemakers, who admire his wines, respect what he's doing in his vineyard, and frequently turn to him for advice. Charlie Tomasello (Tomasello

Winery) has even teamed up with Frank to make a sparkling Rkatzitelli, a consistent award winner. (Rkatzitelli, the most common wine grape in Russia, is grown throughout Eastern Europe and appears to thrive in New Jersey as well.)

Sylvin Farms comprises about 40 acres of land, of which seven are planted. The annual output ranges from 750 to 1,000 cases, depending mostly on how the crops have fared in any given year. Located in a rural, pine-filled section of New Jersey, the winery has a small tasting room, but expansion plans are under way.

Frank Salek

Part philosopher, part scientist, and entirely devoted to vineyards and winemaking, Frank Salek is an inspiration to anyone who has even the slightest affection for wine. His wisdom and sly humor have entertained as well as enlightened many of us over the years. I recently spent several hours with Frank, sampling wines in his tasting room and directly out of barrels in the cellar, asking questions as we made our way through the vintages of the past decade, Here is some of our conversation:

Q: Your Merlot has such unusually soft tannins and long-lasting flavors. How do you achieve this great style?

A: I guess it's due to the fact that I don't have the sophisticated equipment other winemakers have. I mostly just let the wine alone without tampering with it too much. If I do anything special to this wine it's that I give it an extended maceration [the length of time the freshly pressed juice rests on its skins]. And good bottle aging is important too, especially for Burgundy and Bordeaux style wines. They've just got to have enough time in the bottle.

Q: Your Cabernet Franc tastes so ripe and round. This seems to be an especially good grape in Eastern regions, which more and more vintners are beginning to embrace.

A: Yeah, it's a nice wine. I've been growing Cabernet Franc for 20 years. Why in hell hasn't everyone else gotten on to it before now?

Q: To me, many of your wines taste very European. They have the elegance, subtlety, and complexity that one associates with fine European wines.

A: In a way, I am European in outlook, in my feelings about crops and land. My family was from Poland and other Eastern European countries. An uncle of mine had a little place up in Wallington, Bergen County, New Jersey, where he grew everything. I have vivid memories of the vegetables, of the peach trees and other things that grew there. I remember how neatly he dispatched a rabbit for dinner. Even though I was only four or five, I remember the black hen who laid more eggs than any of the others. I don't know, maybe this kind of thing is where I get some of my ideas.

While we were talking, Frank was heating up some Italian bread stuffed with sausage, and we devoured it as we continued making our way through the wines.

(Continued)

Q: The Cabernet Sauvignon was delicious on its own, but I can't believe how the flavors just sing once you put them together with this sausage.

A: It's because the tannins in the wine form a loose chemical bond in the mouth with the proteins in the sausage. I agree with you, this is a very good combination. If you ask me, there's nothing like Cabernet Sauvignon. It's the nearest and dearest thing to my heart.

A: Speaking of tannins, even your very young red wines — the ones we've just tasted right out of the barrel — have surprisingly soft and pleasant tannins. So many wines have a harsh tannic grip in their extreme youth. What do you do to get that softness?

A: I leave the wine on its skins for 21 days. Other than that, I don't do anything special, I don't add anything back in.

Q: Some of your barrels look pretty old and funky. What kinds of barrels do you mostly use?

A: I have both French and a couple of American oak barrels. But the ones you're referring to are old whiskey barrels. I de-charred them and cleaned them so they have virtually no flavor. They're just neutral storage containers.

Q: To my mind, one of the problems with a lot of wines for many years now has been an overbearing presence of flavor from oak. . . .

A: It depends on what you want to taste. It's a question of whether you want to taste the oak or want to taste the fruit and what it will evolve into over time.

Q: Well, if you aren't looking to flavor the wine with oak, what's the point of spending all that money on barrels?

A: Barrel aging is important because it does add certain characteristics to wine besides flavor. Barrels permit wine to soften and lose a certain amount of their boisterous youth. Wines are like children, who, as they grow through adolescence and enter adulthood, become more viable human beings. Of course their basic character stays the same. Chances are that if the damn wine tastes lousy now it will taste lousy five years from now.

Q: How exactly does the barrel-aging process work — does the wine evaporate through the wood?

A: Yes. The molecules for alcohol are long, while water's are short. The short chain leaves the barrel through the porous wood. The wine becomes concentrated, and the dissolved gases dissipate as a result of fermentation.

Q: When it comes to winemaking, do you ever make mistakes?

A. Oh sure, from time to time you do screw up. I once had to dump about 500 bottles of Chardonnay from the 1991 vintage — a really terrific year, too. But I screwed it up and couldn't find any way to save it, so I ended up just pouring it down the drain.

Q: That must have hurt!

A: It did, but it would have hurt more if I'd tried to sell it to people.

Q: I honestly think your Blanc de Noirs [a Brut made from Pinot Noir] is one of the most elegant and complex sparkling wines I've ever had outside the Champagne region itself.

A: I think so too, but I'm going to stop making it.

Q: What! Why?

A: It's too hard to sell. There just doesn't seem to be much of a market for good sparkling wine. You know, it isn't just the money. The way I make wine and the prices I can ask for it — well, let's put it this way, I'm never going to make much money on this. But there's not much point in making a wine like the Blanc de Noirs and not be able to sell it.

Q: The Sparkling Muscat Ottonel must be a success, however, since it just won the New Jersey Governor's Cup Award. [This was, in fact, the Fifth Governor's Cup that Sylvin Farms had won.] Actually, I can't think of much better ways to end an evening than with this wonderful glass of wine.

A: The Muscat pleases me, too. You don't need a whole lot of adjectives to describe it. In the final analysis, the question is simply: do you enjoy it?

Q: I guess that would be the question about making wine too. Despite all the frustrations and difficulties, do you enjoy it?

A: Look, this is an endeavor that requires a great deal of personal interest. When you get right down to it, it's madness. But it's a hell of a lot of fun.

Charles Tomasello in the cellar of Tomasello Winery, Hammonton, New Jersey.

Marguerite Thomas

TOMASELLO WINERY
609-561-0567, 800-MMM-WINE; fax 609-561-8617.
www.tomasellowinery.com.

Frank Tomasello, a local farmer, established Tomasello Winery in 1933. Today, it is run by Frank's grandsons, Charles and John ("Jack"), whose empire is expanding at an astonishing rate.

E-mail: jack@tomasello winery.com.

225 White Horse Pike, Hammonton, NJ 08037.

Directions: From Atlantic City take Rte. 30 west for 18 miles. White Horse Pike is just past mile marker #29. Follow the signs to the winery.

Owners: Charles and John Tomasello.

Open: Mon.–Sat. 9am–8pm, Sun. 11am–6pm.

Price Range of Wines: $8.50 for Steuben to $12 for Estate Chardonnay.

Special Features: Tomasello has four retail outlets, including one in historic Smithville, NJ. Call the winery for exact locations.

- Cabernet Franc
- Cabernet Sauvignon
- Chambourcin
- Villard Noir
- Rkatsitelli
- Epilogue

With 86 acres of vines, Tomasello rivals Renault as New Jersey's biggest grape grower, and it produces 52 percent of the state's wines (about 50,000 cases). An enormous assortment of wine comes from Tomasello, including an excellent Chambourcin, a light, flavorful red that resembles Beaujolais in character. A rich and spicy Villard Noir is one of this winery's most popular products. ("I wish I had a couple hundred more cases of it to sell," says Jack.) The Cabernet Sauvignon is particularly fine, with a nice balance between fruitiness, complex oak flavors, and restrained tannins. Tomasello also is one of the few wineries in the region to produce wine from Concord and Catawba grapes.

The vineyard and winery are actually only part of the Tomasello picture. There is also a Tomasello outlet store in Smithville, where wine tastings take place and gourmet food items are sold. It's a good place to stock up for a canoe trip or a picnic in the Pine Barrens. Tomasello is housed in a modern Mediterranean-style complex built around a court-yard. It includes a banquet room, a pleasant tasting room, and picnic facilities in addition to the winery operation itself.

SYLVIN FARMS

Tomasello Winery

Sparkling Rkatziteli

ATLANTIC COUNTY NEW JERSEY SPARKLING WINE
METHODE CHAMPENOISE

Alcohol 12% by Volume

RKATZITELI GROWN AND CUVEE
PRODUCED BY SYLVIN FARMS
GERMANIA, GALLOWAY TWP., NEW JERSEY
B.W. #276

SPARKLING WINE PRODUCED AND
BOTTLED BY TOMASELLO WINERY
HAMMONTON, NEW JERSEY
B.W. #68

CONTAINS SULFITES

COASTAL VIRGINIA

Two years after they landed in the New World, the settlers of Jamestown harvested, crushed, and fermented wild native grapes to produce America's first grape wine. While the results left much to be desired, the yearning for palatable wine, and for an economically viable industry with which to slake the thirst of this large new market, was strong enough to lead to years of frustrating and futile endeavors.

European grapes were imported into the colonies, and all householders were required by law to plant grapevines. French grape growers were sent by the London headquarters of the Virginia Colony to assist in the development of a wine industry. As late as 1769, despite mounting tensions with England, the colonists were still trying, without success, to make a drinkable wine in Virginia. It wasn't until the late 20th century that science and technology advanced to the point where wine, at last, was produced in the coastal area of Virginia. While Ingleside and Williamsburg have been virtually the two significant wineries in the region, a new winery was being built on the North Neck just as this book was going to press, and others are bound to follow.

HARTWOOD WINERY
Phone & fax: 540-752-4893.
E-mail: jdliving@erols.com.
345 Hartwood Rd.,
    Fredericksburg, VA
    22406.
Directions: From
    intersection of I-95/17,
    go 6 miles north on 17.
    Turn right on Rte. 612
    and go 1.5 miles to
    winery on left.
Owner: Jim Livingston.
Open: Wed.–Sun.
    11am–6pm, closed
    Thanksgiving,
    Christmas, and New
    Year's Day.
Price Range of Wines: $9
    for Rappahannock White
    and Red to $18 for
    Cabernet Sauvignon.

Jim Livingston, who opened Hartwood in 1989, is both the winemaker and the vineyard manager. From Chardonnay to Rappahannock White (medium-dry, made from Vidal) and a light Cabernet Sauvignon, the wines have a strong local following. Less than an hour from Washington D.C., Hartwood attracts Capital consumers who like to take a scenic drive into the countryside to stock up on local wines.

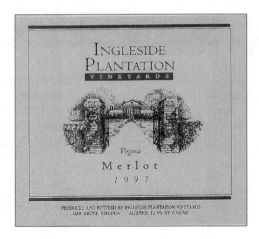

**INGLESIDE
PLANTATION
VINEYARDS**
804-224-8687,
    800-SIP-INGLESIDE;
    fax 804-224-8573.
www.ipwine.com.
5872 Leedstown Rd., Oak
    Grove, VA 22443.
Directions: 2.5 miles south
    of Oak Grove on
    Leedstown Rd.
Owners: The Flemmer
    family.
Open: Mon.–Sat.
    10am–5pm, Sun.
    12noon–5pm.
Price Range of Wines: $9
    for Pope's Creek White to
    $18 for Cabernet
    Sauvignon Reserve.
Special Events: Jazz
    concerts in the courtyard,
    Fall Barrel Tasting,
    Holiday Open House.

- Chardonnay
- Cabernet Franc
- Cabernet Sauvignon
- Merlot
- Viognier

A peninsula formed by the Rappahannock and Potomac Rivers as they empty into Chesapeake Bay, the Northern Neck of Virginia is a region filled with history. For example, both George Washington and Robert E. Lee were born here.

Ingleside Plantation Vineyards belongs to the Flemmer family, whose ancestor purchased the plantation in the late 1800s. The first vines were planted in 1960, and the winery began operation in 1980. Ingleside has 75 acres planted in vines and produces up to 14,000 cases of wine annually. The Chardonnay has nice rich flavors, and Pope's Creek is a simple, sippable white wine blended from Chardonnay, Seyval, Vidal, and Viognier. Ingleside is the only other producer besides Horton to make a Viognier; like Horton's, this one has characteristic floral aromas and appealing flavors. The Cabernet Franc has nice spicy characteristics, but the Merlot is what everybody wants — it sells out quickly, leaving devotees begging for more. Chesapeake Claret (80 percent Cabernet Sauvignon, 20 percent Chambourcin,) is soft but not shy, filling the mouth with flavor. Colonial Red is an interesting Ingleside product: a Chambourcin/Cabernet Sauvignon blend that is based on the wine used for Communion in Washington's day. Today it is sold to local Episcopal churches. It's a fairly sweet wine, especially popular at holiday time as a base for mulled wine.

LAKE ANNA WINERY
540-895-5085;
fax 540-895-9749.
www.lawinery.com.
5621 Courthouse Rd.,
Spotsylvania VA 22553.
Directions: From I-95 take
the Thornburg exit. Go
west on Rte. 606 for 2.5
miles; cross intersection
at Snell to Rte. 208.
Continue on 208
(Courthouse Rd.) 11.5
miles to the winery on
the left.
Owners: Bill and Ann
Heidig.
Open: Wed.–Sat.
11am–5pm, Sun.
1pm–5pm; Jan. & Feb.:
weekends only.

L ocated two miles from scenic Lake Anna, this small family winery makes Chardonnay, Cabernet Sauvignon, and Merlot. With 25 acres under vine, the winery produces 2,000 cases annually.

*Patrick Doffeler, owner of
Williamsburg Winery.*

Marguerite Thomas

**WILLIAMSBURG
WINERY**
757-229-0999;
fax 757-229-0911
www.wmbg.com/winery.
5800 Wessex Hundred Rd.,
Williamsburg, VA 23183.
Directions: From Colonial
Williamsburg take Rte.
31 toward Jamestown.
Go left to Rte. 199 east,
turn right onto Brook-

B elgian-born Patrick Doffeler was a business executive in France and New York, working for Eastman Kodak and Phillip Morris. "After I'd lived as a corporate mercenary for twenty years, my wife, Peggy, said, 'Now do something intelligent,'" recalls Patrick. His answer was to buy a farm in Williamsburg in 1983, which he converted into a vineyard and winery. Why wine? "Because it's the last consumer product that isn't standardized," Patrick explains. "There are too many vari-

wood Lane, then turn left onto Lake Powell Rd. The winery entrance will be on the left.
Owner: Patrick Doffeler.
Open: Mon.–Sat. 11am–5:30pm, Sun. 12noon–5:30pm.
Price Range of Wines: $6.75 for Governor's White to $21 for Gabriel Archer Reserve.
Special Features: Colonial wine bottles on display.
Special Events: December candlelight open house in conjunction with Colonial Williamsburg.

• Chardonnay
• "Governor's White"
• Merlot
• "Gabriel Archer Reserve"

ables in winemaking for it to ever become standardized." Patrick first came to Williamsburg in 1951, when he was a high-school student. "The place stands for our history, for a century of enlightenment, for grace of architecture," he says. "It stands for searching for a way of doing things differently."

By nature, Patrick loves a challenge (one of his great passions is to race vintage automobiles), so embarking on a winemaking project in an area where others had floundered for 300 years was just the sort of thing that interested him. It was also intelligent, as it turns out, for Williamsburg Winery has achieved surprising success. Financially it has enjoyed small but solid sales growth and critically it has received numerous awards and national attention, including praise from such respected writers as Robert Parker.

Williamsburg has 68 acres under vine. It is the largest producer of wines in Virginia — 50,000 cases annually – and it has the state's largest barrel cellar, with more than 600 barrels. It is also Virginia's most aggressive marketer, having succeeded in placing its wines in restaurants from Vermont to Atlanta.

Williamsburg produces some terrific wines, all from vinifera grapes. Steve Warner, the winemaker, graduated from Fresno State University in California. Most of his wines have layers of complex flavors underneath full fruit tones. This leaves a pleasing, long aftertaste at the back of the palate. The whites include Governor's White, Williamsburg's most popular wine, a good sipper made from Riesling and Vidal. John Adlum Chardonnay honors the foremost Virginia winemaker in Thomas Jefferson's day. Acte 12 of Sixteen-Nineteen Chardonnay is named after the law passed by the Virginia House of Burgesses in 1619 requiring every householder to plant and maintain 10 vines.

The full-bodied Merlot has rich flavors of spice and fruit. The Gabriel Archer Reserve, named for the co-captain of the *Godspeed*, which brought the first settlers to Jamestown in 1607, is a Bordeaux-style blend of Cabernet Sauvignon, Cabernet Franc, and Merlot. This wine is produced only in years when the fruit achieves an exceptional degree of ripeness.

An interesting collection of Colonial wine bottles is on display at the winery.

WINDY RIVER WINERY
804-449-6996;
fax 804-449-6138.
www.windyriverwinery.com.

Virginia's only female-operated winery, Windy River is managed by Judith Rocchiccioli while daughter-in-law Katherine is the winemaker. The estate includes 12 acres of vines, the oldest of

20268 Teman Rd.,
Beaverdam, VA 23015.
Directions: From I-95
northbound take Doswell
exit to Rte. 1 north; go 1
mile to Rte. 684, left on
Rte. 684, then 10 miles to
Rte. 738; right on Rte.
738, then 1.5 miles to
winery on right. From I-
95 southbound take
Ladysmith exit; right on
Rte. 639, then 6 miles to
Rte. 738; left on Rte. 738,
then 4 miles to winery on
left.
Owners: Judith and Randy
Rocchiccioli.
Open: Apr.–Dec.:
Thurs.–Sat. 12noon–5pm,
Sun. 1pm–5pm;
Feb.–Mar.: weekends
only; Jan. by
appointment.
Price Range of Wines: $9
for Ruby Blush to $16 for
Cabernet Sauvignon.
Special Events: Rock
Dances, Jazz in the
Vineyard, Theater at the
Winery, Harvest Ball.

- Wolf Blanc
- "The Wolf"

which were planted in 1995. The winery opened in April 1998. Colorful labels often depict femmes fatales in glamorous garb with a wolf lurking in the background (grown-up Red Riding Hoods?). Wolf Blanc, a white blend based on Seyval, has that grape's pleasant aroma with underlying lemony flavors. The Wolf is an easy-drinking red based on Chambourcin. The Cabernet has medium body and color and a hint of Cassis in the mouth — an enjoyable wine, especially considering the youth of the vines.

LAKE ERIE REGION

Grapes, grapes all around, and lots of wine to drink! The Lake Erie region is the largest grape-producing area in the nation outside of California. It starts just west of Niagara Falls and continues almost as far as the Ohio/Michigan border. It's literally awash in vines, mostly the dark-leafed American natives, which cover approximately 40,000 acres and span three states. Increasingly, European vinifera vines are replacing the stalwart natives in winemaking, but wine accounts for less than 10 percent of the grapes grown in this region; the rest go to the grape juice industry, which is based on Concord and other American labrusca grapes.

Although it isn't near the ocean, the area along the shores of Lake Erie has soil and climate reminiscent of the coastal regions. When the glaciers inched south during the Ice Age, the Canadian soil, rocks, and boulders scooped out monstrous holes in the earth. Later, as temperatures warmed and the glaciers receded, the holes filled with glacial melt to form the Great Lakes.

A unique, narrow plateau of gravel and loam that is well suited to grapevines was left behind near Lake Erie. "Our vineyards are where a lake beach was located many, many years ago," explains Gary Woodbury, whose winery bears his family name. As the land rises beyond this plain — sometimes only a mile behind the lake — the soil becomes too heavy for vine roots to thrive.

The deep waters of the lake store warmth from the sun that is reflected back onto the land, raising nearby temperatures in much the same way as the Atlantic Ocean keeps the coastal region temperate. Because of this combination of topography and weather patterns, and with 190 sunny growing days a year, the grape industry flourishes here. Chautauqua County, in the western-most section of New York, for example, supplies almost 60 percent of the state's annual grape production.

In the 19th century, the Lake Erie region was an important wine center — in fact, at the turn of the century, Ohio was the largest wine-producing region in the nation — but Prohibition knocked out Lake Erie's wine industry. Only in the last decade or so has it finally begun to re-emerge as a serious player in the Eastern wine market.

A handful of family-run wineries are still making the traditional, sweet wines their fathers and grandfathers made from labrusca grapes. "It's what the customers want," shrugs Ed Heineman, the fourth generation at Heineman Winery at Put-In-Bay Island in Ohio. "If you're brought up on native American grapes like the folks around here, that's what you prefer. And if you're a beginner, you like something sweet. But the more you drink, the more you'll probably move to drier wine."

As more Americans are becoming familiar with wines from California and Europe, a new generation of winemaker is emerging in the Lake Erie region —

knowledgeable vintners who are willing to satisfy the demand for drier, European-style wines. An impressive number of new wineries have opened in the past couple of years in the Lake Erie region: ten in Ohio alone. And an increasing number of wines emerging from the Lake Erie region are as exciting as any in the East. This is especially true for white wines, but certain reds, especially Cabernet Sauvignon, Cabernet Franc, and perhaps Pinot Noir, seem to be catching up in quality. One indication that Lake Erie is emerging as a *region* rather than just a collection of disjointed wineries is the new "Reflections of Lake Erie" label, used by 13 winemakers around the lake. Each makes an original white wine, using any one or a combination of the seven grape varieties suitable to this region: Riesling, Chardonnay, Pinot Gris, Cayuga, Vidal, Seyval, and Vignoles.

"For today's wine tourist, no other district in America offers historic vineyards and colorful wineries in settings as uniquely spectacular as those that still operate along the shore and on the Wine Islands of Lake Erie," wrote Leon Adams in *The Wines of America* a couple of decades ago. This is all the more true today, with the addition of high-quality wines.

The wineries are spread out almost in a straight line along the lake on Routes 2 and 5, and they're easy to find. As they tend to be clustered together, it's possible to visit several in a day. One of the most colorful experiences of wine-country touring awaits the visitor at the northwestern edge of Ohio, where one can island-hop from wineries to vineyards on the lake.

Even without the wineries, Lake Erie is a great travel destination. Boating, fishing (including ice fishing), and other water sports are a lure, and Niagara Falls is not far away. Cleveland's cultural attractions abound. The bounty of local farm stands and U-pick apple farms, plus the natural beauty of the region's many parks, such as Presque Isle Wilderness Area, offer additional scenic and recreational opportunities. Now that good wine can be factored into the equation, a sojourn to the Lake Erie region becomes irresistible.

NEW YORK

JOHNSON ESTATE WINES
716-326-2191, 800-374-6569; fax 716-326-2131.
E-mail: jwinery@cecomet. net.
Rte. 20, Westfield, NY 14787.
Directions: Two miles west of village on Rte. 20.
Owners: The Johnson family.

The Johnson family has been growing grapes in this location for more than a century; they opened the winery in 1961. This makes Johnson the oldest estate winery in New York State, meaning that it grows all its grapes on its own property, comprising 150 acres.

Johnson winery is a regional winery, producing quality wines (about 15,000 cases annually) from labrusca and French-American hybrids. Until

Open: Daily 10am–6pm.
Price Range of Wines: $6.45 for Blush to $12.50 for Chancellor, $16.50 for Ice Wine.

• Ice Wine

recently, it did not make wine from vinifera grapes. "We felt the best grapes for this region were hybrids and labrusca," says winemaker Mark Lancaster. "Now, with what they're doing with cloning and such, you *can* grow some vinifera as long as you're careful about the rootstock you select." Cabernet Franc is the grape with which Mark starts his foray into vinifera grape growing.

Meanwhile, Johnson Estate continues to produce a variety of successful whites, including Blancs de Blancs Sec and Liebestropfchen, "Little Love Drops," a fruity dessert wine. Reds include Chancellor Noir, with the color of dark velvet and the taste of mixed berries. Ice Wine made from late-harvested Vidal grapes is sweet and tasty. Mark will be releasing a series of sparkling wines over the next few years—the first one is out now.

WOODBURY WINERY & VINEYARDS
716-679-9463, 888-697-9463; fax 716-679-9464.
www.woodburyvineyards. com.
E-mail: wv@woodbury vineyards.com.
3230 South Roberts Rd., Fredonia, NY 14063.
Directions: From I-90, take Exit 59; turn left onto Rte. 60, then left onto Rte. 20, then right onto South Roberts Rd. Follow signs to the winery.
Owners: Gary Woodbury and Joseph Carney.
Open: Mid-June–mid-Sept.: Mon.–Sat. 9am–8pm, Sun. 12noon–8pm; mid-Sept.–mid-June: Mon.–Sat. 9am–5pm, Sun. 12noon–5pm.
Price Range of Wines: $6 for Niagara to $20 for Brut Champagne.

• Seyval

"I met Konstantin Frank in 1967," says Gary Woodbury, referring to the Finger Lakes vintner, who through his own success and powers of persuasion, inspired so many other Easterners to plant vinifera grapes. "It's because of him that we stand here today and talk."

It is the last day of summer, and Gary and I are strolling through the 2.3 acres of Chardonnay, Riesling, and Cabernet vines that he planted after that fateful meeting with Dr. Frank. Another 75 acres of hybrids and native American grapes were planted by Gary's grandfather in 1915. Most of this crop is sold to the Welch Company for grape juice. "When local 'experts' said you couldn't possibly grow vinifera grapes here, that was a challenge to me," smiles Gary. He sold his first bottle of vinifera wine on June 29, 1980.

He has never looked back. As we make our way through rows of vines, we pop a few golden Chardonnay grapes into our mouths, savoring the honeyed sweetness of their juice. Gary's hand-held device for measuring the fruit's sugar content confirms our impression of ripeness: the grapes range from 18 to 22.2 Brix, indicating that this vineyard is just about ready for harvesting.

Back at the winery, we taste Woodbury's Riesling, Chardonnay, a clear and crisp Seyval (Seyval's outstanding virtue, according to Gary, is consistency), and a sweet Niagara. "Just as a supermarket has to have sugar, a winery in New York State has to have a Niagara," observes Gary. Served over ice on a hot afternoon, Woodbury's Niagara makes a pleasant sipping wine.

Woodbury produces nine wines, about 15,000 cases annually from 40 acres of vines. "I try to keep it at a manageable level of confusion," says Gary.

He is confident the Lake Erie region is on its way to success as vines and winemakers mature. "We think our own wines have been getting better as the vines age. Of course, we also got better at making it," he says.

Woodbury Winery offers a unique Adopt-A-Barrel program. Any individual or group can "adopt" a barrel full of wine that will remain in Woodbury's cellars for four years. At the end of that time, each "parent" will receive two cases of wine — and they can keep the barrel.

PENNSYLVANIA

CONNEAUT CELLARS WINERY
814-382-3999,
   800-877-CCWWINE;
   fax 814-382-6151.
12005 Conneaut Lake Rd.
   (Rte. 322), P.O. Box 5075,
   Conneaut Lake,
   PA 16316.
Directions: From I-79 take
   exit 36-B; follow signs
   on Rte. 322 about 7 miles
   to winery on the left.
Owner: Joal Wolf.
Open: Daily 10am–6pm.
Price Range of Wines:
   $5.95 for Princess Snow
   Water to $18.95 for
   Merlot.
Special Events: Open
   House last weekend in
   April, fall picnic 1st Sun.
   after Labor Day.

Conneaut Cellars has fashioned itself after a turn-of-the-century winery, with much of the work done by hand. "We are an old-fashioned winery," says owner-winemaker Joal Wolf. Owning no vineyards of its own, Conneaut purchases its fruit from the Lake Erie region. It produces 5,500 cases of wine a year, including Chardonnay and Cabernet Sauvignon. Other dry vinifera and hybrid-based wines and a sweet American native wine are made as well.

Conneaut is further from Lake Erie than the other Erie wineries (about 30 minutes from Markko Vineyard), but its outlook is tied to the region. "Our philosophy is to produce wine from our own region rather than to copy California or France or Austria," explains Joal. "For that reason we use only American oak, for example. We want to extract the best character from our region."

MAZZA VINEYARDS & WINERY
814-725-8695, 800-796-9463;
   fax 814-725-3948.
11815 East Lake Rd. (Rte.
   5), North East, PA 16428.

Born in Italy, Robert Mazza came to the United States as a young child. He is thoroughly American, but with a hint of European aesthetics. The winery itself has a distinctly Mediterranean look compared to the rural wooden structures that

Directions: 15 miles east of Erie on Rte. 5.

Owner: Robert Mazza.

Open: July–Aug.: Mon.–Sat. 9am–8pm; Sept.–June: Mon.–Sat., 9am–5:30pm, Year-round: Sun. 11am–4:30pm.

Price Range of Wines: $5.95 for table wines to $22.95 for Ice Wine.

• Vidal Ice Wine

predominate in this region. And the wines include European varietals such as Riesling, Chardonnay, and Cabernet, as well as locally popular hybrids and American labruscas.

Robert and his brother Frank started the winery in 1972, after their home-winemaking hobby escalated into a full-time occupation. Although Mazza grows four acres of Vidal Blanc, most of their grapes are purchased from other Pennsylvania growers. Under the terms of the state's farm winery law, no out-of-state grapes may be used to make Pennsylvania wine. Mazza makes a delicious ice wine from Vidal Blanc grapes. Unlike some ersatz versions of German eiswein, which are made from grapes frozen in a freezer, Mazza's grapes hang on the vine in the traditional way, usually until late December, by which time their juice has frozen into concentrated sweetness.

The Mazzas produce 12,000–15,000 cases of wine annually.

PENN SHORE WINERY & VINEYARDS

814-725-8688; fax 814-725-8689.

10225 East Lake Rd. (Rte. 5), North East, PA 16428.

Directions: 15 miles east of Erie on south side of Rte. 5.

Owners: Robert Mazza and other shareholders.

Open: July–Aug.: Mon.–Sat. 9am–8pm, Sun. 11am–5pm; Sept.–June: Mon.–Sat., 9am–5:30pm, Sun. 11am–5pm.

Price Range of Wines: $5.80 for Kir to $8.95 for an oak-aged Chardonnay and $12.95 for a sparkling wine.

Founded as a co-op by local grape growers, the winery today has three owners. Robert Mazza, one of the owners, manages this winery, as well as his own. Gary Mosier, the winemaker at Mazza Vineyards, also handles winemaking for Penn Shore. At this winery he produces a variety of wines that include several crisp, dry whites, such as Chardonnay, Seyval, Vignoles, and a dry red that he calls — Dry Red. The best-selling Kir is a sweet blend of Catawba and Seyval with a touch of cassis flavoring.

PRESQUE ISLE WINE CELLARS

814-725-1314, 800-488-7492; fax 814-725-2092.

www.erie.net/~prwc.

E-mail: prwc@erie.net.

9440 Buffalo Rd., North East, PA 16428.

By the consensus of most of his colleagues, Doug Moorehead has been instrumental in encouraging people to gamble on vinifera grapes. He has also been a pivotal force in encouraging regional vintners to band together to market Lake Erie wines.

Directions: From the west on I-90, take exit 10 (Harborcreek), then go north on Rte. 531 to Rte. 20, then east on Rte. 20 for 3.8 miles. From the east take I-90 to exit 12 (North East), and go west on Rte. 20 for 7 miles.

Owners: Doug and Marlene Moorehead and Marc Boettcher.

Open: Mon.–Sat. 8am–5pm, Sun. during harvest only.

Price Range of Wines: $5 for Creekside White to $13 for Pinot Noir and Merlot.

- Cabernet Franc
- Cabernet Sauvignon
- Chardonnay
- Petite Syrah
- Pinot Grigio
- Riesling

The Moorehead family has been growing grapes in this region for three generations. They own 160 acres of vineyards, with 130 acres planted in Concord and Niagara grapes that are sold to the Welch Juice Company. The remaining acres are planted in wine grapes, supplemented by fruit purchased from "two superb growers on Lake Erie," as Doug describes them.

Doug and his wife, Marlene, first made their mark as suppliers of juice and equipment to home and professional winemakers. This continues to account for about 97 percent of their winery business. But it is that remaining 3 percent — the wines — that will put Presque Isle on the map. Only 3,000 cases are produced now, from both hybrid and vinifera grapes.

Doug clearly believes the future lies with vinifera. "Hybrids are one good pathway," he says, adding that some day in the future, new hybrids may rival and even surpass vinifera. "But for now, anyone who wants to be on the national or world stage — and this is a possibility for our region — will have to do it with vinifera."

While Chardonnay and Cabernet Sauvignon are Presque Isle's best selling vinifera wines, Doug is excited about his Petite Syrah, despite the difficulties involved in producing it. "If we get 100 gallons a year from it we're lucky," he sighs. Why bother with such a problematic variety? "Because the wine is just *so* good," answers Doug. "Making it can be equated to the task of Sisyphus. But every time I get discouraged, I taste another bottle."

In general, Doug believes the region's future in red wine lies in Cabernet Sauvignon. He is cautiously optimistic about the prospects for Lake Erie's wine. "The dilettantes who got into the business in the 1980s have dropped out," he explains, "Most of the people now are serious about making wine."

One of the most important strengths of the region, says Doug, "is the great varietal fruit characteristics we get here." Indeed, his own wines live up to this description. From an elegant Riesling to a fine Cabernet Franc blended with small amounts of Petite Syrah, to a Cabernet Sauvignon with unusual depth of color and flavor, all are excellent.

Presque Isle's setting is as charming as its wines, with picnic tables in the woods next to a small stream.

OHIO

BUCCIA VINEYARDS
440-593-5976.
E-mail: bucciwin@suite 224.net.
518 Gore Rd., Conneaut, OH 44030.
Directions: From I-90, take the Conneaut exit. Follow Rte. 7 to Rte. 20. Go west on Rte. 20 to Amboy Rd., then go north to Gore Rd. Turn left 0.5 mile to winery.
Owners: Fred and Joanna Bucci.
Open: Mon.–Sat., usually all day but call ahead to confirm if traveling a long distance.
Price Range of Wines: $6 for Niagara to $10 for Riesling.
Special Feature: B&B at the winery.

This small winery (4.5 acres), set amidst vineyards and orchards, produces wines from its own hybrid grapes as well as from vinifera purchased locally. Vignoles, Maiden's Blush, and Reflections of Lake Erie are the house specialties.

CHALET DEBONNE VINEYARDS
440-466-3485,
800-424-9463 (OH only); fax 440-466-6753.
www.debonne.com.
E-mail: debonnevyds@mwweb.com.
7743 Doty Rd., Madison, OH 44057.
Owners: Tony Debevc, Sr. and Jr., and their wives, Rose and Beth.
Directions: From Cleveland, take I-90 east, turn south onto Rte. 528 to Griswold, turn left onto Emerson, and then right on Doty, follow signs to winery. From Erie, take I-90 west, turn south onto Rte. 534 to

Chalet Debonne is the most visible winery in the Lake Erie region. Its wines are featured in many local restaurants, and the winery itself hosts a popular series of events.

Anton Debevc planted his first vineyard here in 1916. His son, Tony, tended the vineyard for many years, and was eventually joined by *his* son, Tony. The grapes at that time were used for grape juice. When the price of grapes dropped in the late 1960s, Tony Sr. and Tony Jr. began to make wine. In 1971, they opened the winery.

Rose and Beth (Tony Sr's. and Jr's. wives), produce 25,000 cases of wine annually. They have 80 acres planted in grapes, which is supplemented by additional fruit purchased from other growers.

The winery's appealing wines include a full-bodied Proprietor's Reserve Chardonnay and a soft and pretty Pinot Noir. The winery makes several classic labrusca wines — Delaware, Catawba, Niagara — as

South River Rd. west, which runs into Doty.
Open: Tues., Thurs. & Sat. 12noon–8pm, Wed. & Fri. 12noon–midnight.
Price Range of Wines: $5.89 for River Rouge to $12.79 for Pinot Noir.
Special Features: Gift shop, indoor and outdoor tables, fireplace. A B&B located 0.25 mile down the road from the winery (phone: 440-466-7300)
Special Events: Steak Fries, Hot Air Balloon Race, '50s and '60s Day, Summer Concert Series and more.

- Chardonnay
- Chambourcin

CLAIRE'S GRAND RIVER WINE COMPANY
440-298-9838.
5750 South Madison Rd., Madison, OH 44041.
Directions: From Cleveland, take Rte. 90 east to the Madison-Thompson exit, go 3 miles south to the winery.
Owner: Alan and Joanne Schneider.
Open: Mon., Wed.–Sat. 1pm–6pm.
Price Range of Wines: $6–$8.

HARPERSFIELD VINEYARD
440-466-4739.
6387 State Rte. 307, Geneva, OH 44041.
Directions: From I-90 take exit 212. Go south on Rte. 528 to the first left (Rte.

well as a Riesling and a dessert Vidal. It has recently begun to expand into more vinifera grapes such as Pinot Gris and Cabernet Franc.

The Chalet Debonne winery looks as if it had been transported here straight from the Alps, which may be a reflection of the family's Slovenian roots. Visitors may purchase light fare to be enjoyed with wine in the snack shop. There's also a pleasant indoor area with tables near a fireplace for relaxing, as well as tables scattered throughout the attractive grounds, including under the grape arbor in front of the winery.

New owners Alan and Joanne Schneider purchased the former Grand River Winery in 1998. The winery produces about 5,000 cases of wine annually made from grapes grown on its own 17 acres, as well as those purchased from other local growers. The best offerings are easy-drinking Beaujolais-style wines. The winery's top seller is its Blanc de Renard ("White Fox"), a sweet Niagara; its best-selling dry wine is Vignoles. Half the profits from the wines and from the winery gift shop and café are donated to the Faith Foundation, an organization designed to help retired priests and other underadvantaged citizens. "I hope we can sell millions in order to help other people less fortunate than we are," says Joanne. The winery also makes altar wine for the Youngstown and Cleveland Dioceses. "This is the first time any local winery has been given this permission," Joanne says with pride.

"I believe in doing things small and doing them right," says Harpersfield founder Wes Gerlosky. He is indeed doing things small: he produces merely 2,000 cases of wine annually, but all the wine is made from grapes grown in his own 14-acre vineyard. He is certainly doing things right, as he is turning out some of the most exciting wines in the Northeast.

Defining a Region: Doug Moorehead, Arnulf Esterer & Wes Gerlosky

No vintner can gain recognition if the region in which he or she works doesn't have a reputation for producing good wine. I can think of only one important producer in the world who is turning out premium wines in a vacuum: Serge Hochar, who produces the acclaimed Château Musar wines in Lebanon. Generally, unless a region has prestige and a solid reputation, an individual winemaker stands little chance of attracting attention outside his own vineyard.

It takes strong leadership to develop an identity for a region, and leadership in winemaking — as in the world at large — comes naturally to only a few individuals. In the relatively small Lake Erie area, there are three men with the necessary talent, vision, and drive.

Douglas Moorehead is the pioneer who, after tasting Germany's best wines when he was in the army in the 1950s, resolved to make premium wines back home. He got vinifera vines from Konstantin Frank and hybrids from Philip Wagner, both trail-blazing vintners of New York's Finger Lakes. Convinced that the Lake Erie region was suitable for producing fine wines, Doug encouraged local growers to switch from native American vines to these varieties. He fought for the passage of a Pennsylvania state law that would permit farmers to sell their own wine directly to consumers. When the bill was finally passed in 1969, he opened Pennsylvania's first winery, Presque Isle.

Doug, a soft-spoken man with short, graying hair and a pleasant, intelligent face, has worked hard to persuade his colleagues to band together to improve the overall quality of Lake Erie wines. It would be best for the region's identity, says Doug, to limit the number of grape varieties grown to a few outstanding examples, rather than obscuring the picture with a bewildering number of indifferent wines made from numerous grapes. "We've organized a quality-control group," he says, "and we're starting to sort out the varieties we should be working with."

Like Doug, Arnulf Esterer also learned about raising vinifera vines directly from Dr. Frank. He founded Markko (named after the Finnish policeman who sold him the property) in 1969, and it was the first of Ohio's modern wineries. Like Doug, he believes the Lake Erie region must build its image on the best possible wine that it can produce. "As far as I'm concerned, the Pinot Gris race is on," he says. "Everybody, everywhere makes Chardonnay, and reds are hard for us to produce consistently. But we do well with Pinot Gris, which Dr. Frank said was the greatest early-ripening grape of all. It's just a question now of who's going to make it the best."

While Arnie is encouraged because leading producers are putting their confidence in vinifera rather than in hybrid grapes, he acknowledges that there is still a long way to go. "We have to figure out how to survive the coldest winters, like the one in 1994. That one wiped us out," he says. Despite the problems, Arnie is confident the region has the potential to make a name for itself. "It hasn't happened as fast as I'd hoped," he adds, "but with the second generation coming along, it *will*."

Wes Gerlosky embodies that second generation. A solidly built man with a thick mustache, Wes fills a room with his presence. He is perhaps less a diplomat than the two older men and less willing to compromise when quality is the issue. He dismisses the efficacy of the Quality Control Group, for example, claiming that it is more about marketing than about quality.

"Do you know why Eastern wine is such a hard sell?" he asks impatiently. "Because so many people have been making schlock in the East. The only thing that got California going was that they stopped making jug wine with screw tops. They started using better grapes and making good wine."

Because of such outspoken ideas, Wes says that he and Arnie Esterer are considered radicals by many of their colleagues. "But, in fact, we're the traditional ones," Wes protests. "We're the ones making the kind of wine everyone else in the world drinks. Some guys up here make wines that aren't accepted anywhere on the planet! You've *got* to have a vision beyond the end of your nose, because the world is awash in good wine. We have to change, and then I think we can do as well as Burgundy." Burgundy? He nods. "I think we can be the Beaune of this region. If we do this right, we

Marguerite Thomas

Wes Gerlosky

can make a mark." Anyone who doubts the veracity of Wes's sentiments need only taste his wine to understand what he's talking about.

Like the talented Italian winemakers known as the "Super Tuscans," who were daring and ambitious enough to make wine outside the sanctioned government regulatory structure, the Lake Erie vintners are refusing to settle for business-as-usual in winemaking. They are doing their best to elevate their region's wine into the global realm.

---

307). Travel 4 miles to the winery on the left.

Owner: A corporation, with Wes Gerlosky as manager and winemaker.

Open: Call winery for hours.

Price Range of Wines: $16 for Cabernet Franc to $20 for Reserve Chardonnay.

- Cabernet Franc
- Chardonnay
- Gewürztraminer
- Pinot Gris
- Riesling

Wes stumbled into his winemaking career by accident in the early 1970s, when he took over the management of the apple farm his father had purchased as a retirement project. Inspired by the French wines they had begun drinking, Wes and his wife, Margaret, decided to try their hand at winemaking.

At first, they used the Concord grapes that were growing on the property. "The wine was terrible," he says bluntly. He began talking to people who made wines he liked, particularly Arnie Esterer at Markko Vineyard and Doug Moorehead at Presque Isle. Encouraged by them, he began ripping out apple trees and planting vinifera vines, while refining his winemaking techniques.

In 1985, he built a cellar and decided to start selling his wines. His first vintage was released in 1986. In the beginning, he made only four wines, all of them white: Chardonnay, Riesling, Gewürztraminer, and Pinot Gris. "These early-ripening whites are the strength of our region," he says. Lately, however, Wes has been adding red wine to the production. His first Cabernet Franc has been released, and the Pinot Noir vineyards will be soon be ready to harvest. "Until now, Pinot Noir clones haven't been good enough, yielding undistinguished, raisiny wines," says Wes. "But now good clones from Burgundy are available. It will be a challenge to grow the grapes and to make the wine, but when Pinot Noir is good, it's really good. You never forget a great Burgundy."

Wes attributes his success to his experience of wines. "Even though I had only seat-of-the-pants training, I made it a point to buy and taste good wines. It can be expensive," he says, "but it's really important to be familiar with good wines so you know what you're aiming for. Then what you need is the best possible fruit. It's not easy to persuade growers to leave their fruit on the vine until it's thoroughly ripe, but that is critical."

Wes's long-range goals include emphasizing the influence of the region on his wine and developing a greater consistency. "We want to make a living, not a fortune, by growing grapes and making wine," he says. "I think eventually we'll be able to make something as good as anywhere in the world."

Harpersfield is on its way to reaching these goals. Its four Chardonnays range from lean and delicate to full-bodied opulence. The Riesling has the aromatic amalgam of floral scents and oiliness that one looks for in a great Riesling. The Pinot Gris and Gewürztraminer resemble the deep-flavored lush wines of Alsace. All Harpersfield wines are exceptionally food-friendly. (Wes suggests drinking the Gewürztraminer with rabbit or chicken stew seasoned with paprika.)

KLINGSHIRN WINERY
440-933-6666;
   fax 440-933-7896.
33050 Webber Rd., Avon Lake, OH 44012.
Directions: From I-90 take the Rte. 83 exit, go north on Rte. 83 to Webber Rd., then go left to the winery.
Owners: Allan, Barbara, and Lee Klingshirn.
Open: Mon.–Sat. 10am–6pm.
Price Range of Wines: $4 for a dry Concord to $16.99 for a sparkling wine made with Riesling grapes.

During Prohibition, Albert Klingshirn developed a thriving grape-juice business in this small community on the outskirts of Cleveland. Repeal left Klingshirn with a surplus of grapes. He decided to turn them into wine. In 1935, he opened a winery, which his son, Allan, eventually took over. Allan introduced hybrids into the family business and today, Allan and Barbara Klingshirn's own son, Lee, is gradually adding vinifera vines.

The vineyard is currently divided into nine acres of Concord, plus an additional eight acres of premium hybrid and vinifera varietals. With the addition of purchased grapes, winemaker Lee Klingshirn produces 5,000 cases a year. At present, Lee believes Riesling is the best vinifera grape for the region, but he acknowledges there will always be a strong local demand for traditional American labrusca wines. Klingshirn wines, which are simple, clean, and light, rather than rich and complex, include a dry Concord, a snappy Chardonnay, and a sparkling wine made from Riesling grapes. There are swings outside the tasting room for the kids, as well as fresh grape juice in season.

MARKKO VINEYARD
440-593-3197, 800-252-3197; fax 440-599-7022; www.markko.com.
E-mail: markko@suite 224.net.
4500 South Ridge Rd., Conneaut, OH 44030.
Directions: From I-90 take exit 235, go north on Rte. 193 to Main St; turn right, bear right at South Ridge, and continue 3 miles to winery.
Owners: Arnulf Esterer and Tim Hubbard.
Open: Mon.–Sat. 11am–6pm, appointment recommended.
Price Range of Wines: $7.50 for Covered Bridge, a generic name for several everyday sipping wines, to $30 for Pinot Noir and Late Harvest Riesling.
Special Events: Catch of the Day & Chardonnay, annual Markko Perch Fry, Blessing of the Vines, annual Odds & Ends Sale and Auction.

• Cabernet Sauvignon
• Chardonnay
• Pinot Noir
• Riesling

Stone pillars flank the entrance to the curving driveway that leads to this small winery tucked away in the hills. Markko's pups, a group of friendly, gray-bearded dogs with wagging tails, extend their enthusiastic greeting. Arnulf Esterer, who owns Markko with partner Tim Hubbard, appears in the doorway of the winery to greet me. His own gray beard matches the dogs. We go inside to a cozy tasting room, where I am treated to some astonishingly good wines, all from vinifera grapes grown on Markko's own 14-acre vineyard.

Arnie, who had two previous careers, one in the Navy and the other as an industrial engineer, has been producing wine here since 1968. In fact, Markko was Ohio's first post-Prohibition winery. "Konstantin Frank got me started," he says, explaining that he was one of the many vintners to be convinced by Dr. Frank that vinifera grapes could be grown in the East. Arnie believes that this region is unusually hospitable to grapes. "We have good soils and a longer growing season than the Finger Lakes," he explains. "The Lake Erie region could produce 10 percent of the nation's wine. We could do 30 to 50 million gallons — we already do more juice than that."

After we sample his current Chardonnay, Arnie opens a bottle of eight-year-old Chardonnay that is still youthful and fresh, with the distinctive aroma and flavor of roasted almonds and toasted bread picked up from the oak barrels in which the wine was fermented. I am skeptical when he pours a 20-year-old Chardonnay. But although the wine has lost some fruitiness, it is still vibrant, with no trace of oxidation or deterioration. "It's the acidity that protects the wine," Arnie explains. "This was a hard wine when it was young, but it's softened and taken on another life with age. This is what we can do with white wine in this region."

"It's harder to make consistently good red wines," Arnie says, as he pours a Pinot Noir and a Cabernet Sauvignon. Both wines are excellent. His Riesling comes as close to a Moselle as any American Riesling I've tasted.

As good as these wines are, however, it is the Pinot Gris (in this case blended with Riesling) that Arnie is really excited about. "This is the grape that can define our region," he says. He describes the wide stylistic variations of the grape, a white mutation of Pinot Noir. The wine can range from bone-dry to full, opulent Alsatian Tokay. (Pinot Gris is, confusingly, called Tokay in Alsace.) "We don't know how we should style ours yet," admits Arnie, "but that's the fun of it." If his fragrant and intensely flavorful Pinot Gris becomes the model for the region, the wine world will surely take note.

Markko produces 2,000 cases of wine a year. All of Markko's wines are excellent, dry libations to enjoy with meals. "We don't cater to the sweet-wine crowd here," warns Arnie. The winery is an easy three-mile drive from the excellent beach at Conneaut Park on Lake Erie.

ISLAND WINERIES

In 1870, there were more than 7,000 acres of vineyards in the Lake Erie region, on the mainland and on islands between Toledo and Cleveland. On the Bass Islands alone there were dozens of thriving wineries, including one on Middle Bass Island that was purported to be the largest winery in the nation. By the turn of the century, several wineries in the Sandusky area were winning competitions as far away as Paris.

Vines thrive on the islands because the surrounding water moderates the weather, creating warmer temperatures and a longer growing season than on the mainland. In addition, the islands enjoy approximately 25 percent less rainfall than the rest of the region, because storms break up before reaching them. Even after the lake freezes in winter, the Lake Erie islands are generally the warmest places in Ohio.

During Prohibition, some island wineries continued producing wine legally for medicinal or sacramental purposes, while others made bootleg wine, which led to occasional confrontations with government officials. Local folklore is full of stories of irate vintners wielding shotguns to chase the officials away.

As in the rest of the East, most of the wineries never fully recovered after Repeal. The few that survived concentrated on sweet Catawba, Delaware, and other native American wines, which still have a local following and attract a substantial number of tourists. The interest in refined, European-style wines that swept the East in the early 1990s is just beginning to be felt here. The region is a charming place to visit, and occasionally one happens upon a very good wine.

Put-In-Bay, Middle Bass, and Kelley Islands can be reached by ferry. There . is also a regular jet ferry service. Call 1-800-245-1JET for schedules and prices.

FIRELANDS WINERY

419-625-5474,
  800-548-WINE;
  fax 419-625-4887.
www.firelandswinery.com,
E-mail: info@firelands
  winery.com.
917 Bardshar Rd.,
  Sandusky, OH 44870.
Directions: From Rte. 2, exit
  at Rte. 6 and follow signs
  to winery.
Owners: Paramount
  Distillers.
Open: June–Sept.:
  Mon.–Sat. 9am–5pm,
  Sun. 1pm–5pm;
  Oct.–Dec.: Mon.–Sat.
  9am–5pm; Jan.–May:
  Mon.–Fri., 9am–5pm,
  Sat. 10am–4pm.
Price Range of Wines: $4.99
  for a medium dry Vidal
  to $10.95 for the
  Sparkling Brut and Rosé.
Special Features: Multi-
  media wine education
  presentation, large gift
  shop.
• Cabernet Sauvignon
• Chardonnay
• Pinot Gris

HEINEMAN WINERY

419-285-2811;
  fax 419-285-3415.
Catawba St., P.O. Box 300,
  Put-in-Bay, OH 43456.
Directions: Take the jet
  ferry from Port Clinton to
  Put-in-Bay and follow
  signs on the island to the
  winery.
Owner: Louis Heineman.
Open: Apr.–mid-Nov.:
  Mon.–Sat. 10am–10pm,
  Sun. 12noon–7pm;
  mid-Nov.–Apr.:
  Mon.–Sat. 8am–5pm.
Price Range of Wines: $6
  for Catawba to $12 for
  Chardonnay.

Although Firelands Winery is not on an island, it is located on Sandusky Bay, the gateway to the island wineries. This strip of land is called the Firelands, after the region along the Connecticut coast that was raided and burned by British troops during the Revolutionary War. Citizens whose property was destroyed were granted parcels of land in the Connecticut Western Reserve, now part of northern Ohio.

The original winery here was established in 1880 by Edward Mantey, a German settler who cultivated grapes and made wine for other German immigrant families. The Mantey Winery was eventually rechristened Firelands. It is owned by Paramount Distillers, a small Ohio corporation that produces wine under five different labels: Mon Ami, Lonz, Meiers, Mantey, and Firelands. The total production is 50,000 cases annually.

The Mantey wines are all sweet labrusca. "They are our bread and butter," says Ed Boaz, Fireland's president. The wines under the Fireland's label are a testament to the skills of Claudio Salvador, an Italian winemaker from the Veneto region, who has been at this winery for more than a dozen years. They include an outstanding Chardonnay and Cabernet Sauvignon, as well as a Pinot Noir.

Commodore Oliver Hazard Perry sailed from this island to battle the British fleet in 1813. After the victory, he returned to send his famous dispatch: "We have met the enemy and they are ours." A peace monument commemorating this event rises over the small harbor at Put-in-Bay Island.

In summer, the island is a lively place, but in the tranquility of off-season, one senses what the island was like in 1888 when Gustave Heineman arrived. An immigrant from Baden, a wine-producing area along the Rhine River in Germany, he established the first winery on the island. By 1900, there were 17. About 40 acres of vines are still maintained by a handful of growers, but Heineman, which survived Prohibition by making grape juice, is the only remaining winery.

Ed Heineman, great-grandson of the founder, is the present winemaker. He produces about 10,000 cases of wine a year, using grapes from the family's 15-acre vineyard, as well as from other Put-in-Bay and North Bass Island vineyards. Heineman makes 20 different wines, mostly from native labrusca varieties, which is the only grape grown on the island. Recently, Ed began making a Chardonnay from mainland grapes. This and Riesling are the only vinifera wines produced.

In the German beer-garden setting at Heineman, one can sample traditional sweet American wines, as well as variations of native species made into dry wines. Catawba, for example, and Claret, a mixture of Concord and Ives grapes, are well-made, mildly grapey wines. Although they may not convert partisans of Cabernet Sauvignon, they nevertheless offer an agreeable option for anyone who wants to sample an interesting variety of wines. One of Heineman's specialties is a sweet wine made from Ives grape. It is so popular, says Ed, that he has begun stockpiling Ives. "A lot of my colleagues are switching to vinifera grapes," he adds, "but they aren't having an easy time of it. I recognize that tastes are changing, but if this past summer is any indication of how much people like our wines, we will just keep on growing."

OTHER LAKE ERIE WINERIES

LONZ WINERY (419-285-5411, Middle Bass Island, OH 43446), a gothic stone building embellished with turrets and battlements, sits on the southern tip of Middle Bass Island. It began life as the Gold Eagle Winery during the Civil War, and by 1875 it had become the largest wine producer in the nation. The original winery, twice destroyed by fire, was rebuilt in 1942 by George Lonz, whose father had been producing wines on the island since 1884. George sold his Isle de Fleurs Champagne to revelers who sailed regularly to the island after Repeal. Today, most Lonz wines are produced at the Firelands Winery in Sandusky, but some sparkling wine is still made on the island. The winery is an active place, with wine tastings and tours of the century-old cellars, a snack bar, gift shops, playground, and a picnic area. There are a host of special events — from garage sales and grape-stomping festivals to entertainment by barbershop quartets and dancing on the patio in summer.

PART TWO
The Atlantic Uplands

Dr. Michael Fisher, owner,
Amwell Valley Vineyard

Marguerite Thomas

The Atlantic Uplands lie between the coastal zones that border the Atlantic Ocean and the Eastern mountain ranges. This vast plateau runs north to south, and it is also sometimes called the Piedmont, or "Up Country." Higher above sea level than the Benchlands, the Uplands are characterized by gently rolling hills easing up toward the Allegheny, Blue Ridge, and Appalachian Mountains. These Eastern viticultural Uplands include northern New Jersey, the Delaware River Valley, Pennsylvania (except the central and western mountainous sections), Maryland, northern and central Virginia, western Connecticut, and the Hudson River Valley and Finger Lakes regions of New York.

Because of a long growing season and mineral-laden soils, the best Uplands wines exhibit a beautifully balanced ratio between sweetness, acidity, and alcohol. They are characterized by delicate fruit flavors and, when the grapes come from the region's very best vineyards, have rich and intense flavor components.

The soils that are washed down the mountains are well drained and rich in calcium and the other minerals that grapes thrive on. An increasing number of viticulturists are gaining greater knowledge of the Eastern wine regions, larger capital investments are being made, more vineyards are being planted, and more wineries are opening. Undoubtedly, this extremely promising area will continue to develop as one of the country's most important viticultural regions.

NORTHERN NEW JERSEY AND THE DELAWARE RIVER REGION

A s with most Eastern wine regions, this area is influenced by a great body of water, the Delaware River, which moderates the climate to make it more amenable to grapes. On both sides of the river, the countryside is idyllic, dotted with gracious old stone farmhouses, elegant horse farms, rolling hills, and country retreats. Quaint villages that range from tourist meccas to remote and genuinely charming country hamlets fill the region.

New Jersey's Hunterdon and Warren counties lie on the east side of the river. Their landscape comes as a pleasant surprise to those who think the state is a holding tank for industry and pollution. The vista here is characterized by contentedly grazing horses in spacious green pastures enclosed by white fences, and curving driveways that lead to handsome country estates.

Directly across the river, the Pennsylvania wineries are set in a background that is picturesque enough to attract sightseers from all over the world. Scenic River Rd. (Rte. 32), a narrow road that meanders along the Delaware River through Bucks County, is one of the prettiest drives in the East. It was at the southern end of this road on Christmas Day in 1776 that George Washington and the Continental Army crossed the icy Delaware River to deal a crushing blow to the British.

In addition to wineries, there are numerous recreational activities in the area. Among these are historic mansions, such as Pennsbury Manor, William Penn's 17th-century country estate on the banks of the Delaware, and Andalusia, one of the finest examples of Greek Revival domestic architecture in the nation. Both are open to the public. Art galleries, antique stores, and shopping outlets beckon as well.

The wineries are more widely dispersed in this area than in others, so more time may be needed for travel. But with a wealth of good restaurants and inns, this region offers plenty of opportunities for lunch and overnight breaks.

NEW JERSEY SIDE OF THE DELAWARE RIVER

ALBA VINEYARD
908-995-7800;
   fax 908-995-7155.
269 Rte. 627, Village of
   Finesville, Milford, NJ
   08848.
Directions: Take Rte. 78 west
   to Exit 7 (Bloomsbury).

R udi Marches founded Alba Vineyards in 1983. Subsequent problems forced the winery to close for awhile until 1997, when Rudy and Tom Sharko formed a partnership. With 26 acres under vine, Alba is now up and running at full speed, producing about 4,000 cases a year. After major

Follow Rte. 173 west for 2.3 miles to Rte. 639 west. Go 2.8 miles to Rte. 627 south; travel 2 miles to winery on the right.
Owners: Tom Sharko and Rudy Marchesi.
Open: Wed.–Sun. 12noon–5pm.
Price Range of Wines: $5.99 for Blush to $14.99 for Reserve Port.
Special Events: Music festival, concert series, fireworks.

• Port

AMWELL VALLEY VINEYARD
908-788-5852;
fax 908-788-1030.
80 Old York Rd., Ringoes, NJ 08551.
Directions: From Flemington Circle, take Rte. 202 south. Take the Reaville exit onto Rte. 514 east. The winery is 1.1 miles further. Old York Rd. is Rte. 514.
Owners: Dr. Michael Fisher, Jeffrey and Debra Fisher.
Open: Sat.–Sun. 1–5pm, and by appointment.
Price Range of Wines: $7 for Pheasant Ridge Blush; $17 for Cabernet Sauvignon; $20 for Port.

renovations, the beautiful 1805 stone barn has been recast as an up-to-date winery and hospitable tasting room. Alba's Raspberry Wine wins prizes across the country. . Red Wine Heritage (a blend of grapes predominated by Maréchal Foch) has a popular following. The Vintage Port, a fortified wine made by traditional Port methods, is so popular that Alba has doubled the production each year — and still sells out!

Amwell Valley Vineyard is noteworthy in many respects. Founded in 1978 by Dr. Michael Fisher, a London-born scientist at Merck Sharp and Dohme Research Laboratories, this is the oldest winery in this part of New Jersey. One of Dr. Fisher's important contributions to the industry was his successful campaign to improve New Jersey's archaic winery laws. His efforts resulted in the passage of the Farm Winery Act in 1981. This act helps regulate the quality of wine produced in New Jersey and encourages the preservation of farmland. It has also opened the door to entrepreneurial winemaking. Until the passage of the act, only seven winemaking licenses had been issued in New Jersey since Prohibition.

Dr. Fisher became interested in vineyards after reading an article in *Scientific American* about the various grape-growing regions in the world. He contacted one of the contributing authors, Philip Wagner of Boordy Vineyards in Maryland, who guided the Fishers in their first planting of hybrid grapes. After the initial harvest, they began experimenting with other grapes, and today they raise both vinifera and hybrid grapes on 11 acres of their 30-acre farm. They produce about 2,500 cases of wine, ranging from a pleasant Maréchal Foch (a hybrid) to Gewürztraminer (a vinifera).

"Grapes aren't as hard to grow as I had thought, as long as you select the right kind," says Fisher. "Riesling, for example, is reasonably easy to grow here." But, he adds, there are other factors that help, too: "We have better fungicides and pesticides now than we used to, which makes it all possible. Also, the weather is warmer these days."

Amwell Valley's wines are mostly on the lean side and make nice picnic wines. You can enjoy them either inside the large new tasting room that opened in the summer of 1996, or on picnic benches on the deck, overlooking the vineyards and a sweep of unspoiled land that stretches to the Sourland Mountains in the distance.

Nicolaas Opdam, general manager of King's Road Winery, Asbury, New Jsersey.

Marguerite Thomas

**KING'S ROAD
VINEYARDS
AND WINERY**
908-479-6611, 800-479-6479;
    fax 908-479-1366.
www.kingsroad.com.
360 Rte. 579, Asbury, NJ
    08802.
Directions: From I-78 take
    exit 11. Follow signs to
    Pattenburg on Rte. 614,
    continue another 3 miles,
    then turn right onto Rte.
    579 and go 0.2 miles to
    the winery, on the left.
Owner: Robert Abplanalp.
Open: Wed.–Sun.
    12noon–5pm.
Price Range of Wines: $6.95
    for Royal Blush to $18 for
    Cabernet Sauvignon.
Special Feature: Light
    snacks available.

King's Road Winery, which opened in 1981 on the site of a former pig and cow farm, is a leader on several fronts. It is the first winery in New Jersey to have its wines served on an airline (Kiwi Airlines), and it is one of the first to sell its Chardonnay in California (to the Richard Nixon Library).

King's Road is owned by Robert Abplanalp who, trivia buffs will recall, was President Nixon's pal as well as the inventor of the aerosol spray valve. Dutch-born winemaker and general manager Nicolaas Opdam is proud of his winery and of the state it's located in. "New Jersey is more than just Newark," he insists. "People who come out here are always surprised at how nice it is." He's particularly proud of the special, small stainless steel fermentation tanks he designed and had custom-made in California.

King's Road has a 25-acre vineyard on its 100-acre property. The first planting took place in 1980 with native labrusca grapes. The intention was to sell the grapes to vintners, but when they proved to be

Special Events: Evenings with the Winemaker and other events.

• Chardonnay

poor sellers, the labrusca was replaced with vinifera vines. Today, the winery's total output is 4,000 cases.

King's Road is the largest producer of Chardonnay in the state. It also makes Ensemble, a light and sweet blend of Riesling and Seyval, and the easy-drinking and popular Marcato, a Cabernet Sauvignon/Merlot blend.

The winery is on a small rural road that in Colonial days was known as "The King's Highway"; the road was then a major thoroughfare connecting the northern and southern sections of the state. The winery's tasting room is located in the converted hayloft of a 200-year-old barn. Cheese and other light snacks are sold in the shop, and there are a few café tables where visitors can enjoy a glass of wine.

Richard Dilts, co-owner of Poor Richard's Winery, Frenchtown, New Jsersey.

Marguerite Thomas

POOR RICHARD'S WINERY
908-996-6480.
www.castle.net/poorrich.
E-mail: poorrich@ptdprolog.net.
220 Ridge Rd., Frenchtown, NJ 08825.
Directions: From I-78 take the Clinton/Pittstown exit. Go south on Rte. 513 to Frenchtown; turn left on Rte. 12 to Ridge Rd. From Flemington, travel west on Rte. 12 to Rte. 519, and then go north to Ridge Rd.

This winery is as unique as its wines and its winemaker. Richard Dilts and his partner, Judy Rampel, have devoted themselves to making honest, unpretentious country wines, a task they proved can be done without the luxury of endlessly deep pockets. "Unlike other wineries, we didn't go to the bank, get a million-dollar loan, and then go out of business," Richard explains. "We may not be as dazzling as some places, because we pay as we go along."

Indeed, the operation is simple. Currently 10 acres are under cultivation, and the winery produces about a 1,000 cases annually. Although plans call for expanding the winery and vineyards, for

Owners: Richard Dilts, Judy Rampel, Floyd Turner, and Virginia Record.
Open: Thurs.–Sun. 12noon–5pm, or by appointment.
Price Range of Wines: $6 for Vidal; $8.45 for Reserve Vineyard Red.
Special Events: Spring and summer open house, annual chili competition.

the moment both the tasting bar and winemaking facilities are located in a simple whitewashed underground cellar. The equipment includes plastic "barrels" and a vintage hand-operated corker.

Richard started as a home winemaker, but when the Farm Winery Act was passed in the early 1980s, he decided to go into the wine business full-time. He planted his own vineyard in the early 1980s. Like many vintners in the French countryside, Richard is part man of the earth, part philosopher. He vigorously defends his decision to raise hybrid rather than vinifera grapes. "They are an expression of American tastes," he says. "They are better suited to our soils and climate than vinifera grapes, and the wines go with American food."

Like Richard himself, the wines tend to be straightforward and full of character. The Reserve Vineyard Red, for example, can be a surprisingly well-balanced and assertive hybrid blend that belies the unsophisticated winery equipment. The rugged, hilly vineyards form an appropriately scenic backdrop for the winery.

Pat Galloway in the tasting room at Unionville Vineyards, Ringoes, New Jersey.

Marguerite Thomas

UNIONVILLE VINEYARDS
908-788-0400;
fax 908-806-4692.
www.unionvillevineyards. com.
E-mail: uvineyard@ aol. com.

Unionville Vineyards is one of the youngest of New Jersey's wineries, but the land it occupies has been a productive peach orchard since at least the mid-19th century. "New Jersey was one of the great peach producers in the 1800s," explains Unionville owner Pat Galloway. "Then the peach blight hit, and that's when the industry moved to

9 Rocktown Rd., Ringoes, NJ 08551.

Directions: From Rte. 202/31 about 6 miles south of Flemington Circle, turn east onto Wertsville Rd. At the 2nd crossroads turn right onto Rocktown Rd. The winery is the first drive on the left.

Owners: Patricia Galloway and Kris Nielson.

Open: Thurs.–Sun. 11am–4pm.

Price Range of Wines: $7.50 for Fields of Fire (a popular blush wine) to $21.99 for Cabernet Sauvignon.

Special Events: Summer Fest in August with picnics and live music, October Pumpkin Fest in the fall with live band, hayrides and activities for the kids.

• Chardonnay
• Reserve"
• Riesling
• "Hunter's Red Reserve"
• "Hunter's White

Georgia." In its next incarnation the property became a dairy farm.

Established as a vineyard and winery in 1988 by Pat and her husband, Kris Nielson, Unionville released its first wines in 1992. Since the owners also jointly own an engineering firm, they rely heavily on their winemaker, John Altmaier, who was trained in Ohio, the Finger Lakes, and Germany. Along with vineyard manager Darren Hesington, who has been on the scene since the beginning, this group has come an impressively long way with their winery. The vineyard has expanded from 11 acres of hybrid and vinifera grapes planted on the 90-acre property to 26 acres. "We're planting more and moving more and more towards vinifera," says Darren.

Unionville, clearly one of the best wineries in New Jersey, consistently wins prizes and awards for its wines. The semi-dry Riesling is a perennial favorite. Hunter's White Reserve (an oak-aged Vidal), Hunter's Red Reserve (a fine, oaky Chambourcin), Chardonnay, Seyval Blanc, and Cabernet Sauvignon are all winners, too.

The eye-catching labels depict hunting scenes with foxes and horses, reflecting one of the popular pastimes in this region. The tasting room and winery facilities are located in a former dairy barn, which was handsomely rebuilt by a local Mennonite contractor, using stones from the original foundation.

OTHER WINERIES ON THE NEW JERSEY SIDE OF THE DELAWARE RIVER

CREAM RIDGE WINERY (609-259-9797, fax 609-259-1852; www.cream-ridgewinery.com; e-mail: creamridgewinery@earthlink.net; 145 Rte. 539, Cream Ridge, NJ; Mail: P.O. Box 98, Cream Ridge, NJ 08514). Located halfway between New Jersey's northern Uplands and the Benchlands to the south, Cream Ridge specializes in fruit wines. They also make a credible red table wine from Chardonel grapes and a white wine from Chardonnay. For anyone curious about fruit wines, this is a good place to try them. The

Raspberry Wine, a blend of 75 percent black raspberry and 25 percent red raspberry, is oak-aged and made into an inky, rich, and slightly tannic dry wine that is truly astonishing. It needs hearty food to accompany it — perhaps stewed venison, duck, or a pork roast with prunes.

FOUR SISTERS WINERY (908-475-3671; 10 Doe Hollow Lane, Rte. 519, Belvidere, NJ 07823) This winery is part of a large fruit and vegetable farm owned by Laurie and Robert Matarazzo. The winery, which opened in 1984, is named after the family's four daughters. It produces numerous wines, the most notable being Chardonel. The winery hosts a variety of events and activities, ranging from grape-stomping parties to Native American powwows.

LaFOLLETTE VINEYARD AND WINERY (908-359-8833, fax 908-874-7884; 64 Harlingen Rd., Belle Mead, NJ 08502) Winery owner Mimi LaFollette Summerskill, who is also a writer, and her late husband, John Summerskill, who was President of Cornell University, originally raised Black Angus cattle on their 30-acre farm. This proved to be a daunting challenge, as the cattle often wandered into the gardens of irate neighbors. So, in 1979, they switched to grapes. They decided to concentrate on a single varietal, "instead of trying to be all things to all people," says Mimi. They settled on the Seyval grape and planted 11 acres. LaFollette now produces about 1,500 cases of straightforward Seyval and a small amount of oak-aged Seyval. The wine is served in several Princeton restaurants and at some functions at the Faculty House at Princeton University. LaFollette's small tasting room is housed in a former sheep barn. There are picnic facilities outside.

TAMUZZA VINEYARDS (908-459-5878; fax 908-459-5560; e-mail: tamuzza@ goes.com; 111 Cemetery Rd., P.O. Box 247, Hope, NJ 07844) Although the village of Hope is a historic 1769 Moravian village, the far-reaching marketing strategies of Tamuzza Vineyards definitely reflect the 20th century. It claims to be the largest supplier of personalized wine labels and wedding wine favors in New Jersey. The Cabernet Sauvignon is a decent wine.

PENNSYLVANIA SIDE OF THE DELAWARE RIVER

BIG CREEK VINEYARD
610-681-3959, 717-325-8138; fax 610-681-3960.
E-mail: bigcreek@post office.ptd.net.
Keller Rd., Kresgeville, PA 18333.
Mail: RR 5, Box 5270, Kunkletown, PA 18058.

When the third edition of this book was in preparation, Big Creek was still too young for its wines to be properly evaluated; but if winemaker Dominic Strohlein's vision is fulfilled, this will be an exciting winery. The first grapes were planted in 1995 on the property the Strohlein family has owned for 55 years (25 acres were planted by 1999). The winery and tasting room, installed in

Directions: Follow Rte. 209 to Rte. 534 west and go 0.1 mile to Beltzville Rd. Go 1.3 miles to Keller Rd., then turn left and go 0.3 mile to second driveway on the left.
Owners: The Strohlein family.
Open: Mon.–Thurs. 1pm–5pm, Sat & Sun. 1pm–7pm, Sun. 2pm–5pm.
Price Range of Wines: $6 for Seyval to $14 for Raspberry Champagne.

a 3,500-square-foot, airy, modern space, opened in 1996. The winery produces about 2,000 cases annually. Dominic admits they're "pushing the climate" for grape growing here in the foothills of the Poconos, but this has not stopped him from planting Pinot Noir, Chardonnay, and — are you ready — Sangiovese, Nebbiolo, and Dolcetto. "Why the Italian grapes — do you think you're in Tuscany here?" I ask. "Well, we refer to Tuscany as 'the Kresgeville of Italy,'" jokes Dominic. Then, turning serious, he points out that his vineyard gets lots of southern sun and that the slate and shale soil is extremely well drained. Comparing the site to Germany's Moselle wine region, he says that he expects his vines to be fruitful, with proper pruning, "including keeping the canes two inches above the ground so we can throw dirt up on it for protection in the fall."

"Grapes are funny," he adds. "If they can survive in the first place, they'll adapt to the site." If anyone can get those grapes to survive, I'll bet it's Dominic.

BLUE MOUNTAIN VINEYARDS
610-298-3068.
www.bmvc.com.
E-mail: sales@bmvc.com.
7627 Grape Vine Dr., P.O. Box 492, New Tripoli, PA 18066.
Directions: From Rte. 22 take Rte. 100 north, 9 miles to Rte. 309 north, and go 1.75 miles. Turn left on Rte. 143 and go 0.25 mile to New Tripoli; turn left onto Madison St. and go 1 mile to Grape Vine Dr. Follow signs to winery.
Owners: Joseph and Vickie Greff.
Open: Mon.–Fri. 1pm–6pm, Sat. & Sun. 10am–6pm.
Price Range of Wines: $7.50 for Vidal to $22 for Meritage.

• Chardonnay
• Merlot

Joseph and Vickie Greff began making wines in 1993 and opened their big chalet-like tasting room, with its big deck and sweeping views, in 1995. They have 23 acres under cultivation and produce about 4,700 cases of Chardonnay, Cabernet Sauvignon, Cabernet Franc, Pinot Noir, and Merlot. The Greffs concede that they're right at the edge of the growing region, which gives Joe — who used to own an insurance business but is now fulltime winemaker and vineyard manager — plenty of challenges. "I'm experimenting and learning and trying to come out with the right combination," he says. "Vinifera is hard to grow, but that's the wine I like, so I'll take the chance." My favorites among these promising wines include the Chardonnay and the Merlot, both nicely balanced and with good fruity flavors.

BUCKINGHAM VALLEY VINEYARDS

215-794-7188.
www.pawine.com.
1521 Rte. 413, Buckingham, PA 18912.
Directions: From Rte. 202 between New Hope and Doylestown, take Rte. 413 south for 2 miles to the winery.
Owners: The Forest family.
Open: Mar.–Dec.: Tues.–Sat. 11am–6pm, Sun. 12noon–5pm; Jan.–Feb.: Thurs.–Sat. 11am.–6pm, Sun. 12noon–4pm.
Price Range of Wines: $5.50 for Vidal Blanc; $7.50 for Chardonnay; $12.50 for Champagne.

- Vidal Blanc

Buckingham Valley Vineyards is profitable enough to support an entire extended family: Jerry and Kathy Forest and their grown children, Jonathan, Kevin, and Christopher, who all work at the winery. The Forests started growing grapes in 1966 so they could make wine for their own consumption. One thing led to another, and they now have 20 acres planted in grapes and produce 12,500 cases of wine annually.

Except for small amounts of Chardonnay and Riesling, all the wine is made from hybrid and native grapes, and it is all top quality. The dry reds, which are aged in American oak, tend to be fleshy wines, and the whites are full-bodied, clean, and flavorful. The wines usually show a good balance between fruitiness and the pronounced acidity that characterizes Eastern wines. The sweeter wines have interesting personalities that go beyond mere sweetness.

The winery itself doesn't have a lot of razzle-dazzle. It is basically an addition to a suburban house. A self-guided tour is offered, as well as a help-yourself wine pouring. There are picnic tables outside.

Stormy Skrip at Clover Hill, Breinigsville, Pennsylvania.

Marguerite Thomas

CLOVER HILL VINEYARDS & WINERY

610-395-2468, 888-CLOVER HILL; fax 610-366-1246.
www.cloverhillwinery.com.

Set in the bucolic countryside south of Allentown, Clover Hill got its name when John and Pat Skrip (he was formerly a civil engineer and she was a teacher), decided to buy a farm. As they

E-mail: clover01@fast.net.
9850 Newtown Rd.,
  Breinigsville, PA 18031.
Directions: From New York
  take I-78/US 22 beyond
  Allentown to Rte. 100
  south. Turn right at the
  2nd traffic light onto
  Schantz Rd.; go to
  Newtown Rd. and turn
  left to the winery.
Owners: John and Pat
  Skrip.
Open: Mon.–Sat.
  11am–5:30pm, Sun.
  12noon–5pm; Nov.–Dec.
  holiday season:
  9am–5:30pm.
Price Range of Wines: $6.75
  for native varietals to
  $13.95 for Chambourcin.
Special Events: Seasonal
  open houses.

• Catawba
• Concord
• "Clover Hill Red"
• Niagara

climbed to the top of their highest hill to admire the view, Pat spotted a four-leaf clover at her feet; within seconds, John had found one too. They immediately named the place after these lucky omens, and a cloverleaf became the logo for their wine labels. The original clovers are framed and hanging in the Skrips' home.

The couple planted their first vineyard in 1975; then, while they waited for the vines to mature, John took courses in viticulture. They opened the winery in 1985. Now, almost 15 years later, Clover Hill produces close to 17,000 cases of wine annually. The vineyards have recently expanded to about 60 acres, with a new 10-acre tract that has been planted in Cabernet, Sangiovese, and Chardonnay, and another six-acre site that will be mostly hybrid vines. The Skrips' son, John III, who earned a degree in enology at California's Fresno State College, is the winemaker, while his wife, Stormy, is in charge of public relations. The next generation of Skrips — a boy named, of course, John — was born to John and Stormy in 1998.

Clover Hill's winery is immaculate, reflecting the Skrips' passion for cleanliness. The wines are also clean and bright, with the purity of fruit shining through. The Niagara and the Catawba are native varietals with strong, grapey aromas. Niagara is the most popular wine here. "It's like tasting the inside of the grape's skin," marveled one satisfied tasting-room customer. The Concord is fantastically sweet, yet not heavy or syrupy. My favorite of recent Clover Hill releases is Clover Hill Red, an intriguing and complex wine.

FRANKLIN HILL VINEYARDS

610-588-8708, 888-887-2839;
  fax 610-588-8158.
E-mail: vineyard@epix.net.
7833 Franklin Hill Rd.,
  Bangor, PA 18013.
Directions: From Rte. 22
  take Rte. 611 north to
  Martin's Creek Inn. Turn
  left onto Front St. At the
  top of the hill, go right
  onto Franklin Hill Rd.
  The winery is 1.7 miles
  further on the right.

Franklin Hill Vineyards is hidden away in the hilly farmland that rises above the Delaware River in Pennsylvania. Elaine Pivinski Austen was a Flower Child in the 1960s: "Yes, I was at the original Woodstock," she smiles. She's now the hard-working owner of this winery.

It all began when Elaine and her former husband decided to buy a farm instead of living on a commune. Having no idea what to do with this former barley field, they wrote to Pennsylvania State University for advice. The university suggested planting the new hybrid grapes that people were

Marguerite Thomas

Elaine Pivinski Austen, owner of Franklin Hill in Bangor, Pennsylvania.

Owner: Elaine Pivinski Austen.
Open: Mon.–Sat. 11am–4pm; call for Sun. hours.
Price Range of Wines: $7 for Country Red to $10 for Chardonnay.
Special Features: Wine and gift stores.

• Cayuga

trying to raise. This appealed to the pair, who planted their vineyard in 1976. A winemaker friend taught them the trade, and they released their first vintage in 1982. To their astonishment, it sold out in 15 months. But by 1985, the marriage had broken up and Elaine was left with the winery and three children to tend. "I vowed, when I found myself running this business alone, that I would employ only working mothers," she says.

Bonnie Pysher fit the job description perfectly. She learned how to make wine, run the tractor, spray the vineyards, and fix anything that broke. "She's perfect," sighs Elaine contentedly. Most of the other employees at Franklin Hill are local farmers' wives. "They put their kids on the school bus and then work in the vineyards for a few hours," says Elaine. Eventually she opened one, then two more retail shops where the wines are sold. This is where she spends most of her time now, assisted by her 80-year-old father. Elaine's blue eyes light up when she speaks of him. "He's the world's best salesman. If you come in to buy a bottle of wine, you'll probably leave with a case."

Franklin Hill has 15 acres under cultivation and produces about 5,000 cases annually. Its wines include Seyval Blanc and Chardonel, a Seyval-Chardonnay cross. Both are crisp, dry whites. The rest of the production is mostly hybrid-based semi-sweet and sweet wines. "The Pennsylvania Dutch around here don't like red wine and they don't like dry wine," Elaine explains. She does, however, make a couple of reds, including Chambourcin and Dechaunac. Her own personal favorite is Cayuga White, a very pleasant wine with a fragrance reminiscent of Sauvignon Blanc. Elaine likes it with cheese and crackers, and it's also good with Mexican food and other spicy dishes.

Franklin Hill has 15 acres under cultivation and produces 5,000 cases annually. The tasting room is located among the barrels and fermentation tanks in the winery. Bring your own cheese and crackers for a picnic with a bottle of Cayuga — and, who knows, maybe you'll leave with a case. The retail stores are open every day: **The Wine & Gift Shops** (570-619-7260; Rte. 611, Fountain Springs West, Tannersville, PA 18372); **The Grape Spot** (610-559-7887; 3603 Nicholas St., Easton, PA 18045); **The Grape Arbor** (610-332-9463; 597 Main St., Bethlehem, PA 18017).

PEACE VALLEY WINERY
215-249-9058.
300 Old Limekiln Rd., Chalfont, PA 18914.
Directions: From Doylestown go northwest on Rte. 313 to New Galen Rd. Turn left and go 2 miles, then turn right onto Limekiln Rd. and go one mile to the winery.
Open: Wed.–Fri. & Sun. 12noon–6pm, Sat. 10am–6pm; Dec.: daily 10am–6pm.
Owners: Susan Gross and Robert Kolmus.
Price Range of Wines: $6.99 for New Britain White to $12.99 for Champagne.
Special Events: Nouveau Release (weekend before Thanksgiving), Spring Fling (around Income Tax Day).

Peace Valley Winery is situated in an aptly named place — a tranquil, wooded valley that seems light years away from the traffic and industrial blight of contemporary civilization. The first stage in the creation of the winery began in 1968 when Susan Gross planted grapes in a small vineyard on her property. She found a market among home winemakers, so she kept planting more vines. She's now up to 24 acres of vines.

In 1984, she opened her own winery. While she produces some Chardonnay and is experimenting with Cabernet Sauvignon, the specialty at Peace Valley is wines made from blends — mostly native American and French-American hybrids. "The trend is to switch to varietal wines (wines made from a single grape variety)," grumbles Peace Valley's winemaker, Robert Kolmus. "So we're bucking the trend by blending different grapes. But we feel that's the best way to emphasize fruity flavors."

Peace Valley Winery is a good place to sample native American grape wines, such as Niagara and Fredonia, which aren't produced much locally any more. Visitors can also pick their own grapes and apples here.

PINNACLE RIDGE WINERY
Phone & fax: 610-756-4481.
E-mail: pinridge@aol.com.
407 Old Rte. 22, Kutztown, PA 19530.
Directions: From Allentown: Take Rte. 22/78 to Exit 12 (Kutztown, Krumsville, and Rte. 737). Go north on Rte. 737 to the blinking red

Pinnacle Ridge's first vintage was 1993, and the winery opened in 1995, but already this is one of the most exciting wineries around. The sparkling wines are simply delicious. The Brut Reserve (65 percent Pinot Noir, 25 percent Chardonnay, 10 percent Pinot Meunier) will delight anyone who loves fine Champagne. It's soft and creamy, yet also bright and fresh, a truly fine sparkler. The Brut (Chardonnay spiked with Chambourcin) has a pretty, pale pinkish hue, toasty aromas, and a fruity light in Krumsville. Turn right (east) onto Old Rte. 22 to the winery, 0.8 miles on the left. From Reading: Take Rte. 222 north toward Kutztown. Take the Rte. 737 exit (Krumsville) and travel north on Rte. 737 for 6 miles, to the blinking red light in Krumsville. Proceed as above.

Owners: Brad and Dawn Knapp.

Open: Sat. 10am–5pm, Sun. 12noon–5pm.

Price Range of Wines: $6 for Vidal and Cayuga to $13 for Brut Reserve.

- Chambourcin
- Late Harvest Vidal
- Sparkling Wine

SAND CASTLE WINERY

800-722-9463; fax 610-294-9174.

http://members.aol.com/winesand.

E-mail: winesand@aol.com.

755 River Rd., P.O. Box 177, Erwinna, PA18920.

Directions: The winery is located on River Rd. (Rte. 32), which parallels the Delaware River. It is 12 miles north of New Hope and 2 miles south of the Frenchtown Bridge.

Owner: Joe Maxian.

Open: Mon.–Sat. 10am–6pm, Sun. 11am–6pm.

Price Range of Wines: $11 for Cuvée Blush to $19 for Pinot Noir.

Special Events: Seasonal festivals include an art festival, the Chardonnay Blossom Festival, and the Cellar Sampler Festival.

finish. The Blanc de Blancs, made from Cayuga, is "off-dry" (slightly sweet) and charming. I'm not the only one who likes it: "The combination of sweetness and lower price point makes it our most popular bubbly," says Brad Knapp. Brad, who has a Ph.D. in chemistry, recently left the world of science to devote himself full-time to the winery. Believe me, science's loss is the wine lover's gain. Brad is a serious, gifted winemaker, who will only get better as his vines mature. For now, he has three acres under cultivation, making 2,000 cases — and growing.

S and Castle has the most stunning location in this region; it sits high on a hilltop overlooking the Delaware River. The tasting room has an undistinguished appearance, but there's talk of building a castle just like the one in Bratislava, Slovakia, where owner Joe Maxian, grew up. If and when this happens, it will be a dramatic landmark in this scenic section of the Delaware River Valley.

The underground caves, where wines are stored in barrels and stainless steel tanks, are as spectacular as the setting. Seven thousand square feet of space was blasted out of the shale mountain to create the facility. The winery produces 16,000 cases of wine annually from vinifera grapes that are grown on the estate's 55-acre vineyard. The first vines were planted in 1983, and the winery opened in 1988.

The wines are all traditional European varietals such as Chardonnay, Cabernet Sauvignon, and Riesling.

SLATE QUARRY WINERY

610-759-0286; fax 610-746-9684.

E-mail: sidswine@aol.com.

460 Gower Rd., Nazareth, PA 18604.

Directions: From Rte. 22 take Rte. 191 north toward Nazareth; veer left at the blinking light at the crossroads of Rte. 946; cross over Rte. 248 and travel 0.75 mile further to a group of houses. Turn right onto Knauss Rd. and go 0.25 mile to winery sign. Bear right onto Gower Rd; the winery is 0.25 mile farther.

Owners: Sid and Ellie Butler.

Open: Feb.–Sept.: Fri.–Sun. 1–6pm, or by appointment; Oct.–Dec.: Tues.–Sun. 1–4pm.; closed Jan.

Price Range of Wines: $6 for Vidal to $12 for Champagne.

Special Event: Every autumn Slate Quarry hosts a Vigneron-for-the-day event where attendees participate in crushing grapes, followed by lunch and a wine tasting; people usually return the following year to buy a bottle of the wine they helped make.

• Chambourcin

S late Quarry is known as much for the grapes it grows to sell to other vintners as for its own excellent wines. Sid Butler, a science professor from Lehigh University, originally grew a few grapes and produced just enough wine for his family to enjoy. But now that he's retired, he makes about 1,000 cases of wine a year and oversees his 13 acres of vineyards. He raises mostly hybrids, but has recently added Chardonnay, Cabernet Franc, and Pinot Meunier.

The Lehigh Valley farm dates back to the Colonial days and is located near a slate quarry. The vineyard, with its slate-laced soil, is clearly Sid's passion, and he experiments with a variety of grapes, including several Chardonnay clones — Florental, a little-known Gamay hybrid, and Chardonel, a Chardonnay/Seyval cross that he sells to other wineries in the region. The Butlers believe the mineral-rich soil gives a distinctive character to their wines, and indeed one can detect a hint of mineral in the wine's flavor.

All of the wines the Butlers make are sold at the winery. Most Slate Quarry wines are off-dry (or slightly sweet) wines. Sid explains that people often claim they don't like sweet wine but, "while they talk dry, they usually end up buying sweet." His best-selling wine is "Ellie's Rosé," a medium-sweet pink wine with a Muscat grape aroma. He also makes an above-average Chardonnay, a good Cabernet Franc, and a dry and rich oak-aged Chambourcin, the red hybrid that many Pennsylvania vintners claim as their signature wine. Don't miss the Late Harvest Johannisberg Riesling.

VYNECREST WINERY

610-398-7525, 800-361-0725.

www.vynecrest.com.

E-mail: landisig@ptd.net.

172 Arrowhead Lane, Breinigsville, PA 18031.

Directions: Take Rte. 78/22

V ynecrest and its newly remodeled tasting room are located in an 1840s barn in the gently rolling hills of the Lehigh Valley. John and Jan Landis have been growing grapes here for 25 years; in 1989 they opened the winery and tasting room. They now make about 800 cases of wine, all from

to Rte. 100 south. At 2nd traffic light turn right onto Schantz Rd. Go approx. 2 miles to Arrowhead Lane; turn right to winery on left.
Owners: Jan and John Landis.
Open: Thurs.–Sun. 1–6pm.
Price Range of Wines: $7 for Seyval Blanc to $9 for Baco Noir.

- Arrowhead White
- Seyval

their own grapes. As they have recently added a couple of acres to their original nine, that production may increase. Vynecrest Seyval has a nice crispness and pleasant aftertaste. Arrowhead White is a spicy, mellow semi-sweet blend of Gewürztraminer and Traminette (an aromatic French-German hybrid that is currently finding much favor with Eastern vintners). Arrowhead Red is a semi-sweet blend of Chambourcin and Cayuga. "It's more for folks who like wines to be both red and sweet," Jan explains. Baco Noir has the strong cherry nuances characteristic of that varietal, and Autumn Gold is a late-harvest wine that's good both after dinner or, served ice cold, as a pleasant summer drink.

OTHER PENNSYLVANIA AND DELAWARE RIVER WINERIES

As in many other wine regions in the East, the Delaware River Valley has many commercial wineries that are so small they are just one step up from home winemaking — "professional hobbyists" is the apt description given by the owners of one such winery, Rushland Ridge. Most of these wineries are open only on weekends, since the owners usually have full-time jobs. Visitors who stop in unannounced at other times will most likely be greeted by a "closed" sign on the door.

HUNTERS VALLEY WINERY (717-444-7211; R.R. 2, Box 326D, Rtes. 11 & 15, Liverpool, PA 17045) With a 2.5-acre vineyard, Hunters Valley makes wine from American grapes such as Niagara and Concord.

RUSHLAND RIDGE VINEYARD & WINERY (215-598-0251; 2665 Rushland Rd, P.O. Box 150, Rushland, PA 18956). This small family-run winery raises 13 varieties of French-American hybrid grapes on three acres. They make about 675 cases of wine annually, including Seyval, Vidal, Cayuga, Niagara, Chellois, and Baco Noir.

SOUTHERN PENNSYLVANIA AND MARYLAND

Eric Miller of Chaddsford Winery.

Courtesy Chaddsford Vineyards

Southern Pennsylvania's wine region is located along some of the most scenic routes in the nation. Fortunate travelers will amble through the Brandywine Valley, where they can visit Longwood Gardens with more than 11,000 species of plants, and Winterthur Museum, the former du Pont mansion that now contains an unrivaled collection of American decorative arts and antiques.

Visitors also will savor the peaceful countryside around Chadds Ford, immortalized in paintings by three generations of Wyeths. Many of their paintings are on display at the Brandywine River Museum.

The wineries in Pennsylvania are reached by driving through the unspoiled farmland of Lancaster Country, across mile after mile of rolling, fertile fields and past pristine farmhouses maintained by Mennonite and Amish farmers, who still use teams of horses to plow the land. The absence of billboards, strip malls, and fast food outlets fills one with nostalgia for simpler times.

The same complex soils and moderate climate (with approximately 195 growing days) that make this a good place to grow wheat also provide a hospitable environment for grapes. Pennsylvania produces about 100,000 tons of grapes annually. The wine industry generates thousands of jobs and contributes over a billion dollars to the state's economy.

In Maryland, the undulating countryside is filled with farms and pastures, although throughout the area, horse farms and hay fields, groves of trees, and dairy barns are rapidly disappearing to make way for housing. The poignant contrast between these two landscapes intensifies one's appreciation for the remaining rural regions, where vineyards help preserve agricultural land and where traditional country houses, surrounded by the kind of simple gardens that reflect the most basic human need to keep in touch with the earth, remain as dignified survivors of a time past.

Another type of garden altogether is the Ladew Topiary Gardens, in Jacksonville, Maryland, not far from Boordy Vineyards. One of the finest gardens in the world, it has 22 acres of sculptured hedges, as well as animal and geometric figures.

SOUTHERN PENNSYLVANIA

John Crouch of Allegro Vineyards with a silver medal from the Summit International Competition.

Marguerite Thomas

ALLEGRO VINEYARDS
717-927-9148.
R.D. 2, Box 64, Sechrist Rd., Brogue, PA 17309.
Directions: From I-83 take exit 6 onto Rte. 74, traveling about 7 miles beyond town of Red Lion to Brogue. Turn right at post office onto Muddy Creek Rd. Travel 2 miles and look for winery sign on the left.
Owners: Tim and John Crouch.
Open: Fri.–Sun. 12noon–5pm, or by appointment.

Allegro is the sort of place that inspires musical metaphors. No wonder. Allegro's owners, brothers Tim and John Crouch, are former classical musicians. Allegro wines are among the best in the East (they positively sing!) and well worth the drive to this rather remote spot.

The brothers planted their vineyard in 1973, and the winery building followed in 1980. Today, with 15 acres under cultivation, they annually produce 3,500 cases that truly live up to the brothers' original goal "of making excellent European-style table wines that are reasonably priced."

The Premium White (Seyval plus a touch of Vidal) has the crisp elegance of Bach's keyboard fugues. The balance and finesse of the Reserve Chardonnay is positively Mozartian, while the stylish Riesling,

Price Range of Wines: $6.95 for Premium White to $24.95 for Cadenza.

Special Events: Chef series, musical events, an annual festival, spotlight weekends.

- Premium White
- Sauvignon Blanc
- Traminette
- Vidal
- Proprietors' Red
- "Cadenza"

made like a German Spätlese, conjures up Schubert's *Trout* Quintet (yes, it's a good fish wine). Traminette is heavily perfumed, light and saucy, with lots of personality — the vinous equivalent of Edith Piaf, perhaps? The Premium Red, a Chambourcin/ Chellois/Leon Millot blend, is dry, informal, and joyful — a Louis-Armstrong kinda' wine which, according to the winemaker, is terrific with tomato-based pasta sauces. ("If you don't go with beer, go with Premium Red," he says.) Cadenza is a very fine limited-production Cabernet Sauvignon with a touch of Cabernet Franc, as rich and supple as the voice of Cecilia Bartoli singing Italian love arias.

Many Pennsylvania wine shops sell Allegro wines, and they are on several restaurant wine lists. But half the fun of going to a winery is to buy some wine. Take a bottle out on the deck for a picnic, and while you're surveying the countryside you may even find yourself humming a few bars of Beethoven's *Pastorale* Symphony.

CALVARESI WINERY

610-488-7966.

107 Shartlesville Rd., Bernville, PA 19506.

Directions: From Reading go 10 miles north on Rte. 183; then go right at the elementary school in Bernville to the winery, which will be 0.5 mile on the right.

Owners: Tom and Debbie Calvaresi.

Open: Thurs.–Fri. 1–6pm, Sat. & Sun. 12noon–5pm.

Price Range of Wines: $5.50 for Aurora and Niagara to $10.95 for Cabernet Franc and Pinot Gris.

- Baco Noir
- Aurora

This small, unassuming winery northwest of Reading is owned by Tom and Debbie Calvaresi. Like many other small-scale vintners, Tom started out as a home winemaker whose hobby became his profession. Tom began making wine in his basement in Reading. Eventually, the Calvaresis moved to the country, where they built a new home and a simple winery with a tasting room in one corner.

The Calvaresis have only a token five-acre vineyard, because Tom believes that most people aren't both good vineyard managers and good winemakers, and he wanted to concentrate his energies on winemaking rather than vine growing. Calvaresi produces a variety of wines (3,000 cases annually) from all-Pennsylvania grapes purchased from vineyards around the state, and long-term contracts with local growers have paid off as evidenced by the good recent vintages. These are true *vins de pays* — regional wines that are inexpensive, uncomplicated, and have a strong local following. Hybrid and native grape varieties are particularly good bets, although Calvaresi's Pinot Gris shows distinct promise and may lead to future successful endeavors with vinifera. The selection includes Chardonnay, Riesling, Seyval, and Baco Noir, a semi-dry, fruity red that, according to the Calvaresis, local people like with pasta. Aurora and Niagara, two grapey wines, are "just like the grapes grown in Grandma's backyard," says Tom.

CHADDSFORD WINERY
610-388-6221;
  fax 610-388-0360.
www.chaddsford.com.
E-mail: cfwine@
  chaddsford.com.
632 Baltimore Pike (Rte. 1),
  Chadds Ford, PA 19317.
Directions: From
  Philadelphia take I-95
  south to Rte. 322 west;
  turn left onto Rte. 1 and
  travel 6 miles to the
  winery.
Owners: Eric and Lee
  Miller.
Open: Daily 12noon–6pm;
  Jan.–Mar.: closed Mon.
Price Range of Wines: $7.99
  for Chaddsford White to
  $30 for Merican.
Special Events: Labor Day
  Bash (jazz) and Memorial
  Day Bash (blues), wine
  classes, December
  Candlelight Christmas in
  Chaddsford.

- Cabernet Franc
- Cabernet Sauvignon
- Chambourcin
- Chardonnay
- "Merican"
- Riesling

Chaddsford Winery proves that the old real-estate dictum "location, location, location" applies to wineries as well. Situated on Highway One in the beautiful Brandywine Valley, Chaddsford each year receives thousands of drop-in visitors who cruise the gift shop, take advantage of the winery's self-guided tour, taste the wines, and buy. (By Eastern standards, this is a large winery, with an annual production of 32,000 cases.) Of course, to succeed, wineries, unlike real estate, also need long-range goals, marketing skills, and a talented winemaker.

Chaddsford has been blessed with all of the above. Owners Eric and Lee Miller opened the winery in 1982, in what Eric describes as their big old Yankee barn. Eric's palate was trained in Burgundy, where he lived when he was growing up, and his winemaking skills were honed in upstate New York, where he was the winemaker at Benmarl, his father's winery.

When they decided to start their own winery, Eric and Lee might have gone straight to California, but Eric preferred the more restrained, complex wines of Burgundy to the low-acid, high-alcohol wines that California was then making. "But California has come around magnificently since then," Eric is quick to acknowledge. After searching for a place where they could make the Burgundy-style wines Eric loves, the Millers finally settled on Chadds Ford.

"The soils in the Brandywine Valley are similar to those in Burgundy," says Eric, "and the two regions have almost the same number of growing days — there are 195 here compared to 190 in Burgundy." The rolling hills, with lots of southern exposure, also remind him of Burgundy's terrain.

Eric has no illusions about replicating Burgundy here — "I'm not going to be making Montrachet," he smiles — but the wines he turns out are distinctive, characterized by a bracing thread of acidity, accompanied by a strength and depth of character that make them among the best in the East. Chaddsford makes a mind-boggling number of different wines. Among my favorites are the dreamy Stargazers Chardonnay and the Pinot Grigio, which strikes a nice balance between the roundness of Pinot Gris from Alsace and the more austere Italian interpretation of this grape. I like the regular Chardonnay, which is bright and fresh, and the plump and plummy Cabernet Franc. Merican — a Bordeaux/Meritage-style blend of Cabernet Sauvignon, Cabernet Franc, and

Eric Miller

Eric Miller is among the few contemporary East Coast winemakers whose name is well known to his colleagues. His wines are recognized by national wine writers and are served in important restaurants in Philadelphia, Washington, D.C., New York, and even California.

An ambitious marketing program has contributed to the steady growth of the winery. Production has expanded in a dozen years from 3,000 to 32,000 cases. I ask him how he accounts for this success. "The most important thing to me, as a winemaker, is also being a wine drinker," he says, only half jokingly. "The problem with many Eastern winemakers is that they may be foodies, but they aren't drinkers." Liking your product is one essential; good planning is another. "I'm trying to become a better businessman, and one thing I've learned is that you have to have a goal. In winemaking, it's the same thing. You have to have a vision of what you're going to make."

Knowing from the outset that he would never be able to create exact replicas of Burgundian white wines, Eric identified specific characteristics about them that he liked, and that he felt were achievable here. Then, by carefully selecting his grapes and using the right vinification techniques, he has kept his goal in mind. "I like lean, not fat wines," he says. "I like the fruit to be secondary, with nice vanilla showing through, and sometimes, toast. And honey, especially honey. I like a good, firm texture, which is something this region gives us, and I also like a wine that's minerally."

Eric's aim was to establish a regional image for his wines rather than to play David to California's Goliath. "I want my product to have a regional signature," he explains. "I can't out-market the big boys — the Mondavis and those people — but I can make something that is really good and unique to this area. You have to claim your own uniqueness and quality," he adds. "It's all you've got."

Another reason for his success, Eric admits, is that many people are simply curious about anything new. "It's in our human nature to poke around, to try new things," he says. An individual might resist tasting a new wine, explains Eric, because he likes French wine, or he's grown up drinking native American wine: "But then he'll get curious. 'How would it go with the local cuisine?' he might ask. Then he'll say, 'Hmmm, that crisp, dry, earthy Chardonnay from Stargazers Vineyard sure does taste a lot better with this Chesapeake crab cake than that sticky old Concord. I'll have to try it again sometime.'"

Like his wines, Eric's personality is colorful and intense, yet balanced by a playful streak that keeps peeking through. His conversation darts from idea to idea in the same way a hummingbird works a row of flowers.

"There are two distinctly different characteristics of white wine," he might announce suddenly, having run out of nectar from the previous conversational topic. "First, there are the big, rich wines for keeping, then there is the second category of lean, fresh, flowery wines that are meant to be drunk young. People don't distinguish between the two, but they're as different as vegetables and beef." He explains that people don't go into a store and ask for a nice, *old* apple. Instead, they want it to be fresh and crisp. Eric believes that we don't think about wines in those terms enough. "Of course," he admits, "price is a factor — those light, lean wines are admittedly less expensive. . . ." There he goes, whirring off toward another subject. I think I'll pour myself a glass of Chaddsford Chambourcin, finish up the last of the delicious cassoulet Eric has made to go with it, and do my best to follow wherever this new discussion leads.

Merlot — has complex aromas, robust and long-lasting flavors, and well-balanced tannins. In a great year it's a stunning wine.

FRENCH CREEK RIDGE VINEYARDS
610-286-7754.
200 Grove Rd., Elverson, PA 19520.
Directions: From the west follow PA Turnpike, take exit 22 onto Rte. 23 east. Go 6 miles and turn right onto Grove Rd. to winery on the left. From the east take exit 23 off PA Turnpike onto Rte. 100 north. Take 23 west, go approx. 6 miles, then turn left onto Grove Rd. to the winery.
Owners: Fred and Janet Maki.
Open: Thurs.–Sun. 12noon–5pm
Price Range of Wines: $10–$17.

• Cabernet Franc

A relatively new winery (Fred and Janet Maki bought their farm and planted the vineyards in 1991), French Creek Ridge is already showing promise with such good wines as Cabernet Franc and Vidal Ice Wine. Sparkling wine, Pinot Noir, and Cabernet Sauvignon also look good for the future. Production is currently about 1,000 cases, a number that's destined to grow.

NAYLOR VINEYARDS & WINE CELLAR
717-993-2431, 800-292-3370; fax 717-993-9460.
www.naylorwine.com.
4069 Vineyard Rd., Stewartstown, PA 17363.
Directions: From I-83 take exit 1 in Shrewsbury to Rte. 851 east and go 4 miles to Stewartstown. Take Rte. 24 (Main St.) north for 2 more miles to winery.
Owner: Richard H. Naylor.
Open: Mon.–Sat. 11am–6pm, Sun. 12noon–5pm.
Price Range of Wines: $6.50 for Niagara; $16.95 for Cabernet Sauvignon Reserve; $25 for Seductivo.

Nestled among the rolling hills and lush green valleys of southern York County, the warehouselike winery sits on a hill overlooking a 32-acre vineyard where Eastern labrusca, French-American hybrid, and European vinifera grapes grow. This plateau, rising 1,000 feet above sea level, was known as "The Barrens" during the Revolutionary days because it was devoid of trees. Early Indian tribes had burned them off so that grass could grow to provide a habitat for game. For a brief period in 1777–1778, York, the nearest city, served as the site of the Sixth Continental Congress.

The area was settled by Scotch, Irish, and German immigrant farmers in the late 1700s and has been primarily used as farmland ever since. In 1975, Richard H. Naylor began planting vines on his property. The winery, which was founded in 1978, currently produces 8,000 cases of wine annu-

Special Events: Big bands Sat. nights, Jun.–Sept; June Grape Blossom Festival, October Harvest Festival (including a grape-stomping contest), other seasonal festivals.

- Cabernet
- Chardonnay
- Pinot Gris
- Riesling
- Chambourcin
- Vignoles

ally, including more than 20 varieties of table wine.

A visit to Naylor Wine Cellars provides more than a sampling of wines. It's also an opportunity to stock up on wine accessories, gift baskets, and home winemaking supplies, as well as to receive a colorful and entertaining education. Dick Naylor's wine labels literally talk to consumers. For example, the Riesling label reads as follows: "Hi, I'm Dry Riesling . . . The scent of spring blossoms across a sunlit meadow quickens your senses in anticipation of an ultimate sensation. Then there's a gentle brush of flavor like a lover's lips, as you sample the essence of my lively, green, gold nectar. I'm crisp, fruity, yet very smooth . . . I prefer salads or lite soups, sandwiches and quiches . . . my favorite dish is broiled seafood . . . As you can see I'm very flexible and so much fun to be with socially." Quickened senses or not, it's a nice wine. So is the big, exuberant Chardonnay, the Pinot Gris (a good value at $9.95) and the Reserve Cabernet Sauvignon. Naylor's Chambourcin is a benchmark of this grape's potential — the best examples are as dark and mysterious as a well-made fruitcake. "Intimacy," a beautifully packaged after-dinner wine, is the soul of sweetness tempered by the acidity that characterizes Vignoles at its best.

NISSLEY VINEYARDS AND WINERY ESTATE
717-426-3514,
  800-522-2387 (PA only);
  fax 717-426-1391.
140 Vintage Dr.,
  Bainbridge, PA 17502.
Directions: From Lancaster take Rte. 30 west to Columbia and exit onto Rte. 441. Follow 441 north for 8 miles; turn right on Wickersham Rd. and continue 1.5 miles, following signs at the intersection to the winery.
Owners: The Nissley family.
Open: Mon.–Sat. 10am–5pm, Sun. 1–4pm.
Price Range of Wines: $7.75 for Niagara or Apple to $11.75 for Chambourcin.

Nissley is a family-run winery that makes fresh, clean, fruity wines from hybrid and native American grapes. Set on a 300-acre estate that's enhanced by a row of stone arches, the winery has been a favorite tourist destination for almost two decades. Forty-six acres of the estate are given over to vines, for an annual production of 2,000 cases. Wines range from Niagara to "Red Wine," a blend of red hybrid grapes with some white added to keep the potion light and simple.

A picnic area and lawn concerts on Saturday evenings in July and August provide additional pleasures for visitors.

SEVEN VALLEYS VINEYARD AND WINERY

Phone & fax: 717-235-6281.
www.yorkbiz.com/seven
valleyswinery.
885 Georges Ct., Glen Rock,
PA 17327.
Directions: From I-83 take
Exit 1 in Shrewsbury, and
go west on Forest Avenue
(Rte. 851) to the stoplight
at Main St. Turn right and
go 0. 2 mile to Clearview
Dr. Turn left and go 1.3
miles to Gantz Rd.. Turn
right and follow signs to
the winery.
Owners: Fred and Lynn
Hunter.
Open: Weekends
10am–5pm and by
appointment; Jan.–Feb.
by appointment only.
Price Range of Wines: $7.50
for Limerick (blend of
Vidal, Seyval, Cayuga,
and Steuben) to $12.85
for Late Harvest Vidal.
Special Feature: Wineshop:
27 N. Main St., Shrews-
bury, PA 17361; 717-227-
0257. Open Wed.–Sun.

After driving along country roads, one comes to an idyllic, isolated small valley where Seven Valleys Winery is situated. Fred and Lynn Hunter had looked at 106 other farms before agreeing that this old homestead was the right place for their winery. They chose this site because they believed its elevation, its well-drained soil, and its extended growing days were right for growing grapes. For several years the Hunters commuted to Phila-delphia, where they were psychologists. In the interim, they planted vines on their property and sold grapes to Pennsylvania wineries. Finally, on Labor Day in 1994, they opened their own winery in an old stone-walled cellar containing old-fash-ioned horse stalls. They now grow nine varieties of grapes on their 25-acre vineyard and produce 500 cases annually.

Seven Valley's wine production is still limited and still very young, but the Hunters' foresight is paying off — the wines get better and better every year. The Riesling and Gewürztraminer are pleas-ant, slightly sweet wines that are still dry enough to accompany a wide range of foods. Country Red, a blend of Chambourcin, Cabernet Sauvignon, and Chancellor is an assertive wine. "I'm not an expert at any of this," says Lynn candidly. "Just like everyone else, I taste the wine and if I like it, then it's good."

SMITHBRIDGE CELLARS

610-558-4703.
www.smithbridge.com.
E-mail: highgate@csrlink.net.
159 Beaver Valley Rd.,
Chadds Ford, PA 19317.
Directions: From the intersection of Rtes. 1 and 202,
go south on Rte. 202 for
2.2 miles. Then go right
on Beaver Valley Rd. 0.5
mile to the winery.
Owner: The Highgate
Corportation.
Open: Sat. & Sun. 12noon–
6pm; longer on holidays.
Price Range of Wines: $9
for Valley White; $20 for
Cabernet Sauvignon.

New owners Geoffrey and Frances Harrington and the Highgate Corporation took over Smithbridge Cellars in 1998. Since they'll be using the grapes from the vineyard that original owner Trip Stockli planted in 1983, the potential for mak-ing excellent wines is certainly there. About 1,200 cases, including Chardonnay and Cabernet, are being produced now annually from seven acres. This is definitely a winery that bears watching.

TWIN BROOK WINERY
717-442-4915.
5697 Strasburg Rd., Gap, PA 17527.
Directions: From Rte. 202 take Rte. 30 Bypass (around Exton, Downington, and Coatsville). At end of bypass continue west on Rte. 30 for 2.1 miles to Swan Rd.; turn left and follow signs 3 miles to winery.
Owners: Richard Caplan and Cheryl Caplan.
Open: Apr.–Dec.: Mon.–Sat. 10am–6pm, Sun. 12noon–5pm; Jan.–Mar.: Tues.–Sun. 12noon–5pm.
Price Range of Wines: $7.50 for Clock Tower White to $25 for Limited Merlot.
Special Events: Art exhibits throughout the year, outdoor concerts Sat. evenings in summer.

• Chardonnay
• Cabernet Franc
• Pinot Gris

The 70-acre parcel of land where Twin Brook Winery sits has a rich history. It's said that it was once the site of an Indian village, and in 1748 William Penn's brother granted the land to the Sadsbury Quakers. The stone and frame barn where the winery is located, was originally constructed in the 1800s, although it was partially destroyed by fire in 1933. A notation found on a board indicates it was rebuilt "in 9 days by 56 men and Charlie Celos." Today, the winery building is distinguished by its original hand-hewn beams — one of which is more than 65 feet long — and by the stained-glass windows that were salvaged from a demolished church. The Lancaster Historic Preservation Society recognizes Twin Brook as a significant historic site.

Named for a pair of brooks that run through the property, Twin Brook Winery was founded in 1988 by two lawyers, Richard Caplan and Cheryl Caplan. The winery's grapes all come from the estate's 30-acre vineyard. Twin Brook produces about 4,200 cases of wine annually, with 75 percent coming from vinifera grapes and the rest from hybrids.

If other wineries can produce wines as good as Twin Brook's Pinot Gris and Chaddsford's Pinot Grigio, Pennsylvania's reputation will continue to rise. Twin Brook's Cabernet Franc and Cabernet Sauvignon are also good. Several local restaurants pour Twin Brook wines.

MARYLAND

BASIGNANI WINERY
410-472-4718.
15722 Falls Rd., Sparks, MD 21152.
Directions: Take I-83 north to Shawan Rd. west (exit 20B). Go 3 miles to Falls Rd., turn right and go about 6 miles north to winery on the left.

Although his winery became bonded in 1986, Maryland native Bert Basignani only recently left the construction business. Now he's headed into winemaking full-time. This is good news for wine lovers. Bert currently makes 1,500-1,800 cases of wine, which he hopes to expand in the near future. (He owns 10 acres of vines next to the winery and leases other local vineyards.) The winery and tasting room are located on a pretty, wooded

Owners: Bert and Lynn
  Basignani.
Open: Sat. & Sun.
  12noon–5pm,
  or by appointment.
Price Range of Wines: $7.50
  for Seyval to $22 for
  Lorenzino Reserve
  (Cabernet blend).

• Cabernet Sauvignon
• Chardonnay
• "Elena"
• "Lorenzo"
• Riesling
• Seyval
• Vidal

slope. Generally considered Maryland's premier winery, Basignani produces wines that are featured in many local restaurants and retail wine shops. The Chardonnay is lush and long-lasting on the palate, the Seyval is unusually complex, and Elena — a white blend — is crisp and dry. The outstanding Cabernet tastes of spice and ripe fruit. Lorenzo, a Bordeaux-inspired red blend, has graceful aromas, body, and flavor.

Marguerite Thomas

The 19th-century stone and wood barn at Boordy Vineyards, Hydes, Maryland.

BOORDY VINEYARDS
410-592-5015;
  fax 410-592-5385.

Philip Wagner, the founder of Boordy Vineyards, is one of the most important figures in

www.boordy.com.
E-mail: boordy@aol.com.
12820 Long Green Pike,
Hydes, MD 21082.
Directions: From the
Baltimore Beltway take
exit 29 (Cromwell Bridge
Rd.) east to Glen Arm
Rd. Go left and travel
3 miles to Long Green
Pike. Turn left, and go
2 miles to winery.
Owner: Rob Deford.
Open: Mon.–Sat.
10am–5pm, Sun.1–5pm.
Price Range of Wines: $6.25
for Boordy White to
$15.25 for Sparkling
Wine.
Special Events: Spring
Champagne Release
Celebration, Mother's
Day Picnic, Father's Day
Pig Roast, summer
concert series, Fall
Harvest Party.

- Chardonnay
- Seyval
- Vidal

the contemporary chapter of winemaking in the Eastern United States. He was the London correspondent for the Baltimore *Evening Sun* in the 1930s when he was introduced to the hardy French hybrid grapes, which he felt produced a more appealing wine than native American grapes. A home-winemaker himself, Wagner was intrigued enough by these vines to bring some back and plant a vineyard at his home in Maryland. He was soon convinced that French hybrids were the solution to the problems American vintners faced in trying to grow European vinifera grapes in an era before technology made such an endeavor possible.

Wagner and his wife, Jocelyn, tirelessly promoted the establishment of an American wine industry in the East. They provided fledgling vintners with everything from vines to advice. In 1943, the Wagners founded Boordy Vineyards (they always insisted the name has no meaning). Today, Boordy is the oldest and largest winery in Maryland.

In 1980, Rob Deford, a friend of the Wagners and one of Boordy's grape suppliers, bought the winery and moved it to his 250-acre beef and grain farm a few miles away from the original site. Located in the scenic Long Green Valley, an area listed in the National Register of Historic Places, the winery is housed in a charming 19th-century stone and wood barn. To supplement the grapes grown on the estate's 16-acre vineyard, additional fruit is purchased from the Eastern Shore of Maryland, the central Piedmont region, and the Catoctin Mountains.

Boordy recently acquired 33 additional acres of vineyard in the western part of the state. The annual output of Boordy Vineyards is now 11,000 cases. The Chardonnay tends to be dominated by toasty, oak-infused aromas and flavors. Seyval has a mild herbal quality, while the Vidal smells and tastes like apples. Boordy Red, a blend of Chancellor, Chambourcin, and Cabernet Sauvignon is a good pasta wine.

CATOCTIN VINEYARDS
Phone & fax: 301-774-2310.
805 Greenbridge Rd.,
Brookeville, MD 20833.
Directions: From Frederick,
take I-70 west to Rte. 29;
take Rte. 29 south to

"**W**inemaking with vinifera grapes is still in the experimental stage on the East Coast," insists Bob Lyon, Catoctin's winemaker and one of its five owners. Bob knows as much as anybody about the comparative challenges of winemaking in the East. His background is in California winemaking,

Columbia; then take Rte. 108 northwest to Ashton; then take Rte. 650 (N. Hampshire Ave.) 4 miles to the winery, on the right.
Owners: Bob Lyon; Jerry, Ann, and Molly Milne; and Shahin Bagheri.
Open: Sat. & Sun. 12noon–5pm, Mon.–Fri. by appointment.
Price Range of Wines: $5–$20.

ELK RUN VINEYARDS & WINERY

410-775-2513;
    fax 410-875-2009.
www.elkrun.com.
E-mail: elk_run@msn.com.
15113 Liberty Rd., Mt. Airy, MD 21771.
Directions: From Baltimore: Take I-70 to Mt. Airy. Go right on Rte. 27 north and proceed 8 miles to Taylorsville. Go left on Rte 26 2.5 miles to the winery on the right. From Washington: Take I-270 to Father Hurley Blvd. Go right on Rte 27 north and proceed as above.
Owners: Fred and Carol Wilson.
Open: Wed.–Sat. 10am–5pm, Sun.1–5pm, or by appointment.
Price Range of Wines: $6.99 for Blush to $35 for Cabernet Sauvignon.
Special Events: Champagne release, barrel-tasting series, chocolate & wine cookoff (Feb.).

including a degree from U.C./Davis and work at Chateau Montelena and Byrd Vineyards. But he is also aware of the East's advantages. "This is the perfect climate for Cabernet Sauvignon. It's hot, but not too hot," he nods towards the 50-acre vineyard at the base of the Catoctin Mountain.

Bob's aim is to make classic-style Cabernet Sauvignon, with little fining, and aging in French oak for two years. The wines have good color and a pleasing intensity. The vineyard was planted in 1975 and the winery opened in 1983. It now produces some 3,500 cases annually, with half vinifera and the rest hybrid. Catoctin Vineyards provides a nice rural setting for a picnic.

This small winery and vineyard, located in rolling farmland, was the site of some of the earliest winemaking in the country: English, French, and German settlers turned apples, berries, native American grapes, and whatever other fruits they could raise into wine in the 1700s. Today, Fred and Carole Wilson make wine from the vinifera grapes that are Europe's traditional wine grape, including Chardonnay, Cabernet Sauvignon, Cabernet Franc, Merlot, Rielsing, and Gewürztraminer. They also make Vine de Jus Glacé, a much-admired late-harvest Gewürztraminer. They have 20 acres under cultivation and produce 4,000 cases annually.

FIORE WINERY AND LA FELICETTA VINEYARD

410-836-7605, 410-879-4007.
www.fiorewinery.com.
3026 Whiteford Rd.,
Pylesville, MD 21132.
Directions: From I-95 take
exit 77B to Rte. 24 north.
Travel 22 miles to Rte.
136. Go east 1 mile to the
winery.
Owners: Mike and Rose
Fiore.
Open: Wed.–Sun.
12noon–5pm, or by
appointment.
Price Range of Wines: $6
for Blush to $19.50 for
Caronte.
Special Events: August
wine festival, jazz and art
festival.

• Chambourcin
• "Caronte"
• Chardonnay
• "L'Ombra"
• Vignonles

Fiore and La Felicetta remind one of small, family-run wineries in Italy. Mama sits in the shade of the terrace on a hot summer morning while Mike Fiore is heading for the vineyards on a tractor. Bees buzz in the roses, the trees are filled with birds whistling Verdi, and one expects the smell of espresso to waft from the house. But Rose Fiore isn't in the kitchen brewing coffee. She's been pruning vines. She zips up now on a golf cart, wearing shorts, a tee shirt, blue eye shadow and a film of vineyard dust.

As we taste wines, Rose tells me the vineyard was named in honor of the La Felicetta Vineyard in the Calabria region of Italy, where the Fiore family has been making wine since the 16th century. Mike grew up in Italy, working in a vineyard planted by a Fiore whose ancestor came to America 200 ago to help Thomas Jefferson grow grapes. At the age of 17, Mike was the youngest cellarmaster in Italy.

The Fiores planted their first grapes here in 1982 and opened the winery in 1986. In 1998, Mike left his day job to work full-time at the winery. Fiore now has 14 acres of vines and produces 7,000 cases of wine annually. The Fiores believe the attractive Seyval and Vidal Blanc wines owe their distinctively dry and fruity flavor to the influence of the nearby Susquehanna River and the Chesapeake Bay. The soil composition here, where marble and slate quarries abound, also adds a distinctive, minerally flavor reminiscent of rain-dampened pebbles. Good though the white wines are, Mike's passion is for red. "White wines are okay when you don't have red," he shrugs.

Luckily, the local soils seem ideal for red wine grapes. Fiore Chambourcin, fermented on Cabernet stems to give it sturdier tannins and length of flavor, has the rich aroma of cedar and licorice. The Fiores are convinced that Chambourcin does better in the Mid-Atlantic regions than elsewhere in the East. "It's too cold in upstate New York and too hot in Virginia," says Rose. Caronte, a blend of Merlot and Cabernet Sauvignon, tastes of ripe cherries and plums. L'Ombra, a Seyval/Vidal blend that spends two months in French oak, is semi-dry and delicious. Fiore's brand-new tasting room has beautiful views over the vineyards and surrounding pastoral countryside.

WOODHALL VINEYARDS & WINE CELLARS

410-357-8644;
fax 410-357-8650.

Woodhall Vineyards makes only dry table wines. As Chris Lang, a former airline pilot, explains (referring to partner Al Copp), "Al hates

17912 York Rd., Parkton, MD 21120.

Directions: From I-695 take I-83 north to exit 27. Turn right on Mt. Carmel Rd. to York Rd.; turn left to winery, which will be on the left.

Owners: Chris and Patricia Lang, Al Copp.

Open: Tues.–Sun., 12noon–5pm, or by appointment (except major holidays).

Price Range of Wines: $7 for Simply Red and Angler Red to $25 for Copernica Reserve.

- Chardonnay
- "Parkton Prestige"
- Late Harvest Vidal

sweet wine, so we don't make any. People say that selling sweet wine is how you make money. I guess we'll never have any money."

Woodhall Chardonnay is nice and fruity with round overtones from time spent in oak barrels. Parkton Prestige, a Bordeaux-style red wine made from 65 percent Cabernet Sauvignon, 25 percent Merlot, and 10 percent Cabernet Franc is ripe and rich. The Late Harvest Vidal is a sweet, after-dinner charmer.

OTHER SOUTHERN PENNSYLVANIA AND MARYLAND WINERIES

ADAMS COUNTY WINERY (717-334-4631; 251 Peach Tree Rd., Orrtanna, PA 17353) Located minutes from Gettysburg, this winery is a good example of a small local winery that produces a variety of table wines from vinifera and hybrid grapes.

CYGNUS WINE CELLARS (410-374-6395; 3130 Long Lane, Manchester, MD 21102). Maryland's newest winery, Cygnus is a small family establishment located in the historic town of Manchester.

NORTHERN AND CENTRAL VIRGINIA

Ruins of the house once belonging to James Barbour, Governor of Virginia, near Barboursville. Thomas Jefferson was the architect.

It's an abrupt transition from bustling, cosmopolitan Washington, D.C., to the nearby graceful farmlands of northern Virginia. This is steeplechase and fox-hunting country, and the beautiful horse farms, peaceful country roads, and alluring villages provide one set of compelling reasons to visit the area. Another is the numerous Civil War and historical sites. American history lives in this bucolic region snuggled between the coastal plain and the Blue Ridge Mountains, which Virginians call the Piedmont.

The vineyards are interspersed among all of it. Fifty-three Virginia wineries are now in operation, a remarkable number considering that the first successful vinifera grape wines were made here less than 25 years ago

Manassas National Battlefield Park, where the Civil War battles of the First and Second Manassas (better known as Bull Run) were fought, is a few miles from peaceful vineyards. It's in the hills around Manassas that Stonewall Jackson got his name, when Bernard Bee, the Confederate general, rallied his men by calling out, "There is Jackson standing like a stone wall. Let us determine to die here, and we will conquer."

The town of Culpeper, where George Washington received his surveyor's license, was also the place from which Minutemen marched to battle carrying flags inscribed "Don't Tread On Me" and "Liberty or Death." And almost 100 years after the Revolutionary War, the town was the headquarters for the Union Army.

The countryside near Charlottesville is graced by many historic estates, including Monticello, Thomas Jefferson's estate. James Madison's home, Montpelier, is nearby. This is also Virginia's heartland and the center of her wine industry.

Virginia is potentially the most promising Eastern wine-producing state. Lying between the cold weather extreme of the Northeast and the intense heat and humidity of the South (where Pierce's Disease, a deadly vine ailment, thrives), this region may prove to have the most grape-friendly climate. Remarkably supportive state legislation encourages growers and wineries. Virginia has one of the most liberal farm winery laws in the nation. Unlike many other states in the East, wine can even be sold in Virginia's food stores. Another bonus is the affluent and educated population in the Washington, D.C., area, which supports the local wine industry.

Luca Paschina, manager, Barboursville Vineyards.

Marguerite Thomas

BARBOURSVILLE VINEYARDS
540-832-3824;
  fax 540-832-7572.
www.barboursvillewine.
  com.
E-mail: bvvwine@
  barboursvillewine.com.
17655 Winery Rd.,
  Barboursville, VA.

Barboursville is a Virginia winery with an Italian accent. It is owned by the Zonin family, Italy's largest wine producer; the Zonins own eight wineries in Italy. And an Italian winemaker guides it: Luca Paschina, a graduate in viticulture and enology from the Institute Umberto Primo in Alba, who came to Barboursville in 1990.

Barboursville was one of the pioneering Virginia wineries, founded in 1976 by Gianni Zonin. In

Mail: P.O. Box 136, RR 777,
Barboursville, VA 22923.
Directions: At junction of
Rtes. 20 & 33, take Rte. 20
south for 200 yds.; turn left
on Rte. 678 and travel for
0.5 mile, turn right onto
Rte. 777 (Winery Rd.), turn
right at the 1st driveway
and follow the signs.
Owners: The Zonin family.
Open: Mon.–Sat.
10am–5pm,
Sun. 11am–5pm.
Price Range of Wines: $7.49
for Rosato; $24.99 for the
1991 Cabernet Sauvignon
Reserve; $45.99 for the
1988 Cabernet Sauvignon
Reserve.
Special Events:
Shakespeare in the Ruins,
Autumn Explosion &
Barrel Tasting, Old
World Christmas
Celebration, and Guest-
Chef Dinner Series.

- Chardonnay
- Pinot Grigio
- Traminer
- Pinot Noir
- Merlot
- Barbera
- Cabernet
- "Philéo" (a dessert wine
made from Muscat)

BREAUX VINEYARDS
540-668-6299;
fax 540-668-6283.
www.breauxvineyards.com.
E-mail: breauxvin@aol.
com.
36888 Breaux Vineyards
Lane, Purcellville, VA
20132.
Directions: From Rte. 9 go
through Hillsboro, travel
2 more miles to Harpers

addition to establishing an outstanding winery, Zonin's great contribution to the Virginia wine industry was to bring a gifted young agronomist named Gabriele Rausse from Italy to manage the Barboursville property. Despite the skepticism of everyone, Gabriele was the first to show that vinifera grapes could be raised successfully in Virginia. Paschina, his successor, continues the tradition of creating outstanding wines. The Tuscan-style tasting room includes a large brick fireplace, an Italian terracotta floor, and a long tasting bar.

The winery is part of a lovely 830-acre estate (120 acres of vines) that also includes the picturesque ruins of a plantation house that once belonged to James Barbour, who was Governor of Virginia from 1812–14, a U.S. Senator, and a Secretary of State. Barbour's close friend Thomas Jefferson designed the house.

Such Italian classics as Pinot Grigio, Sangiovese, and Barbera are made here. In addition to the Italian varietals, the winery also makes French varietal wines such as Cabernet Franc, Pinot Noir, and Cabernet Sauvignon. All the red wines are characterized by deep color, complex and inviting flavors, and a long aftertaste that lingers satisfyingly in the mouth. Malvaxia Reserve, a dessert wine produced from late-harvest Malvasia grapes, explodes in the mouth like a comet of sweet golden fruit (the Malvaxia bottle is a reproduction of an antique olive-oil bottle discovered in the ruins of the plantation house). Philéo, a blend of Muscat, Riesling, and Malvasia grapes, is wonderfully fragrant.

Annual production of all wines is 25,000 cases.

The first vintage of this new and already very exciting winery was in 1997. Winemaker David Collins helped the original owners plant the vines in 1985, several years before the Breaux bought the property. David then went on to Willowcroft Vineyards, where he perfected the art and science of winemaking. When Alexis and Paul bought the vineyard and nurtured it back to health after it had been neglected for several years, they hired David to come back as winemaker. Perhaps he feels a

Ferry Rd. Bear right to winery, 1 mile on right.
Open: Thurs.–Mon. 11am–5pm.
Owners: Paul and Alexis Breaux.
Price Range of Wines: $10–$18.
Special Features: Informal café, outdoor patio seating.
Special Event: Spring Cajun Festival, with live music and Louisiana cuisine.

- Chardonnay
- Cabernet Franc
- Cabernet Sauvignon
- Sauvignon Blanc
- Riesling
- Vidal

sense of parental connection to the grapes, or maybe this site is particularly suitable for vines. Having the unconditional and enthusiastic support of the owners surely inspires him ("Paul poured his heart and pocketbook into this venture," he says). Whatever the reasons, David's evident passion for this vineyard and winery translates into some mighty superior wines. I wouldn't hesitate to recommend all of Breaux's wines, from the spicy, ripe Seyval to the rich Barrel Fermented Chardonnay, whose flavors linger hauntingly in the mouth. Madeleine's Chardonnay is as charming as the owners' young daughter, after whom the wine was named. The delicious "Lafayette" Cabernet Franc — whose crawfish label is a reminder of the Breaux's Cajun origins — delivers a jolt of fruity aftertaste.

Breaux produced only about 3,500 cases in 1998 but, thank heavens, the short-term goal is to increase to about 10,000 cases. The more of these fine wines the better, as far as I'm concerned. The winery is located near historic Harpers Ferry and is only a couple of miles from Hillsboro, a picturesque village of stone houses.

BURNLEY VINEYARDS
540-832-2828;
    fax 540-832-2280.
4500 Winery Lane,
    Barboursville, VA 22923.
Directions: From
    Charlottesville, go north
    15 miles on Rte. 20 to Rte.
    641. Turn left and go 3
    miles to winery. From
    intersection of Rte. 33 &
    20, take 20 south 2 miles;
    turn right on Rte. 64 and
    go 3 miles to winery.
Owners: Lee, Dawn, C.J.,
    and Pat Reeder.
Open: Apr.–Dec.: daily
    11am–5pm; Jan.–Mar.:
    Fri.–Mon. 11am–5pm, or
    by appointment.
Price Range of Wines: $10
    for Rivanna Red to $15
    for Cabernet Sauvignon.

- Rivanna White
- Rivanna Red
- Cabernet Sauvignon

Burnley is a small family winery (about 5,000 cases) with a big selection of wines: at least 12 different choices. The Reeder family began planting vines in 1977, making this one of the oldest vineyards in the Monticello viticultural area (27 acres in all). Eventually, they began making wine, and in 1985 they opened their own tasting room. The rustic barn-like space affords lovely views of the countryside. (In cool weather, a woodburning stove provides a cozy ambience.) Rivanna White is a pleasant Vidal, and Rivanna Red is an unusual blend of Chambourcin, Maréchal Foch, and Cabernet Franc. The unfined and unfiltered Cabernet Sauvignon is full bodied and full of personality.

Government and Grapes – Governor Jim Gilmore and State Enologist Bruce Zoecklein

That Virginia wineries are the healthiest and fastest growing among the Eastern states is probably due more to the political climate than to weather patterns and soil types. "Virginia's wine industry is becoming widely recognized as one of the best in the nation," states Governor Jim Gilmore. "Its success is due in no small measure to the commitment by the state government to foster a climate in which it has been able to thrive."

"A couple of progressive governors started the ball rolling," recalls state enologist Bruce Zoecklein. "They saw that it wasn't just beverage alcohol they were looking at, but value added products that impact on the state in the form of agricultural production, marketing, tourism and tax revenues." People who may have been initially hesitant — from government to higher education — got on board. "When I first arrived here in 1985, it would have taken an Act of Congress to get a local restaurant to pour Virginia wines," says Bruce. "Now we have peo-

(Continued)

ple who are genuinely interested in the industry, including restaurateurs, retailers, and customers."

Without vigorous state support, Virginia's wine industry would be nowhere near as strong as it is. "We provide tax advantages to our wineries and fund research and marketing for the industry," explains Governor Gilmore. Bruce Zoecklein's contributions through Virginia Tech are among the most striking examples of what forward-thinking support can achieve. A large part of Bruce's job is to identify and address problems of climate, fruit chemistry, technical deficiencies, and the economics of growing grapes and making wines. His strategies are fivefold:

- To conduct a wide-ranging program for grape growers and winemakers, including short courses, seminars, and symposia that brings in producers and researchers from all over the world.

- To organize winery roundtables to be attended by the vintners. ("How many vintners come to these?" I asked Bruce. "Why, all of them," he replied. "Virtually every commercial vintner in Virginia has attended.") Wines of particular regions and styles are tasted and evaluated sensorialy and blindly, then discussed. "This has had a major impact on creating a sense of community," says Bruce. It has also upped the winemaking ante by exposing vintners to styles of wine they might otherwise never encounter; if you aren't intimately familiar with fine wines, you'll never be able to make them yourself.

- To oversee a laboratory that provides free analytical support of chemical, physical, microbiological, and sensorial grape components.

- To conduct on-site visits to wineries. "It's harder to do that now that we have so many wineries," Bruce acknowledges, "but it allows me to keep my finger on the pace of development."

- To publish a bimonthly journal providing news and information to vintners.

Working with his counterpart, Virginia Tech viticulturist Tony Wolf, Bruce explains that a nice synergism is at work. "The state realized that if the industry is going to be competitive it needs to have help. We get more support commensurate to our size than our California counterpart with UC Davis." The results of this support are clear, in quantity and quality. When Bruce arrived in 1995, Virginia produced 30,000 cases of wine a year. Today, with 53 wineries operating and more in the wings, 200,000 cases are produced.

"I am very proud of our wine industry, and enthusiastically support its success," beams Governor Gilmore. Would that all state leaders felt this way.

DOMINION WINE CELLARS
540-825-8772;
fax 540-829-0377.

Largely an arm of Williamsburg Winery, this winery offers all the products from the parent company. Additionally, Dominion produces Raspberry Merlot, Blackberry Merlot, and a Late

1 Winery Ave., P.O. Box 1057, Culpeper, VA 22701.

Directions: From Rte. 29 Bypass, take Culpeper exit onto Rte. 3; turn right on McDevitt Dr. and continue to Winery Ave.

Owner: Williamsburg Winery.

Open: Apr.–Oct.: daily 11am–5pm; Nov.–Dec.: Wed.–Sat.11am–4:30pm, Sun. 12noon–4:30pm; Jan.–Mar.: Fri.–Sat. 11am–4:30pm, Sun. 12noon–4:30pm.

Price Range of Wines: $8 for dry red wine to $14–$18 for dessert wines.

Harvest Dessert Wine. The modern winery, comprising nine acres, is located in an industrial park with views over the scenic countryside.

FARFELU VINEYARD

540-364-2930.

E-mail: cjran@mnsinc.com.

13058 Crest Hill Rd., Flint Hill, VA 22627.

Directions: Take Rte. 522 to Flint Hill. Turn onto Crest Hill Rd. and go 3.5 miles to winery.

Owner: C.J. Ran.

Open: Sat. & Sun. 11am–4:30pm, or by appointment.

Price of Wines: $7 for Red or White Picnic to $10 for Chardonnay and Merlot.

Farfelu's vines were planted in 1967. Its wines first went on sale in 1976 after it became the first licensed winery in Virginia (in 1975). The tasting room is in a weathered gray vintage barn, and the vineyards are beautifully situated on rolling hills overlooking the Rappahannock River. Soft, appealing red and white "picnic" wines made primarily from hybrids are produced here, as well as a pleasant Chardonnay (I wasn't able to taste the Merlot, as it was sold out). "Since I've been doing this for 30 years — and am now doing it full-time — you'd think I'd know what I was doing," says C.J. Ran. "But it's not true. If you don't keep learning, you're in trouble."

One of the things he'll soon be learning is how well the Syrah and Mourvèdre vines he recently planted will perform in this environment. While vintner Dennis Horton is making a name for himself with these and other Rhône Valley varietals, there hasn't yet been what you might call a rush to plant them here in Virginia. Why, I asked C.J., did he do it? "Bullheadedness" was the answer. "Plus, I've always liked Syrah," he added. "No one else is doing it, so I decided I would."

Since I've always liked Syrah, too, I'll be looking forward to tasting these when they're released in a couple of years.

Cheryl and Al Kellert in the gazebo at Gray Ghost Vineyards.

Marguerite Thomas

GRAY GHOST VINEYARDS
Phone & fax: 540-937-4869.
14706 Lee Hwy.,
   Amissville, VA 20106.
Directions: From
   Warrenton take Hwy.
   211 west for 11 miles to
   the winery, which will
   be on the left.
Owners: Al and Cheryl
   Kellert.
Open: Fri.–Sun., Mon.
   federal holidays,
   11am–5pm; other days
   by appointment.
Price Range of Wines: $9
   for Vidal Blanc; $12 for
   Chardonnay; $20 for
   Merlot.

• Cabernet Franc
• Chardonnay
• Vidal

This winery is named for John Mosby, the Confederate colonel who headed the only unit that never surrendered during the Civil War and who, by disappearing like a ghost, persistently avoided capture. Colonel Mosby was also a wine drinker. Al and Cheryl Kellert, the owners and winemakers at Gray Ghost Vineyards, share both an interest in the Civil War events that unfolded near their property and a passion for wine.

Al began making wine when he was a college student. Later, he and Cheryl planted vines in their suburban garden near Washington, D.C. In 1986, they bought this farm, which had earlier been an apple orchard and a horse farm, and they moved their vines here. They now have 11 acres of vineyards, planted mostly with vinifera grapes, supplemented by small amounts of Vidal and Seyval.

Al still works for the U.S. Postal Service in Washington, while Cheryl, who trained at several Virginia wineries, runs Gray Ghost. The 2,000 cases of wine produced annually include a gentle Chardonnay that is fermented in new French oak barrels and an unfiltered, nicely balanced Cabernet Franc.

Gray Ghost reds have a distinctive, pleasantly smoky aroma. "We've noticed that too," Al remarked. "We suspect it might be something in the soil." Hmmm, I wonder if John Mosby smoked. . . .

HORTON VINEYARDS

540-832-7440, 800-829-4633; fax 540-832-7187. www.hvwine.com. 6399 Spottswood Tr. (Rte. 33), Gordonsville, VA 22942.

Directions: From Rte. 29 take Rte. 33 east for 8 miles to the winery entrance, which will be on the left. From Gordonsville, take Rte. 33 west for 4 miles to the winery entrance, which will be on the right. The winery is 0.5 mile from the town of Barboursville.

Owners: Dennis and Sharon Horton; Joan Bieda.

Open: Daily 11am–5pm; closed Thanksgiving, Christmas, New Year's Day.

Price Range of Wines: $7 for Vidal Blanc to $25 for Touriga Nacional.

Special Event: Annual Pig Roast in June.

- Grenache
- Malbec
- Marsanne
- Mourvèdre
- Norton
- Syrah
- Viognier

Like many winery proprietors in the East, Dennis Horton started in 1983 by planting a small vineyard at his home. As his interest and knowledge grew, he began to realize that the humid conditions in the East favored grapes with thick skins and loose clusters. In his search for the ideal grape, he gravitated to the Rhône Valley in southern France, where he was impressed by the refined wines produced despite hot summer weather that rivaled Virginia's.

Viognier, a thick-skinned, loose-clustered, heat-loving grape used for Condrieu and Chateau Grillet wines, particularly struck his fancy. When Dennis and his business partner Joan Bieda began planning their vineyard, they concentrated on Viognier and other Rhône varieties, such as Marsanne, Mourvèdre, Syrah, Grenache, and Malbec. The vineyard was planted in 1988 under the supervision of Dennis's wife, Sharon.

But the Rhône was not Dennis Horton's only fixation. He also had a crush (so to speak) on Norton, a true Virginia grape propagated in 1835 in Richmond, Virginia, by D. N. Norton, who wanted to develop a grape suitable for Virginia's climate. The Norton was so successful that it became the backbone of the Monticello Wine Company in Charlottesville, and as early as the late 1800s, the Monticello Company made Virginia the capital of the Eastern Wine Belt. It retained its position until the state's entire wine industry collapsed under the pressure of Prohibition.

Dennis, who had found a few Norton survivors in his home state of Missouri, became interested in reviving this historic grape. Perhaps Horton's Norton (do you think the name is one reason Dennis loves this grape?) will help Virginia regain its earlier leadership. The wine has an astonishingly dark, inky color and a pronounced aroma reminiscent of cherries and plums. Horton Viognier also has an intense aroma — putting nose to glass is like burying your face in a hedge of honeysuckle. It has the dryness and depth one associates with fine Viognier, and a satisfying long finish. Robert Parker wrote about the 1993 vintage, "While it will not replace a great Condrieu from the likes of Marcel Guigal or André Parret, it represents a major breakthrough in what can be achieved in specific microclimates in the mid-Atlantic region . . . Bravo!" Horton's total production, including that of its affiliate winery Montdomaine, is 30,000 cases.

JEFFERSON VINEYARDS
804-977-3042, 800-272-3042;
fax 804-977-5459.
1353 Thomas Jefferson
Pkwy. (Rte. 9), P.O. Box
293, Charlottesville, VA
22902.
Directions: On Hwy. 53
between Monticello and
Ashlawn-Highland just
southeast of
Charlottesville.
Owner: Stanley Woodward
Jr.
Open: Daily 11am–5pm
except Christmas and
New Year's Day.
Price Range of Wines: $9.95
for dry Seyval to $26.95
for Fantaisie Sauvage.

- Cabernet Franc
- Cabernet Sauvignon
- Chardonnay
- Estate Reserve (Malbec, Merlot, Cabernet Sauvignon)
- Late Harvest Vidal
- Pinot Gris
- Merlot
- Seyval

In 1774, Filippo Mazzei, an Italian viticulturist and a friend of Thomas Jefferson, planted vinifera wine grapes on this site. Mazzei's efforts to grow grapes and make wine were ultimately unsuccessful, but today, 17 acres of vines that were planted in the same spot in 1981 have fared well. "We have one of the best vineyard sites in the state," declares winemaker Michael Shaps. "It's on a southeast-facing slope. It's hot, but it gets a good breeze coming down the mountain so we don't have much of a problem with humidity and mildew. Because of the heat, the fruit ripens very fast."

Michael came to Jefferson in 1995, and under his guidance the wines have improved dramatically. Sales have doubled since he's been here and production has doubled from 4,000 to 8,000 cases. On weekends the tasting room and deck are packed. People come here because of the winery's proximity to Monticello and because of the excellent wines. The Seyval Blanc is clean and refreshing, the Pinot Gris soft and mouth filling. Since the first vintage of Chardonnay Reserve (1997) sold out in less than six months, Michael tripled the '98 to 1,500 cases, which also went fast. There's an even shorter supply (120 cases) of the creamy, aromatic Fantaisie Sauvage, the Chardonnay made from native yeasts. The red wines tend to be huge, deep, and intense with ripe fruit and earthy tones. The Late Harvest Vidal (made from grapes that have been frozen to concentrate the juice) is a sweet delicacy that Michael describes as "pure candy." These are terrific wines that come from vineyards set in the same countryside that Thomas Jefferson loved so much.

The view from Loudoun Valley Vineyards is spectacular.

Marguerite Thomas

LOUDOUN VALLEY VINEYARDS
540-882-3375.
www.loudounvalley
vineyards.com.
E-mail: wine@loudoun
valleyvineyards.com.
38638 Old Wheatland Rd.,
Waterford, VA 20197.
Directions: From Leesburg
take Rte. 7 west for 2
miles to Rte. 9 west. Go 5
miles to the winery on
the right.
Owners: Dolores and
Hubert Tucker.
Open: Apr.–Dec.:
Wed.–Sun. 11am–5pm;
Jan.–Mar.: Sat. & Sun.
11am–5pm.
Price Range of Wines: $8
for table whites to $20 for
Native Yeast Virginia
Oak Chardonnay.
Special Events:
Winemaker's dinners,
Oktoberfest, Winter Soup
Day.

• Chardonnay
• Merlot
• Seyval

Loudoun Valley Vineyards sits on a plateau over-looking vineyards and farms, with the Blue Ridge Mountains to the west and the Catoctin Mountains to the east. The view is spectacular enough to have inspired neighboring artist Rowan LeCompte to create several paintings, one of which is reproduced on Loudoun's labels. LeCompte also designed stained-glass windows and mosaic murals for the National Cathedral in Washington.

Hubert Tucker, an aeronautical engineer with the Federal Aviation Administration, and his wife, Dolores, are the winery owners. Hubert is the winemaker as well. He grows a variety of grapes in his 29-acre vineyard, producing about 5,000 cases of wine a year. He also operates a nursery from which he sells grafted vinifera rootstock to winer-ies.

Loudoun's Chardonnay is crisp and flinty, reflecting the vineyard's rock and clay soil. The Vintner Select Chardonnay, made with native yeasts and fermented in barrels made from native oak (harvested in Virginia, air-dried in California, and coopered in France), is an elegant wine indeed. The Seyval is soft, yet finishes as dry as a Pinot Grigio. The Riesling is a classic semi-sweet wine with a lemony finish.

The winery has a small kitchen behind the tast-ing room, where light fare such as cheese and bread plates, pâtés, and baked Brie are prepared.

These can be enjoyed on a wraparound deck as you drink some wine and drink in the tranquil view as well.

Owner and winemaker Archie Smith of Meredyth Vineyards.

MEREDYTH VINEYARDS
540-687-6277.
Rte. 628, Middleburg, VA.
Mail: P.O. Box 347, Middleburg, VA 20118.
Directions: From Washington, D.C.: Take I-66 to exit 31. Go north on Rte. 245 to Rte. 55, then go right for 1 block. Turn left on Rte. 626 and travel 3.75 miles. Turn right on Rte. 679 and go 1 mile to Rte. 628. The winery will be on the left. From Middleburg: Turn south at the traffic light. Go 2.5 miles to Rte. 628, then turn right and go 2.5 miles to winery.
Owner: Archie Smith.
Open: Daily 11am–5pm except Thanksgiving, Christmas, New Year's Day.
Price Range of Wines: $10 for Blush; $15 for Cabernet Sauvignon.

One approaches Meredyth Vineyards along lazy country roads that skirt the Bull Run Mountains. A long driveway leads up through fields and vineyards, past the ruins of an old farmhouse, to the winemaking facility and tasting room. Meredyth's vineyards were planted on the family farm in 1972 and the first harvest was in 1975, making it the second-oldest winery in Virginia.

Winery owner Archie Smith was teaching philosophy at Oxford when his father summoned him back to help with the Meredyth winery in the mid-1970s. After commuting to England for a while, Archie finally moved back to Virginia to become a full-time winemaker.

The 216-acre farm includes 58 acres of vines, both vinifera and hybrid grapes. Archie defends the hybrids energetically, arguing that they are well suited to the Virginia climate. "Our vines represent both our Old and the New World heritage," he maintains. "A wine like De Chaunac [a hybrid] is hard to sell off the supermarket shelf, but it's interesting from a winemaker's point of view. If grown right, it's chock full of fruit flavors, but it doesn't have much tannin. Personally, I like a wine like this. I don't like wine that sticks to your teeth." The downside of De Chaunac is that it oxidizes easily. "It can taste like rubber boots," Archie acknowledges. Others apparently share his enthusiasm, since the wine consistently sells out.

One of Meredyth's popular Old World/New World wines is Harvest Red, a blend of Cabernet Franc and Maréchal Foch grapes. It's fresh and light, with a faint rose-petal aroma. ("We call it our white wine in drag," smiles Archie.) For those of us who like "wine that sticks to your teeth," Meredyth's Cabernet Sauvignon is softly tannic, with good flavors. From 10,000 to 12,000 cases of wine are produced at Meredyth annually. Picnic tables look out toward the mountains.

Tareq Salahi, winemaker at Oasis Vineyards.

Marguerite Thomas

OASIS VINEYARDS
540-635-7656, 800-304-7656.
www.oasiswine.com.
E-mail: oasiswine@aol.com.
14141 Hume Rd., Hume,
  VA 22639.
Directions: Going west on
  I-66, take exit 27 at
  Marshall, follow Rte. 647
  south for 4 miles to Rte.
  635, turn right and go 10
  miles to winery.
Owners: Dirgham and
  Corinne Salahi.
Open: Daily 10am–5pm,
  except Thanksgiving,
  Christmas, New Year's
  Day.

Oasis Vineyards claims to own the oldest plantings of Chardonnay and Cabernet Sauvignon grapes in Virginia. It was also the first in the state to focus exclusively on vinifera grapes and the first to make a sparkling wine.

From its initial vintage in 1980, when 186 cases of wine were produced, Oasis is now up to about 20,000 cases and still growing. The winery owns 80 acres of vineyards at the winery site, plus 20 additional acres. The proprietors are Jerusalem-born Dirgham Salahi and his Belgian wife, Corinne, who are in the process of handing over many of the business responsibilities to their son, Tareq. Tareq graduated in enology from the University of California at Davis and then worked at Napa's Domaine

Price Range of Wines: $9.50 for Dogwood Chardonnay; $38.50 for Meritage; $55 for Millennium Champagne.
Special Features: Indoor or outdoor café-style seating; heated pavilion seating 2,500.
Special Events: Spring Open House with hors d'oeuvres and live music, Polo Wine and Twilight Dine, Murder & Winemaker Dinner, August Blessing of the Vineyards.

- Chardonnay
- Gewürztraminer
- Merlot
- Cabernet Sauvignon
- Sparkling Wines

PIEDMONT VINEYARDS & WINERY
540-687-5528;
    fax 540-687-5777.
Rte. 626, P.O. Box 286, Middleburg, VA 20118.
Directions: From Washington, D.C., take I-66 to Rte. 50 west, following it to Rte. 626 south. From Middleburg, it's 3 miles south on Rte. 626.
Owner: Gerhard von Finck.
Open: Daily 10am–5pm, except major holidays.
Price Range of Wines: $15 to $30 (Chardonnay).

- Chardonnay
- Native Yeast Chardonnay
- Cabernet Sauvignon
- Merlot

Carneros, which is known for its sparkling wines. Oasis Vineyards sparkling wines are excellent — the Brut is delicate, the Cuvée D'Or somewhat more full-bodied. The Chardonnays tend to be neat and dry, the Riesling leaves a crisp impression even though it is somewhat sweet, and the Gewürztraminer has a characteristic spicy quality. The red wines — Merlot, Cabernet Sauvignon, and the Meritage blend — tend to be soft and discreet in style.

Oasis has a small café that offers Virginia cheeses, smoked trout, and other informal foods. This is a lovely spot for a picnic, with splendid views of the surrounding mountains.

Piedmont Winery was started in 1975 by 73-year-old Elizabeth Furness, who converted her former dairy farm to a winery when she realized grapes were more profitable than milk. Today Piedmont is owned by German investor Gerhard von Finck. Winemakers are John Fitter and Alan LeBlanc Kinne, one of Virginia's top winemaking consultants. Twenty-eight acres are under cultivation, and the winery produces 3,500 cases annually.

Piedmont's many different Chardonnays begin with the elegant, dry Hunt Country label and work up to the glorious Native Yeast Chardonnay, made from fruit that comes from 25-year-old vines — possibly the oldest vinifera vines in Virginia. This wine would easily hold its own against fine Napa or white Burgundy wines. While white wines represent 80 to 85 percent of Piedmont's production, red wines are also beginning to put in an appearance here. Recent Merlot and Cabernet Sauvignon vintages appear excellent indeed, with both showing well-balanced ripe fruit flavors.

PRINCE MICHEL AND RAPIDAN RIVER VINEYARDS
540-547-3707, 800-869-8242; fax 540-547-3088.
www.princemichel.com.
E-mail: info@prince michel.com.
Rte. 29, Leon (near Culpeper), VA.
Mail: HCR Box 77, Leon, VA 22725.
Directions: 10 miles south of Culpeper on Rte. 29.
Owner: Jean Leducq.
Open: Daily 10am–5pm.
Price Range of Wines:
Rapidan River: $9.95 for Riesling to $18.95 for Gewürztraminer.
Prince Michel: $12.95 for Chardonnay to $19.95 for Cabernet/Merlot Reserve.
Special Features: Wine museum, gift shop, restaurant, suites for guests.

• Cabernet Sauvignon
• Chardonnay
• Gewürztraminer
• Merlot
• Merlot/Cabernet
• Sauvignon Reserve

Prince Michel, established in 1983, and its affiliate, Rapidan River Vineyards, are owned by French businessman Jean Leducq. The winemaker is Tom Payette. The combined acreage, which includes 100 acres at Prince Michel and 50 acres at Rapidan, makes this one of the largest vineyard holdings in Virginia. Furthermore, Prince Michel's 30,000-case annual production is one of the largest in the state. It is among the few Virginia vineyards to machine-harvest its grapes.

Jacques Boissenot, a noted wine consultant from Bordeaux, is often called upon to share his expertise at Prince Michel. Among Boissenot's other clients are some of France's most illustrious châteaux, including Pichon-Longueville, Léoville-Barton, and Château-Margaux. Global winemakers such as Boissenot, who is also affiliated with Lafite-Rothchild's operations in Chile, and Bruno Prats, the owner of France's prestigious Cos d'Estournel winery who also consults at Millbrook Winery in New York's Hudson River Valley, are exerting a positive influence on the quality of American wines.

Rapidan River Riesling and Gewürztraminer are fruity and semi-dry, which is to say, somewhat sweet; they would both make good aperitifs as well as accompaniments to spicy dishes and turkey. The Chardonnay tends to be rich and bold. The reds usually all have good aroma, color, and strength.

Prince Michel has a small but interesting wine museum and a superior gift shop. Visitors are encouraged to take an informative self-guided tour of the winery, where detailed explanations of each aspect of winemaking are clearly illustrated. The restaurant is outstanding (and expensive).

SWEDENBURG ESTATE VINEYARD
540-687-5219.
Rte. 50, Middleburg, VA.
Mail: 23595 Winery Lane, Middleburg, VA 20117.
Directions: From Middleburg, take Rte. 50 for 1 mile east to the winery.
Owners: Wayne and Juanita Swedenburg.

Swedenburg Estate Vineyard is part of a working farm that was established 225 years ago by a royal grant instructing the lessee "to build a dwelling house twenty feet long and sixteen feet wide." That original house is now part of the Swedenburg family residence.

Wayne Swedenburg, whose parents were Swedish, was in the Foreign Service when he and his wife, Juanita, bought the farm in 1976, 10 years before Wayne retired. First they raised a few head

View of the fields at Swedenburg Estate Vineyard.

Marguerite Thomas

Open: Daily 10am–4pm.
Price Range of Wines: $8 for Riesling; $11 for Chardonnay; $14 for Cabernet Sauvignon.

• Riesling

of cattle and some hay. Then, in 1980, feeling grapes would be more profitable, they planted a few vines. Eight years later, they opened the winery.

Swedenburg now has about 15 acres of grapes. All are vinifera except for a small amount of Seyval. It produces about 3,000 cases of wine each year.

Swedenburg makes German-style wines. All of the winery equipment is German, and many German practices are followed in the vineyard, including trellising. Swedenburg Riesling, for example, which has more appeal than the average American Riesling, has a lower alcohol content (about 9.5 percent), similar to its German counterparts. While it may be too sweet to accompany most fish dishes, it makes a pleasant sipping wine. The oak-aged Chardonnay is harmonious, and the Cabernet Sauvignon, a grape that does well in the region's limestone soil, is very drinkable.

TARARA VINEYARD & WINERY
703-771-7100.
www.tarara.com.
13648 Tarara Lane, Leesburg, VA, 20176.
Directions: From Leesburg, take Rte. 15 north about 8 miles to Lucketts. Turn right onto Rte. 662 and go 3 miles to the winery sign. The driveway is on the left.

Margaret and Whitie Hubert named their 475-acre farm after the Tarara River, which flooded the area in 1985, the year they bought their property. Tarara is also "Ararat" spelled backwards, which was the name of the mountain where Noah landed after the great flood (the first thing Noah then did was to plant a grapevine). It's hard to believe that this idyllic spot overlooking the Potomac River is only 60 minutes from the turmoil of Washington, D.C. The site offers a hospitable environment for vines as a constant breeze from the river moderates the temperatures. To provide a

Owners: Margaret and Whitie Hubert.

Open: Daily 11am–5pm; weekends only Jan.–Mar.

Price Range of Wines: $7.99 for Blush to $15.99 for Cabernet Sauvignon and Merlot.

Special Features: Winery in a large cave, picnic deck overlooking the Potomac, hiking trails, softball diamond, volleyball court, horseshoe pit, a B&B.

Special Events: Vintners' dinners, wine festivals, wine seminars.

- Cabernet Franc
- Merlot
- Pinot Gris

cool, stable climate in which his wines could age gracefully in their French barrels, Whitie (a retired contractor and developer) blasted a 6,000-square-foot cave out of the land. In the tasting room above the caves, samples are poured from bottles with colorful labels designed by the Huberts' daughter, Martha, a San Francisco artist.

Doug Fabbioli, who was part of the winemaking staff at California's esteemed Buena Vista Winery, came to Tarara in 1997 and has already raised the quality of the wines to a new level. "I'm trying to marry my passion and wine knowledge from California with the climate and soils of Virginia," he explains. The unusual Pinot Gris is stylistically halfway between austere Pinot Grigio and lusher Alsace. Chardonnay is nicely balanced and Merlot is soft and well structured. Terra Rouge, an easygoing blend of Chambourcin and Vidal Blanc with a touch of sweetness, is Doug's "favorite Sunday afternoon sipping wine."

The winery has 55 acres under cultivation and produces 7,000 cases annually.

WILLOWCROFT FARM VINEYARDS
703-777-8161;
    fax 703-777-8157.
E-mail: willowine@aol.com.

The approach to Willowcroft is along a dirt and gravel road that dips and sweeps across the side of Mt. Gilead, offering dramatic views of hayfields, countryside, and distant mountains. When

38906 Mt. Gilead Rd.,
    Leesburg, VA 20175.
Directions: From Leesburg
    go south on Rte. 15. At
    Rte. 704, turn right and
    then immediately left
    onto Rte. 797 (a dirt
    road). The winery will be
    in 3.1 miles on the right.
Owner: Lew Parker.
Open: Wed.–Sun.
    11am–5pm; Jan.–Feb.:
    weekends only by
    appointment.
Price Range of Wines: $8
    for Seyval to $16 for
    Cabernet Sauvignon.

- Cabernet Franc
- Chardonnay
- Merlot
- Seyval

Lew Parker's children were growing up, this was a small farm with a few chickens, goats, and horses. The farmhouse was originally an 1800s log cabin, although it has seen many renovations in the interim.

Lew planted his first grapes early in the 1980s. In 1984, he opened the winery in the old Civil War–era barn, where he makes most of the wines himself. Willowcroft now owns 13 acres of vines and produces about 2,000 cases of wine. The Chardonnay and Seyval are both lean and firm, good matches for food. The Cabernet Franc has a nice spicy quality and is also a good food wine. "My policy is to stay small, make high quality wines, and sell them all," declares Lew. He appears to be succeeding at all of this.

OTHER VIRGINIA WINERIES

TOTIER CREEK VINEYARD & WINERY (804-979-7105, 800-683-6174; 1652 Harris Creek Rd. (Rte. 720), Charlottesville, VA 22902) This established vineyard (planted in the early 1980s) and winery closed at the end of 1998. It remains to be seen whether new owners will bring it back to life.

WESTERN CONNECTICUT

Hopkins Winery, New Preston, Connecticut.

Marguerite Thomas

Connecticut is a tough state in which to grow grapes and produce wine. This is partly because of lack of local support from both the public and the government. Connecticut, in fact, has some of the most unfriendly rules in the nation regulating the sale and distribution of wine.

The western section of the state also has to cope with more challenging weather than any of the surrounding region because it doesn't have the advantage of a large body of water to moderate the climate. Wineries have come and gone since the passage of the state's Farm Winery Act in 1978, but the four current wineries in western Connecticut have survived for twenty-some years.

It's difficult to maintain healthy vinifera vines here, so the wineries have built their image on wines made from hybrid grapes. In recent years, however, some vintners have begun to flirt with vinifera by purchasing grapes from Long Island or the Finger Lakes region. Most recently, they have been discovering ways to raise Chardonnay, Cabernet Franc, and other vinifera varietals themselves.

They have also turned to more refined winemaking techniques, such as the judicious use of oak aging. The wines produced in the past few years have generally shown a great improvement over the lackadaisical quality of earlier efforts. People who are partisans of hybrid wines will find much to interest them in this region, but even the confirmed consumer of European wines will be in for some pleasant surprises. Furthermore, the rural scenery, the splendid old houses, and the charming villages in this part of Connecticut are well worth the trip.

The Connecticut vintners hold several events annually, including a Connecticut Wine and Food Festival. Call any Connecticut winery for information.

Marguerite Thomas

The vineyards at Haight, Litchfield, Connecticut.

HAIGHT VINEYARDS
860-567-4045,
　800-577-WINE (CT only);
　fax 860-567-1766.
www.ctwineries.com.
29 Chestnut Hill Rd.,
　Litchfield, CT 06759.
Directions: From Rte. 8 take
　Exit 42 and then go west
　on Rte. 118 for 3 miles to
　the top of the hill. Just
　beyond intersection with
　Rte. 254, turn left. Winery
　is on the left.
Owner: Sherman P. Haight.
Open: Mon.–Sat.
　10:30am–5pm, Sun.
　12noon–5pm.
Price Range of Wines: $7.98
　for Covertside White to
　$11.98 for Merlot.
Special Events: Spring:
　barrel tasting with food
　and music; Summer:
　Taste of the Litchfield
　Hills, with food from
　local restaurants and
　inns, music, hayrides;
　Fall: crafts fair.

Textile manufacturer Sherman P. Haight was one of a handful of men who successfully fought for the passage of Connecticut's 1978 Farm Winery Law. In anticipation, he planted a vineyard in 1975, and the winery that bears his name opened in 1978. Today, Haight produces 6,000 cases annually and has a 30-acre vineyard. It is planted in approximately 20 percent of vinifera vines.

Among the Haight wines, Covertside White, a predominantly Seyval blend that outsells all others three to one, is proof that sweet wine still has a large and enthusiastic audience. The wine, incidentally, is named for the coverts — thickets where foxes live — that are found near one of the vineyards. Morning Harvest Red is a sweetish red wine aged in American oak barrels. Haight's first Merlot — and except for an off dry Riesling its only wine made from vinifera grapes — is a resounding success. Aged in French oak, it's the sort of mellow, pleasant wine we can hope to see more of from this winery.

HOPKINS VINEYARD
860-868-7954;
　fax 860-868-1768.
www.ctwineries.com.

Hopkins Vineyard may have the most scenic location of any vineyard in the East. It's on the slope of a hill overlooking Lake Waramaug, a

Gerald Corrigan of Hopkins Vineyard.

Marguerite Thomas

E-mail: hopkinsvineyard
@msn.com.
25 Hopkins Rd., New
Preston, CT 06777.
Directions: Take Rte. 202 to
New Preston. Then take
Rte. 45 north for 2.5
miles; take the first left
after passing North Shore
Rd., and then take the
second right onto
Hopkins Rd. Winery is
on the right.
Owner: William Hopkins.
Open: Mon.–Fri.
10am–5pm, Sat.
10am–6pm, Sun.
11am–6pm; Jan.–Feb.:
Fri. & Sat. 10am–5p.m.,
Sun. 11am–5pm.
Price Range of Wines: $7.99
for Westwind White to
$18.25 for Sparkling
Wine.
Special Features: Hay Loft
Wine Bar.
Special Event: Annual
Spring Barrel Tasting.

• Cabernet Franc

large, tranquil lake surrounded by hills and woods
and a scattering of picture-perfect country houses.
The original farm has been in the Hopkins family
for more than 200 years. Hopkins, the oldest continuously operating winery in Connecticut, was
founded by William Hopkins, who started out as a
home winemaker before switching from dairy
farming to vineyards in the mid-1970s. The winery
now produces 7,000 cases of wine a year, all from
grapes grown on its own 35 acres of vineyards.

This is still a family enterprise, with Bill Hopkins
and his son-in-law, Gerald Corrigan, making the
wines. Vinifera planting (notably Chardonnay and
Cabernet Franc, along with a smattering of experimental Pinot Gris) has increased over the past couple
of years to account now for about 50 percent of the
total. "If we grow grapes here, we might as well grow
the best ones we can," explains Gerry. "We're seeing
lots more serious, dedicated wine drinkers now than
we ever did before." The Cabernet Franc is a good
example of the success of recent new vineyard practices (guarding against overcropping, for example) as
well as more sophisticated winemaking. This is a
winery that has leapt forward in quality in the last
few years and will undoubtedly continue to do so.

The Hopkins Hay Loft is a new and attractive
wine bar that serves wines by the glass or bottle
along with light fare such as pâtés and cheeses.

There are also a few antiques and a broad selection of teas for sale here. The tasting room itself is in a renovated 19th-century barn.

McLAUGHLIN VINEYARDS

203-426-1533;
  fax 203-270-8722.
www.ctwineries.com.
Albert Hill Rd., P.O. Box 778,
  Sandy Hook, CT 06482.
Directions: From I-84 take exit 10 and go in the direction of Sandy Hook. Take the first left onto Walnut Tree Hill. Go 2 miles to the island and bear left onto Albert's Hill Rd.; winery is 100 yards on the right.
Owners: The McLaughlin family.
Open: Daily 11am–5pm.
Price Range of Wines: $9.99 for White Table Wine to $14.99 for Garnet, a Cabernet/Merlot blend.
Special Features: Estate-produced maple syrup for sale in the tasting room, hiking and eagle-watching on the property.
Special Events: Jazz Under The Stars, a summer-long series.

- Blush
- White Table Wine

The most isolated winery in this region, McLaughlin is located at the base of a mountain where eagles and hawks soar. In an odd twist of events, the McLaughlin family owns this winery as well as another in Colorado. Morgen McLaughlin oversees the Connecticut facility, while her parents, Bruce and Taffy, operate the Colorado facility. Morgen's father inherited his parents' 160-acre Connecticut farm in the 1970s and he decided to plant a vineyard on it. Later, her mother inherited *her* family's dairy farm in Colorado, where they elected to replicate the experience. Morgen initially resisted joining the family business, but after one summer stint at the winery, she was seduced by the lure of the grape and never left.

McLaughlin's is a good place to taste hybrid and vinifera wines side by side and sometimes blended together. If all blush wine were as tasty as McLaughlin's off-dry but crisp Seyval/Cabernet Sauvignon blend, even wine snobs would give it thumbs up. The White Table Wine, a blend of Aurora, Seyval, and Vidal, shows off the strengths of hybrids with a full, enticing aroma and a rich flavor that fills the front of the mouth. McLaughlin wines also offer a good example of a well-made hybrid's ability to age. I sampled a 10-year-old Seyval that had gained in richness and complexity, unlike the average Chardonnay, which usually declines after a few years. It maintained a freshness, with a slight trace of bubble-gum fragrance. The only flaw was a slight tendency, common in older wines made from hybrids, to lose flavor at the back of the palate. It is short, meaning that it lacks the pleasant aftertaste that characterizes the finest wines. Overall, McLaughlin wines have a distinct personality and are appealing examples of good regional wines.

The winery tasting bar is embellished with a collection of arrowheads dug up from the property when the vineyard was planted. In addition to home-grown maple syrup, the gift shop offers other locally made gastronomic treats. Serious bird watchers may want to visit McLaughlin during November and March when, according to the owners, more eagles come to perch and feed at their farm than at any other site on the Housatonic River.

The winery has 15 acres of vines and produces 2,200 cases annually.

OTHER WINERIES IN WESTERN CONNECTICUT

DiGRAZIA VINEYARDS AND WINERY (Phone & fax: 203-775-1616; www.ctwineries; 131 Tower Rd., Brookfield, CT 06804) Known principally as a producer of sweet wines, DiGrazia also does make a dry Seyval, called Winner's Cup, and a Seyval/Vidal blend, called Vintage Festival. Paul DiGrazia, who has been the owner and winemaker at this family winery since 1978, also pursues a full-time medical practice. One of Dr. DiGrazia's best-selling wines is Honey Blush, which is made by using honey rather than sulfites as a preservative. It is popular among people who are troubled by sulfites. Brookfield is a picturesque small town with a historic district.

THE HUDSON RIVER VALLEY

John Dyson, owner of Millbrook Vineyards and Winery, Millbrook, New York.

Courtesy Millbrook Winery

The Hudson River Valley has one of the most impressive winemaking histories in America. It is the oldest commercial grape-producing region in the United States. As early as the mid-1600s, the Hudson River was recognized as a major trading artery for the New World. English, German, and Dutch farmers in upstate New York used the river to ship their products to the booming market in New York City.

When the French Huguenots arrived in the valley in the 1670s, they established vineyards along the river. Once they learned that European vinifera grapes couldn't tolerate East Coast diseases and climates, they raised table rather than wine grapes.

In 1877, Andrew Caywood moved from Modena, New York, to Marlboro, in the Hudson Valley, where he developed many successful hybrids, most notably the Dutchess grape. Caywood's contributions marked the beginning of this region's foray into commercial winemaking. Prohibition put a temporary halt to the industry, which was revived by Mark Miller when he replanted Caywood's original vineyards in the 1960s (now called Benmarl Vineyards).

The Hudson River Valley is a famously scenic region that attracts antiques hunters, art aficionados, history buffs, and nature lovers who come for the hiking trails and water sports. The homes of several of the famous 19th-century Hudson River painters who lived and worked here are open to the public. Historic sites such as the 17th-century stone Huguenot houses in New Paltz and the museum at George Washington's Headquarters in Newburgh are also well worth a visit. And, of course, wine lovers can spend a day or a week visiting wineries and sampling local wines in delightful settings.

WEST SIDE OF THE HUDSON RIVER

ADAIR VINEYARDS
914-255-1377;
fax 914-691-9584.
E-mail: adairwines@
aol.com.
52 Allhusen Rd., New
Paltz, NY 12561.
Directions: Winery is 6
miles south of New Paltz.
From Rte. 32, turn left on
Allhusen Rd.
Owners: Marc Vincent and
Lori Stopkie.
Open: May–Oct.: daily
11am–6pm; Nov.–Dec.
and Mar.–Apr.: Fri.–Sun.
11am–6pm, otherwise by
appointment.
Price Range of Wines: $7.50
for Seyval to $16 for
"Champagne Brut."

Marc Vincent and Lori Stopkie bought the winery from founder Jim Adair in February 1997. The winery first opened in 1983, in the handsome red barn that has a National Historic Landmark plaque at the entrance. From a window in the tasting room, visitors can look out at a splendid oak that resembles the tree on the Adair wine bottle. (The tree on the label is actually a replica of *The Solitary Oak,* a 19th-century painting by Asher B. Durand, a leader of the Hudson River School.)

Adair has 10 acres under cultivation, with another 10 planned in the next five years. The winery produces 1,700 cases of wine that include a crisp, dry Seyval, Picnic Red (a light Beaujolais-style red), and Landmark Red, a more deeply flavored dry wine made from Maréchal Foch and Millot grapes. Mountain Mist is a late-harvest Vignoles dessert wine with a faint hint of botrytis, the so-called "noble rot" that gives French Sauternes their personality. (Marc is working to bring botrytis back into the Vignoles vineyard, which should result in even more richly flavored dessert wines.) Marc, a Pennsylvania native who studied winemaking and viticulture in Napa, is experimenting in his vineyards with other grape varieties, notably Pinot Gris and Cabernet Franc. "It's more challenging to make wines on the East Coast," he says ruefully. "New York is in its infancy stage right now." I'm betting that Marc's wines continue to evolve over the next few vintages. Meanwhile, a bottle of Adair Picnic Red is just the thing to accompany an al fresco lunch in the shade of that arty oak.

BALDWIN VINEYARDS
914-744-2226;
fax 914-744-6321.
E-mail: bb2@frontiernet.net.
176 Hardenburgh Rd, Pine
Bush, NY 12566.
Directions: From NY State
Thruway (I-87) take exit
17 in Newburgh and
follow Rte. 52 east to Pine
Bush; from the light at
the intersection of Rtes.
52 and 302 make a right

Jack Baldwin never even tasted wine until 1974 when he and his wife, Pat, took a trip to France. His epiphany came in the Côtes-du-Rhône region over a bottle of Châteauneuf-du-Pape. From that moment on, Jack was a man obsessed with becoming a winemaker. He began reading everything he could find about the subject, and he bought grapes to vinify at home. Soon the couple founded a chapter of Les Amis du Vin in New Jersey, where they were then living, to pursue their hobby with other like-minded individuals. They also started looking and follow signs north 1 mile to winery.

Owners: Jack and Pat Baldwin.

Open: July–Oct.: daily 11am–5:30pm; Apr.–June & Nov.: Fri.–Mon. 11:30am–5pm; Winter: Sat. & Sun 11:30am–4:30pm, or by appointment.

Price Range of Wines: $5.99 for Seyval to $16 for Merlot.

Special Events: Fourth of July Strawberry Wine release party, September Raspberry Wine release, November Nouveau party, Christmas party.

• Merlot

for a piece of property where they could raise vines. Eventually they found a 200-year-old former dairy farm in the Hudson River Valley that included a charming stone house, plus an enormous old barn that might be adapted to winemaking. They moved to their dream house in Pine Bush in 1982 and planted a vineyard the same year.

For the first two-and-a-half years Jack commuted 150 miles each day to his job in the marketing research division of the pharmaceutical firm Hoffmann-LaRoche. Like many others who pursue a utopian goal, the Baldwins were not entirely prepared for the staggering amount of work involved in starting a farm, or for the ups and downs of the grape and wine market, or for the sheer exhaustion that went along with it all.

Happily, there were rewards as well. Sales doubled and tripled each year from the Baldwins' first production in 1983 until the stock market crashed in 1987. Today Jack and Pat impress anyone who visits their tasting room as people who are truly happy with the life they've chosen, especially now that their daughter, Wendy, and her husband, Alex, have joined the business.

Jack makes a variety of wines including Chardonnay, Riesling, Gewürztraminer, and Pinot Noir. He is particularly proud of his Strawberry and Raspberry wines, which are nectar to lovers of fruit wine and are popular in Canada and even as far away as England.

It isn't at all unusual to see repeat customers stop by the tasting room. When I was there recently a young couple dropped in for their second case of Raspberry Wine. "Baldwin's the best!" they exclaimed.

For the most part, all the wines produced here are decent *vins de pays* — good regional country wines. The Merlot has a strong aroma of American oak barrels, but it tastes rich and well balanced. Baldwin currently produces about 3,000 cases annually from its 10 acres of vines.

If you plan to picnic under the trees next to the old barn at Baldwin Vineyards, think about bringing some brownies to enjoy with the Strawberry or Raspberry Wine — chocolate, say the Baldwins, has found its ultimate gastronomic partner with these wines.

BENMARL WINE COMPANY
914-236-4265;
fax 914-236-7271.
156 Highland Ave.,
Marlboro, NY 12542.

"This is the oldest vineyard in America," says owner Mark Miller. As he gazes out over the magnificent panorama of mountains and valleys bisected by the mighty Hudson River, he declares — quite correctly — that this is also one of the

Directions: From I-84 take exit 10 north; then take Rte. 9W north for 4 miles to Conway Rd.; turn left and then bear right and travel 1 mile to the winery.
Owner: Mark Miller.
Open: Daily 12noon–5pm.
Price Range of Wines: $7 for Summerwhite, a blend of white grapes, to $15 for Estate Red, a combination of Baco Noir, Chellois, and Maréchal Foch.
Special Features: Hiking trails, art gallery.
Special Events: Concerts, art shows focusing on contemporary Hudson Valley painters, picnics, and medieval events.

world's most beautiful sights. He ought to know. He's lived in some classically beautiful places, including a chateau in Burgundy.

Born in Oklahoma and reared in a farming family, Mark Miller followed his own muse, first as Hollywood costume designer, and later, during the 1950s and 1960s, as the world's most widely published magazine illustrator. It was during these years, while living in France, that Mark discovered that the ultimate destiny of a grape is not necessarily grape juice.

When Mark and his wife, the late Dene Miller, moved to the Hudson River property they had purchased years earlier, his newly developed passion for wine led him to take an interest in the property's historic vineyards. The vineyard had been cultivated successfully for hundreds of years because of its proximity to the Hudson River, which made transportation easier and had a moderating influence on the local microclimate.

With the help of France's famous wine consultant, Emile Peynaud, Mark replanted the vineyard, concentrating principally on hybrids, which he defends staunchly. "We are a hybrid nation. I don't want to spend my life making Chardonnay when the French already do it so well," he once said, although recent Benmarl vintages have included Chardonnay, Merlot, and Cabernet Franc made from local grapes. He promotes New York State wines tirelessly, and he was instrumental in the passage of New York's Farm Winery Act. (By lowering the price of winery licenses and by liberalizing many laws including prohibitive regulations concerning tasting rooms, the 1976 Farm Winery Act made it possible for small producers to operate commercial wineries.) Mark and his architect-wife built the winery compound that is focused on a courtyard inspired by their homes in French chateaux.

"Konstantin Frank and Philip Wagner are the grandfathers of the Eastern wine industry," he says. "I am the father." He is also the father of Eric Miller who, after working as winemaker at Benmarl during the 1970s, struck out on his own to found Chaddsford Winery in Pennsylvania. Mark clearly regrets that Eric left Benmarl, but he is also pleased to have passed the torch along to his son.

Most of Benmarl's wine is distributed to members of its private Societé des Vignerons. Wine drinkers who become members of the Societé receive wine every year as part of their membership, a system through which members help support the 36-acre vineyard. The winery produces about 6,000 cases of wine a year, including Seyval and an Estate Red.

In addition to the wines, visitors can also enjoy a gallery where Mark Miller's delightfully romantic illustrations are displayed, and they can picnic under the pines. There are walking paths and trails through the estate's 12 acres of woods.

BRIMSTONE HILL VINEYARD

914-744-2231;
  fax 914-744-4782.
61 Brimstone Hill Rd., Pine
  Bush, NY 12566.
Directions: From NY State
  Thruway (I-87) take exit
  17 in Newburgh and
  follow Rte. 52 east to Pine
  Bush; turn right onto
  New Prospect Rd. and
  follow signs to winery.
Owners: Valerie and
  Richard Eldridge.
Open: May–Oct.:
  Thurs.–Mon.
  11:30am–5:30pm;
  Nov.–Apr.: Sat. & Sun.
  11:30am–5:30pm, or by
  appointment.
Price Range of Wines: $6
  for still wines to $12 for
  sparkling wines.
Special Event: Bastille Day
  celebration with fruit,
  quiche, and Valerie's
  homemade bread, as well
  as French art and music.

Valerie and Richard Eldridge are Hudson River Valley pioneers, having planted some 20 varieties of French hybrid grapes when they moved here in 1968. In recent years, they added vinifera grapes, speculating that these will do well in their vineyard's heavy, rocky soil. "It's hard soil to plant and cultivate," says Valerie, "but it tends to retain the heat." "Whites do pretty well here," adds Dick, "But red wine grapes are more of a challenge."

The Eldridges aim to produce reasonably priced quality table wines with a French character, much like the wines from France's upper Loire Valley where Valerie was born. The white wines, including Seyval and Chardonnay, tend to have the delicacy typical of wine from cool climates, although they lack the elegance and finesse of good Loire wines. The reds, including Baco Noir and Vin Rouge (a blend of various red hybrid grapes) are light, with pleasant aromas. Brimstone Hill's young Cabernet Franc seems promising enough to Dick to have encouraged him to plant another half acre. Brimstone Hill produces a dry sparkling wine called Domaine Bourmont, Valerie's family name.

Valerie is still a full-time academic at a local university, but Dick recently retired to devote himself full-time to the 10-acre vineyard and to making the 800–850 cases of wine produced here annually. This is strictly a family operation, and you'll find the Eldridges themselves in the tasting room.

BROTHERHOOD WINERY

914-496-9101;
  fax 914-496-8720.
www.wines.com/
  brotherhood.
E-mail: browinery@
  worldnet.att.net.
100 Brotherhood Plaza, P.O.
  Box 190, Washingtonville,
  NY 10992.
Directions: From NY State
  Thruway (I-87) take exit
  16, then travel Rte. 17

Brotherhood Winery is the oldest continuously operating bonded winery in America. John Jacques, a former New Jersey shoemaker, founded it in 1839. Shortly after he moved to the area, Jacques decided to plant a vineyard, having noted that his neighbors were receiving high prices for their grapes. By the time his own vines matured, however, the price of grapes had dropped, so Jacques decided to go into the wine business. The next owners were the Emersons — part of Ralph Waldo's family — who renamed the winery Brotherhood after a nearby commune. The Emersons enlarged

Cesar Baeza

Cesar Baeza and I were in the tasting room sampling Brotherhood Winery's most recent vintages of Merlot and Cabernet Sauvignon when a white-haired gentleman approached. "Where would I find a bottle of Niagara?" he asked. "I used to get that here, and I like it a lot." Cesar studied the man briefly, then suppressed a smile as he said, "You haven't been here for a while. When's the last time you stopped by?" "Oh, 'bout twenty years or so ago," the man answered.

Brotherhood hasn't made Niagara for years, Cesar confided, as we watched the dejected Niagara fancier retreat. This was a pretty typical moment in Cesar Baeza's life as he tries to promote up-to-date, dry wines in a historic, tradition-bound setting that until very recently was the dominion of sweet wines. Cesar is probably better suited to this job than any winemaker I can think of. First of all, he is enviably well-educated, having studied viticulture and enology in his native Chile, and in some of the world's other important winemaking centers as well, including France's University at Montpellier, the University of Madrid, and the University of California at Davis and at Fresno. He has extensive vineyard and winemaking experience both in California and in Europe, including Eastern Europe, where he is credited with creating the Premiat wines of Rumania and the Trakia wines of Bulgaria. He has all-important managerial skills too, having spent a decade as research director for Pepsico's International Wine and Spirits Division.

Cesar's first affiliation with Brotherhood was in 1973, when the then-owners asked him to make their first European-style wine from hybrid grapes. (Until then, Brotherhood wines had been made exclusively from native grapes.) Two years later he returned to California, and subsequently joined Pepsico. In 1987, Cesar found himself back at Brotherhood, this time as winemaker/partner along with five other investors.

Although he was far from naive about the challenges he'd face, even Cesar is sometimes confounded by it all. "It's harder to sell New York wine than Bulgarian wine," he says. One of his first decisions was to sell off Brotherhood's vineyards, which were planted exclusively in native and hybrid grapes. "As a viticulturist by profession, I know what's involved with growing grapes here, and I think it's tough to do that and make wine too," says Cesar, whose opinion is that too many local vintners are better at growing grapes than making wine. Right now the problem for Cesar, as for many others in the East, is the scarcity of grapes. Land is so desirable for real-estate development, he explains, that grape growing — like other forms of agriculture — is being squeezed out. While he has started a program working with local growers to produce quality grapes, he acknowledges sadly that Hudson vineyards are fast disappearing.

Despite the undeniable problems, Cesar Baeza is optimistic about Hudson River Valley wines. The region's volcanic soil, he says, is similar to the Rhine's. And, he adds, that Pinot Noir raised here for sparkling wine is qualitatively not unlike Champagne's (Brotherhood's 6,000 cases of Grand Monarque Sparkling Wine invariably sell out quickly). "In terms of quality, we're the equal of the best places," he says. "We no longer have to be ashamed of our wines. Restaurants are no longer afraid to put local wines on the menu. Writers who wouldn't dream of writing about New York wines a few years ago are no longer afraid their reputations will be compromised if they do." The future, says Cesar, looks good. I couldn't agree more.

west to exit 130; take Rte. 208 north for 7 miles to Rte. 94 east, turn right and then take the first left onto North St.; follow signs to winery. From I-84 follow signs to Stewart Airport on Rte. 207; go 2 miles and take a left at the sign onto Toleman Rd.; go 3 miles to winery entrance on left.

Owners: A partnership.

Open: Daily 11am–5pm; closed Christmas and New Year's Day.

Price Range of Wines: $6.99 for Seyval; $18.39 for Mariage (a Rioja-style blend of Cabernet Sauvignon and Chardonnay); $22.99 for sparkling Monarque.

Special Features: Brotherhood Village (a complex of shops, an art gallery, café, wine museum), winery tours.

Special Events: Outdoor music polka fests, car shows, art shows, Murder Mystery Dinners, September Grape Stomping Festival, and more.

• Chardonnay

the original cellars and winery structure. Today, some of the historic stone buildings house a café and art gallery, while the hand-dug cellars remain the largest natural temperature-controlled wine-aging cellars in the United States.

When Prohibition forced most American wineries to close in 1919, Brotherhood Winery switched to making sacramental and medicinal wines. This production was sanctioned by the government, and enabled the winery to ride out the rocky years. During its long history, Brotherhood has changed ownership only three times. The most recent purchase, in 1987, included winemaker Cesar Baeza among the partners.

Brotherhood owns no vineyards. Instead, it purchases grapes from various Hudson Valley growers, as well as from the Finger Lakes and Long Island. Altogether, the winery produces 50,000 cases of wine under its own label. (Brotherhood also produces and bottles wine for enough other wineries to make it New York's third-largest winery.) In the past few years Cesar Baeza has managed to transform mundane wines into competitive products, and with a little more time and updating of barrels and other equipment, the wines promise to be impressive indeed. The white wines tend to be light, refreshing, and, mercifully, not over-oaked. (The Riesling's popularity soared once it was put in blue bottles a couple of years ago — "Sales tripled," says Cesar in wonderment.) Pinot Noir is light-bodied but aromatic, while Merlot and Cabernet Sauvignon are weighty and rich. Mariage, a Rioja-style blend of Cabernet and tannin-softening Chardonnay, tends to be uneven in quality, but will surely be a winner once the winery gets new barrels.

Brotherhood Village, a complex of shops, an art gallery, café, wine museum, and more, used to be the draw that attracted 100,000 visitors a year. Now the wines themselves are an equally justifiable lure. Incidentally, winery tours here are entertaining and informative. (Brotherhood claims to have invented the concept of winery tours in the 1950s, before California even thought about them.) The café offers simple but tasty lunch fare, or you can stock up on simple picnic supplies at the general store.

RIVENDELL
914-255-2494; mail orders:
1-800-646-5585;
fax 914-255-2290.
www.rivendellwine.com.
E-mail: somewine@
mhv.net.
714 Albany Post Rd., New
Paltz, NY 12561.
Directions: Take NY State
Thruway (I-87) to exit 18.
Turn left off exit onto
Rte. 299. Go west
through town, over
bridge; take first left onto
Libertyville Rd., about
5.5 miles to winery on
right.
Owners: The Ransom
family.
Price Range of Wines: $9
for Seyval Blanc and
Riesling to $15 for
Chardonnay.
Special Events: Vintage
New York store
showcasing wines from
diverse NY state
wineries; art exhibitions;
annual New York State
Chili Cook-off; Sept.
Lobster Fest.

• Seyval
• Chardonnay
• Riesling
• Après

ROYAL KEDEM WINERY
914-795-2240.
1519 Rte. 9W, Marlboro,
NY 12542.
Mail: 420 Kent Ave.,
Brooklyn, NY 11211.
Directions: From I-84 take
the first exit on the west
side of the Beacon-
Newburgh bridge, go
north on Rte. 9W for 1.25
miles beyond Marlboro
to the winery.
Open: Fri.–Sun. 10am–5pm.

Rob Ransom and his family purchased the Chateau George Winery in 1987. Renamed Rivendell, the winery is once again open for tastings, tours, picnics, and general enjoyment of the scenic 65-acre property. Eventual plans are to replant Rivendell's own vineyard, but for the moment grapes are acquired locally and from the Finger Lakes and Long Island. Current production is 10,000 cases annually.

Rivendell concentrates on white wines. The tank-fermented Seyval has a lemony zing plus a nice persistence on the palate. The richness and fruitiness of the Chardonnay may make some people think of a California wine. The German-style Riesling has alluring floral and tropical fruit aromas. Après is a dessert wine that may be a fraction lighter-bodied and less sweet than benchmark sweet wines, but its great bouquet, flavor, and finesse are irresistible. "It's really a pre-dessert dessert wine," jokes Rob Ransom, but I can personally recommend it as an accompaniment to vanilla ice cream topped with quartered and peeled ripe pears and a drizzle of honey.

Rivendell's cozy tasting room and scenic rural setting will remind Tolkien fans of this passage in *Lord of the Rings:* "Rivendell . . . a perfect house, whether you like food or sleep or storytelling or just sitting and thinking best, or a pleasant mixture of them all. Merely to be there was a cure for weariness, fear, or sadness . . . a refuge for all folks of goodwill."

Eight generations of Herzogs have been making kosher wines since 1848, when they were the sole purveyors to Emperor Franz Josef I of Austria. The Herzog family survived World War II because their own loyal employees hid them from the Nazis. But in 1948 they fled the Communist takeover of Czechoslovakia and settled on New York's Lower East Side. In their new country, the Herzogs did what they knew how to do best: they made wine. The word *kedem* comes from a Hebrew expression that means going forward, which aptly describes the Herzogs.

Tasting Room
914-795-2240.
Dock Rd., Milton, NY
12547.
Directions: From the
Kedem Winery in
Marlboro, take 9W north
to first traffic light. Turn
right into the village,
continuing across Main
St. to the stop sign; turn
right on Dock Rd. and go
to the river.
Open: Sun.–Thurs.
10am–4:30pm.
Price Range of Wines: $3.50
for extra-dry Chablis to
$5.50 for a dryish
sparkling wine.
Owners: The Herzog
family.
Special Feature: Tasting
room in old railway
station overlooking the
Hudson River.

Eventually, they expanded to New York's Hudson River Valley, where they now produce a staggering amount of kosher wine — a quarter million cases annually, plus another quarter million cases of kosher grape juice, which makes them the world's largest supplier of kosher wines. In addition to the U. S. market, the wines are widely distributed in Europe, Russia, Taiwan, Hong Kong, and Latin America.

Kedem owns merely 20 acres of vineyards and purchases most of its grapes from other growers. The grapes are vinified at the Marlboro facility, and then the wine is shipped to the Herzog's Brooklyn plant for final "polishing" — filtration and bottling. The family also produces a line of premium kosher wines, called Baron Herzog, in California.

Although many excellent, dry kosher wines are produced in the world, including Baron Herzog, people continue to associate kosher with sweet, grapey wines. But, according to the Kedem winery itself, "kosher" simply means that the wine is made with no additives, preservatives, or artificial color, and with a rabbi on the premises to supervise the process. "*No* preservatives?" I ask. What about sulfites? Well, yes, it seems that it's okay to add a minimal amount of sulfites (one tenth of a gram).

The Kedem Winery in Marlboro has a small tasting room. A few miles away, in Milton, there is a large Kedem tasting room in an old railroad station at the edge of the Hudson River. Café tables are set up in the former waiting room, and a variety of kosher snacks are for sale. An enormous number of wines are available to taste, including selections from the firm's wineries in California, Israel, France, and Italy. The New York wines are mostly sweet and strong flavored, although there is an extra-dry Chablis and a dryish Sparkling Wine. Visitors might as well try the sweet wines here. That's what the Hudson River winery is all about. Try the Cream White or Red, which show off the essence of Concord grapes. Incidentally, Kedem grape juice is outstanding.

OTHER WINERIES WEST OF THE HUDSON

RIVERVIEW has had many ups and downs in the past few years. While Tim Biancalana is still making sparkling wine from Pinot Noir and Chardonnay grapes, the Charbot family, the original owners, appear to have left the project. One can only hope that this once-promising winery will soon find its way back to full production.

WHITE CLIFF is a brand-new winery on the West Side of the Hudson, with 16 acres of vineyards. There's lots of positive local buzz about these newcomers; this is definitely a winery to keep an eye on.

APPLEWOOD WINERY and **WARWICK VALLEY WINERY** are both located in the southwestern part of the Hudson Valley region, close to the New Jersey border. While both specialize in ciders and fruit wines, a small amount of wine from grapes is also produced.

EAST SIDE OF THE HUDSON RIVER

CASCADE MOUNTAIN WINERY
914-373-9021;
  fax 914-373-7869.
Flint Hill Rd, Amenia, NY 12501.
Directions: From Taconic Pkwy. take the Millbrook-Poughkeepsie exit and follow Rte. 44 east through Millbrook to Amenia. Turn north onto Rte. 22 and follow signs to winery.
Owners: William and Margaret Wetmore.
Open: Daily 10:30am–5pm.
Price Range of Wines: $5 for Heavenly Daze (a spiced wine) to $15 for Private Reserve Red (Cabernet Sauvignon aged in oak).
Special Feature: Restaurant (lunch 12noon–3pm daily, except weekends only Jan. & Feb.; dinner Sat. only, 5–8pm.)
Special Events: Wine dinners.

• Reserve Red

Novelist William Wetmore left New York City for the serenity of the Hudson Valley. He did indeed find a quiet atmosphere in which to write there, but in 1972, he planted a vineyard. A winery followed in 1977; then came a restaurant. So much for the peaceful life. Cascade, located in a pastoral mountain setting, includes 10 acres of vineyards high on a hill overlooking fertile farmland. The French-American varietals grown here are supplemented by fruit purchased from growers in the Hudson Valley and in the Finger Lakes. Twelve thousand cases are produced annually. Wines include Harvest Rosé and Coeur de Lion, a very good blend of 25 percent Cabernet Sauvignon and 75 percent Maréchal Foch. Summertide is a semi-sweet Seyval/Vidal blend, and Cascade also produces a sparkling wine that's as clean and bracing as a mountain breeze. Heavenly Daze, a spiced red wine, is perhaps the most popular wine, but my own favorite here is the Reserve Red, a Cabernet blend.

The attractive wooded setting is a fine place for hikes. It would be a nice place to picnic, except that Cascade's own restaurant is so good that I recommend eating there instead.

Hudson River Valley Cheeses

COACH FARM (518-398-5325; 105 Mill Hill Rd., Pine Plains, NY 12567. Open: Daily 3–5pm to watch the milking.)

Some people plant a vineyard because they want to help preserve agricultural land. Miles and Lillian Cahn were concerned about saving the rural character of the 300-acre farm they purchased in the Hudson Valley, but instead of planting a vineyard, they started a goat farm. At first, the Cahns continued to run their successful leather company, Coach Leatherworks, while they commuted back and forth from Manhattan. When they sold the leather business to the Sara Lee Corporation, however, they turned to raising goats and producing cheese full-time.

A French cheese-maker was brought in as consultant. He taught the staff at Coach Farm how to pasteurize the fresh goat milk, how to add a culture and enzymes to cause the milk to curdle, and then how to mold the fresh goat curd into rounds and pyramids, logs and loaves, and the tiny, delectable lumps called buttons. The farm now has 900 goats and produces over 4,000 pounds of goat cheese a week, ranging in style from soft and fresh to dry and aged. It's all delicious and an excellent accompaniment to wine. The United States will never rival France, a country where virtually every community produces its own distinctive cheese. Nevertheless, we have progressed from a nation where cheese was mostly processed in a factory, ready for store shelves in perfect, odorless, tasteless, sandwich-sized slices, individually wrapped in plastic, to one where increasing numbers of entrepreneurs are making flavorful, fresh regional cheeses. Coach Farms is leading the way.

OLD CHATHAM SHEEPHERDING COMPANY (1-888-SHEEP-60; 155 Shaker Museum Rd., Old Chatham, NY 12136; Open: for visits to the creamery, Mon.–Fri. 9am–5pm; Retail Shop, Sat. & Sun. 9am–5pm; to view the milking, daily 6:30am or 3:30–4pm. Closed during Jan.)

Located on 500 acres of rolling pasture in the beautiful Hudson River Valley, this is the largest sheep dairy farm in the country, with about 1,000 East Friesland crossbred sheep. The sheep are fed estate-raised hay and whole grains as well as the lush pasture grasses. The high-tech creamery boasts state-of-the-art computerized equipment, but happily the cheeses still have the delicious, handmade, flavorful and wholesome allure one expects from the world's best cheeses. Look for both fresh and aged cheeses, including Camembert, Shepherd's Wheel, Pyramid, and Mutton Button (small, aged cheese with distinctive flavor). Try any of the cheeses with fresh, fragrant white wines such as Sauvignon Blanc or Pinot Blanc. The aged cheeses also match well with red wines, particularly those with soft tannins. Fresh ricotta and the most delicious yogurt imaginable are also made at Old Chatham. Cheeses may be mail-ordered.

Old Chatham Sheepherding also includes a charming inn and excellent restaurant, both often booked weeks or months in advance.

EGG FARM DAIRY (914-734-7343; fax 914-734-9287; John Walsh Blvd., Peekskill, NY 10566. Open Mon.–Fri. 10am–5pm, Sat. 9am–5pm.)

Egg Farm Dairy is owned by Charlie Palmer, chef and owner of the acclaimed Aureole Restaurant in Manhattan, and cheesemaker Jonathan White. Jonathan started out producing cultured butter and clabbered cream for the finest restaurants and hotels in the New York metropolitan area but gradually began making cheese as well. Today the products are distributed to retailers, caterers, and bakeries, as well as restaurants, nationwide. Egg Farm Dairy turns out nine different cow's milk cheeses, five of which are molded into wheels and pyramids. There is also Amelia (a small goat's milk button) and Delphina (a soft and fragrant sheep's milk wheel), as well as ricotta, mascarpone, buttermilk cheese, and "quarg," a low-fat yogurt-like cheese. The strip-mall setting is less than bucolic, but Egg Farm Dairy's cheeses and butters are superb. A mini-market is held there on Fridays and Saturdays.

CLINTON VINEYARDS
914-266-5372;
fax 914-266-3395.
Schultzville Rd, Clinton Corners, NY 12514.
Directions: From Taconic Pkwy. take the Salt Point Turnpike exit. Turn right and go straight through Clinton Corners. Take a sharp left onto Schultzville Rd. at the 10-mph sign and proceed to winery.
Owners: Ben and Phyllis Feder.
Open: Fri.–Sun. 10am–5pm, or by appointment.
Price Range of Wines: $10 for Apple Wine; $25 for Peach Champagne.
Special Feature: Walking trails on 100-acre estate.
Special Events: Press release party, summer picnics, harvest party.

- Seyval Blanc
- Sparkling Wines

Like several other Eastern vintners, Ben Feder, formerly a New York City graphic designer, went into the cattle business before turning to grapes. When he did succumb to the lure of Bacchus, Ben decided to plant only Seyval grapes. Recently, however, he added one acre of Riesling to his 15 acres of Seyval, but since the Riesling appears to be too temperamental for his site, it's doubtful he'll expand the plantings.

Clinton Vineyards produces 2,500 cases of wine annually. The crisp, fruity Seyval Blanc is vaguely reminiscent of Sancerre and Muscadet from France's Loire Valley. Ben also makes a small amount of a charming, dry, and very drinkable sparkling wine. Peach Gala is a novel peach-flavored sparkling wine, the Hudson River's answer to Italian Bellini. Romance, first released in the summer of 1998, is Clinton's version of white Port, in this case a fortified wine enhanced by the same peach-flavored *dosage* as the Peach Gala. A small amount of Riesling (from zero to 40 cases, depending on the vintage) is also made here.

MILLBROOK VINEYARDS & WINERY
914-677-8383, 800-662-WINE; fax 914-677-6186.
Wing Rd., R.R. 1, Box 167D, Millbrook, NY 12545.
Directions: From Taconic Pkwy. take the Millbrook

One of the best and most innovative wineries in the East, Millbrook was the first vineyard in the Hudson River region to concentrate exclusively on vinifera grapes. The concept for Millbrook Vineyards began in 1976, when John Dyson, then New York State Commissioner of Agriculture, met Dr. Konstantin Frank, the Russian-born winemaker exit to Rte. 44. Take Rte. 44 east to Rte. 82 north, go 3 miles to Shunpike Rd. (Rte. 57); turn right, go 3 miles to Wing Rd., turn left to the winery.

Owner: John Dyson.

Open: Daily 12noon–5pm.

Price Range of Wines: $9.99 for Hunt Country Rosé; $16.99 for Cabernet Sauvignon Reserve; $21.99 for Reserve Chardonnay.

Special Events: Summer concerts, weekend vineyard grill, annual Harvest Party on Columbus Day weekend.

- Cabernet Franc
- Hunt Country Rosé
- Tocai Friuliano

who operated Vinifera Wine Cellars in the Finger Lakes. Frank's success with European vinifera vines greatly impressed John Dyson, who reasoned that the same grapes might also do well in the Hudson Valley, where he owned a farm. He planted an experimental acre and found that his Chardonnay, Cabernet Sauvignon, and Pinot Noir did perform remarkably well. Today he has 52 acres under cultivation, producing 15,000–16,000 cases annually.

Armed with the success of this experiment, plus the knowledge that vinifera grapes offer considerably higher gross returns than other crops, John bought an old dairy farm in 1979, where he planted 50 acres of vines. (John firmly believes that vineyards can help save family farming in the East.) He converted the dairy barn into a state-of-the-art winery. Next, he invented and patented a new trellising system, and then he hired John Graziano, a talented graduate of Cornell University, as his winemaker.

God may have rested after creating the world, but John Dyson just keeps going. In 1989, he purchased two top-quality vineyards in California's Central Coast region, where he grows grapes for important California wineries such as Glen Ellen, Robert Mondavi, and Joseph Phelps. As none of these vineyards has winemaking facilities, John began shipping grapes from his California properties to Millbrook to be made into wine, which he markets under the "Mistral" label. In the mid-1990s, Dyson added Villa Pillo, a vast wine and olive-oil estate in Tuscany, to his holdings. Scarcely pausing for breath, he then stunned the wine world by purchasing Williams and Selyem, the prestigious California winery.

Among the Millbrook wines that carry Hudson Valley and New York State appellations, Cabernet Franc is particularly outstanding, with a rich aroma of berries followed by a blast of long-lasting complex flavors. Hunt Country Rosé, a blend of Pinot Noir and Chardonnay, smells sweetly of strawberries; while it may look like a blush wine, this rosé leaves no perception of sweetness in the taste. The Tocai, a grape native to the Friuli region of Northern Italy, is redolent of tropical fruit aromas and flavors and has a luscious full body. Millbrook Proprietor's Reserve Chardonnay is also full-bodied and understandably popular with wine drinkers who appreciate very oaky wines. To my taste, however, the contribution from oak barrels — particularly the cedary hints of American oak — mask the fruit flavors too much.

Set deep in the countryside, Millbrook's handsome winery and beautiful setting are in themselves worth a visit. But even without all this, the wines alone are enough of a lure for anyone who loves fine wine. Picnic tables overlook the scenic ponds that John created to provide a modifying influence on the climate.

THE FINGER LAKES

The restaurant at Knapp Winery, Romulus, New York.

Marguerite Thomas

Most of the wineries in upstate New York are clustered around three of the Finger Lakes. Cayuga is the longest of the lakes. Keuka, the most scenic, is known as "the jewel of the Finger Lakes" because its waters are unusually clear and clean. The deepest lake is Seneca. Wineries line both shores of Seneca in such profusion that one may easily visit several of them in a single day.

The whole region is one of spectacular scenic beauty, where vine-covered hills roll down to the edge of the water. Hundreds of examples of the Greek Revival architecture that once dominated the Finger Lakes region remain. Many of them are open to visitors, including Rose Hill Mansion, one of the most beautiful Greek Revival houses in America (Rte. 9A, Fayette, NY).

Originally, the Finger Lakes region was home to the Seneca and Cayuga Indians of the Six Nations, whose lands were devastated by the Clinton-Sullivan military expedition of 1779. The area opened up for settlement after the American Revolution. When the Erie Canal linked Cayuga and Seneca Lakes in 1830, the population grew and industry flourished.

More recent history has played its role here as well. The region prides itself on being the birthplace of women's rights: the first Women's Rights Convention was held in Seneca Falls in 1848. Locals also claim that this is the birthplace of American aviation because Glenn Curtiss pioneered the first flying airplanes here in 1908. It is also the birthplace of the modern wine industry in the Eastern United States.

The Finger Lakes are blessed with soil that is a good host for grapes and with a climate moderated by the lakes themselves. It has another advantage as well. "One of our great secret weapons is Indian summer," says Willy Frank

Riesling

Of the many vinifera grape varieties thriving in the Finger Lakes region today, Riesling stands out as the brightest star in the firmament. For a variety of reasons, Riesling is a misunderstood and under-appreciated wine in this country. Part of this has to do with a belief that all Riesling is sweet. Indeed, a lot of Riesling *is* sweet, ranging in style from spineless schlock to some of the greatest dessert wines in the world, such as Germany's Trockenbeerenauslese. But the trend worldwide — Riesling is grown in virtually every wine-producing country on earth — is toward a drier wine, a wine that is adaptable to a variety of foods.

The Riesling grape is believed to have originated in Germany, where the Romans probably cultivated it. Many connoisseurs consider it to be the noblest of all wines. Today, Germany, Austria, and Alsace produce the ultimate Rieslings, recognized throughout the world as unrivaled in style and taste. But in the last few years, a handful of Eastern vintners, particularly in the Finger Lakes region, have begun to produce Rieslings that may soon take their place beside the great European Rieslings.

One of the charms of an excellent Riesling is its beguiling aroma which, in youth, is fresh and floral, and becomes more subtle and intriguing with maturity. As it ages, it may even develop a gasoline-like bouquet known as "petrol," one whiff of which is enough to quicken the pulse of any true devotee of Riesling.

Riesling's character depends, more than most other grapes, on *terroir*, or the site on which it is grown. Mediocre Riesling can vary from watery and insipid versions to those that are cloyingly sweet. Fine Riesling, on the other hand, will range from the light and delicate elegance found in Rieslings from Germany's Moselle region to a full, vivacious elixir, such as that from the Rheingau region. In the mouth, all fine Rieslings, whether dry or sweet, show a notable streak of acidity backed up by a suggestion of honey, flower blossoms, or fruit concentrate.

One of Riesling's many attributes is its ability to age well. Unfortunately, today most top-grade Riesling is consumed in its infancy, before it has the chance to develop the full charm and multifaceted personality of an adult wine.

Riesling is one of the best wines to drink with food. "A dry Riesling is the most versatile wine you have in the house," declares Vinifera Wine Cellars' Willy Frank. Dry Rieslings are excellent matches for grilled food, for most poultry, for sausage and other pork dishes, and for such classic dishes as *choucroute* (sauerkraut). Slightly less dry Rieslings are excellent accompaniments for spicy Cajun, Mexican, and Thai cuisine. When it carries a hint of sweetness, Riesling is a far more satisfying aperitif than most bone-dry wines — "Better than a dry martini," says Willy Frank, "and late-harvested or other dessert-style Rieslings are uniquely satisfying at the end of a meal."

There is nothing mysterious about the promise of Eastern Riesling. Despite small, tightly clustered berries that are vulnerable to injury and disease, Riesling vines also have thick bark and a habit of budding late that enables the plant to resist freezes. Riesling grapes depend on cool nights to develop a bracing thread of acidity and warm days for their characteristic honeyed sweetness. They do particularly well when the growing season is long enough for flavors to develop slowly. If the weather is too warm, as in many parts of California, the grapes ripen before the full balance of fruitiness, acidity, and finesse is complete. In California they have to add acidity to make a palatable wine. On the other hand, when Riesling is grown in a climate that is too cool, the grapes don't ripen completely and lack sufficient alcohol to produce a harmonious wine.

Also favoring Finger Lakes Riesling are substances called monoterpenes. These various compounds, which are responsible for the perfume of certain aromatic grapes such as Riesling and Gewürztraminer, are particularly prevalent in this region's grapes.

Finger Lakes vintner Scott Osborne says: "We can get the acids we need here to balance the sugars. That's what makes Riesling great. The fact that we can get up to 12 percent alcohol adds to the overall balance."

"The Finger Lakes is Riesling country," claims Willy Frank. "We produce some of the most delicate and elegant Rieslings in the world." Fox Run's winemaker, Peter Bell, concurs. "We can make Rieslings that can exceed anyone else's."

Most winemakers in the Finger Lakes agree with these sentiments. So, increasingly, do consumers.

(son of the legendary winemaker Konstantin Frank), describing the exceptional warm period that arrives in late fall to extend the growing season. Because of these conditions, the Finger Lakes region has produced strong-flavored, sweet wines made from native American labrusca grapes such as Niagara and Catawba for generations. It was universally believed that Chardonnay, Riesling, and other European vinifera grapes could not survive New York's freezing winter climate; native labrusca was what everyone focused on.

The first vintner to challenge the labrusca tradition was Charles Fournier, who at the end of Prohibition left his post as chief winemaker at the French Champagne firm of Veuve Cliquot to come to the Finger Lakes to work at the Urbana Wine Company, later known as the Gold Seal Wine Company. Fournier experimented with the hybrid grapes that had been developed in France to withstand phylloxera and other vine diseases. As a result of his work, other vintners began focusing on hybrids. Fournier's most lasting contribution, however, was the trust he put in Dr. Konstantin Frank, the Russian emigré whom he hired in 1953 to help plant vinifera grapes at Gold Seal.

Konstantin Frank had managed vineyards in the Ukraine, where it was not unusual for winter temperatures to drop to 20 or 30 degrees below zero; if vinifera grapes could survive those temperatures, Frank reasoned, there was no reason for them not to do well here. First at Gold Seal, and later at his own winery at Keuka Lake, Frank proved that vinifera vines could be grown in upstate New York. Frank's influence on the entire Eastern wine industry is inestimable. He inspired, encouraged, and educated leading trailblazers Philip Wagner (Maryland's Boordy Vineyards), Louisa and Alex Hargrave (Hargrave Vineyard on Long Island), and John Dyson (Millbrook Winery in the Hudson Valley), among many others.

The second important pioneering European immigrant was German-born Hermann J. Wiemer, who arrived in the Finger Lakes in 1968. He first made wine from hybrid grapes at Bully Hill Vineyards, but switched to vinifera when he acquired his own vineyard and winery in 1979. He also established one of the nation's largest grape nurseries. In addition to producing some of the region's most successful wines, Wiemer provides rootstock, not just to the Finger Lakes but to vineyards all over the country, including California.

Many of the Finger Lakes' leading vintners are descended from growers who began raising labrusca grapes for the Taylor Wine Company and who then replanted with hybrids to keep pace with demand. For years, the powerful Taylor Wine Company was the major player in the Eastern wine business, and most Finger Lakes viticulturists sold their grapes to this giant. When Taylor was taken over by Coca-Cola, many growers resisted becoming a link in the impersonal and exploitative chain of corporate farming. By contrast, the family-run Taylor Company was widely perceived as being benevolent and fair.

By the early 1980s, tastes in New York State, as elsewhere, had shifted from sweet wines towards drier, European-style wines, with an analogous decline in the labrusca and hybrid grape industry. Many of the growers who did not make the switch have had trouble staying afloat economically. "One of the unspoken reasons why hybrid wines are still around is that the grapes are a cinch to grow," one vintner told me. "Vinifera is definitely harder work, and a lot of growers just don't want to make the extra effort."

Today, a new generation of talented winemakers and knowledgeable wine drinkers are changing the character of Finger Lakes wines. Growers have decided to take control of their own destiny by founding wineries themselves. As a result, the Finger Lakes district is unique among Eastern wine regions in that, rather than being dominated by wealthy "outsiders," many of the upcoming stars here are vintners who know the land intimately from working it for generations. They have experienced all the ups and downs of the region's winemaking history, and they are determined to make the kind of serious wines that will garner world recognition. Among the Finger Lakes' visionary vintners are Peter Bell and Scott Osborne (Fox Run), Rob Thomas (Shalestone), and David Whiting (Red Newt).

The strength of the Finger Lakes region rests in the type of wines that are characteristic of cool weather regions, notably Riesling, Pinot Noir, Chardonnay, and Champagne-style sparkling wine. Other currently popular varietals such as Merlot are also doing well here, and Cabernet Franc plantings are on the increase. Red wine grapes are clearly a greater challenge to grow here than in places such as Long Island, where the growing season is longer and the extremes of temperature not as great.

In the past couple of years, as vinifera vines mature, and winemakers and vineyard managers learn more about the region's idiosyncrasies, there have been enormous changes in the quality of Finger Lakes wines. Riesling continues to evolve impressively, but one of the biggest surprises is the exceptional quality of the last few vintages of Chardonnay. An advanced trellising technique that allows more sun to reach the fruit is one of the reasons the best producers are now turning out crisp but flavorful Chards that are well balanced and utterly pleasing. While red wines are not quite up to the standards of the whites, they will probably catch up within a very few years. Many of the reds still have a green, cedary flavor that is a result of many factors, including the youth of the vines, grapes that aren't fully ripe, and the use of inexpensive American oak barrels that can impart an aggressive flavor. The potential for good Finger Lakes red, however, seems indisputable.

SENECA LAKE

ANTHONY ROAD WINE COMPANY
315-536-2182,
800-559-2182 (NY only);
fax 315-536-5851.
1225 Anthony Rd., Penn Yan, NY 14527.
Directions: From I-90 take exit 42 to Rte. 14 south, turn west on Anthony Rd. to the winery.
Owners: John and Ann Martini, and Derek and Donna Wilber.
Open: Mon.–Sat. 10am–5pm, Sun. 12noon–5pm.
Price Range of Wines: $5.99 for Seyval to $15.99 for Late Harvest Vignoles.

• Seyval
• Late Harvest Vignoles

Many exciting things are happening at Anthony Road. The first is that the tasting room has moved further up Anthony Road so that it is now visible from the highway, and thus more accessible. Winemaking facilities are also improving and expanding — production has doubled in the past couple of years to 9,000 cases and will continue to grow. Among recent additions to the winery are the locally made stainless-steel tanks from Vance Metal Fabricators.

Most impressive of all is the continued improvement in the wines. The flavorful Seyval is as good as any I've tasted. The Late Harvest Vignoles is also exceptional.

John and Ann Martini bought their farm on Seneca Lake in 1973. They planted grapes and sold them to other wineries. John, meanwhile, continued working as the field research coordinator at the New York Agricultural Station. In 1989, the Martinis joined forces with winemaker Derek Wilber, a Cornell University graduate in Pomology (the science of fruits), and founded Anthony Road Wine Company.

Derek, who was born in Penn Yan, has been around vines most of his life. His father managed Windy Heights, a 200-acre vineyard that grew grapes that were sold to the Taylor Wine Company. When Coca-Cola bought Taylor, Windy Heights and many other local vineyards were forced out of business. Derek tried to wean himself away from the wine business by studying oceanography in Florida, but he finally succumbed to the lure of Bacchus. He returned to his origins, working as a winemaker for various wineries. A couple of years ago, I stopped by the crowded tasting room to find John pasting labels on bottles. "We sold so much wine yesterday we ran out of labeled bottles," he explained. "That's good, of course. After all, selling wine is our goal." Then he looked up and grinned. "Well, that and having fun." Now Anthony Road has an automatic labeling machine as well as a bottling line and other high-tech equipment. But the four partners still seem to be having fun.

ARCADIAN ESTATE VINEYARDS
607-535-2068, 800-298-1346; fax 607-535-4692.
www.arcadianwine.com.
E-mail: arcadian@ex.trope.net
4184 Rte. 14, Rock Stream, NY 14878.
Directions: From Rte. 17 take exit 32 to Rte. 14. Travel north for 16 miles to Watkins Glen. The winery is 4 miles north of Watkins Glen.
Owners: Mike and Joanne Hastrich.
Open: Mon.–Sat. 10am–5pm, Sun. 12noon–6pm.
Price Range of Wines: $6 for Red Table Wine to $12 for Pinot Noir or Chardonnay.
Special Feature: Cross-country skiing.
Special Events: Cinco de Mayo Celebration, Folk & Blues Music event, Reggae event, Chocolate and Wine Pairing, Venison and Wine Pairing, and much more.

Arcadian, formerly the Giasi Winery, released its first vintage in 1979. Mike and Joanne Hastrich have owned it since 1991. They are determined to build their reputation on red wines, although it's still too early to predict the outcome. They have 72 acres of vines, producing 15,000 cases annually.

The tasting room, located in a refurbished 170-year-old barn, was warm and cozy on the gray, stormy day I visited. It was the perfect setting for the stories Mike told about the resident ghost, a Civil War soldier who, it seems, hangs around the winery pining for his lost love.

The current production of the winery is at 15,000 cases. There's a deck for picnics in nice weather. Buy a bottle of Arcadia's Dechaunac, or the nice Pinot Noir or Chardonnay to go with a picnic. And if a shadowy figure in a blue uniform flits by, you might offer him a glass of wine too.

CASTEL GRISCH ESTATE WINERY
607-535-9614; fax 607-535-2994.
3380 County Rte. 28, Watkins Glen, NY 14891.
Directions: From Rte. 17 take exit 32 to Rte. 14

Castel Grisch was founded in 1982 by a chemist named Alois Baggenstoss, and his wife, Michelle. The Baggenstosses, who had been searching for a spot that reminded them of their native Switzerland, felt they had arrived home when they saw this site looming high above the lake. They

The main house at Castel Grisch in Watkins Glen, New York.

Marguerite Thomas

north. From Watkins Glen follow Rte. 104 (4th St.) west to Rte. 28. Turn right to the winery.

Owners: Tom and Barbara Malina.

Open: Mother's Day–Nov.: daily 10am–6pm; other times of year: daily 10am–5pm.

Price Range of Wines: $5.99 for Seneca Dream White or Red to $24.99 for Cabernet Franc.

Special Features: B&B, restaurant.

Special Event: Oktoberfest, including hay rides and live music.

CHATEAU LaFAYETTE RENEAU
607-546-2062, 800-469-9463.
Rte. 414, Hector, NY 14841.
Directions: From Rte. 17 take exit 32 to Rte. 14 north. In Watkins Glen take Rte. 414 north. The winery is 7.4 miles northeast of Watkins Glen.

planted vines and produced their first vintage in 1984. They also built a chalet-style winery and opened a restaurant on the spot.

In 1992, Tom and Barbara Malina bought Castel Grisch. Tom, who had previously been a regional sales manager with Banfi Vintners, a Long Island-based wine importer, is delighted to be living in such spectacular surroundings. The couple enjoys overseeing the restaurant, winery, and the 135-acre estate, of which 35 acres are planted in vines. The Malinas have also converted the manor house, where the Baggenstosses lived, into a bed and breakfast.

While the Malina's imprint on the wines is only beginning, the future looks good. At present, 6,000 cases of wine are produced annually, including oak-aged Chardonnay, Baco Noir that is aged in Hungarian oak, Cayuga, and Gewürztraminer.

One of the hazards of visiting the Finger Lakes region is that people are sometimes so charmed that they end up buying a vineyard here. That's what happened to Dick and Betty Reno a few years ago. They purchased their lakeside parcel in 1985 and commuted to the site on weekends while they replanted the old vineyard and rebuilt the winery.

The Renos hired winemaker David Whiting, whose stylish, well-crafted wines helped place

Owners: Dick and Betty
  Reno.
Open: Mar.–Oct.: Mon.–Sat.
  10am–6pm, Sun.
  12noon–6pm; Nov. &
  Dec.: Sat. 12noon–5pm,
  Sun. 12noon–4pm; Jan. &
  Feb.: by appointment.
Price Range of Wines: $6.49
  for Vidal Blanc to $20 for
  Pinot Noir.
Special Events: Hayrides
  through the vineyards,
  barbecues, and a fall
  pick-your-own-grapes
  event.

Chateau LaFayette Reneau near the top of the
region's quality producers. While David has since
gone on to open his own winery (Red Newt),
Reneau continues to win awards and has become
particularly well known for its red wines. The current winemaker is Tim Miller.

The winery maintains 38 acres of vines, from
which the Renos produce about 9,000 cases annually. Among their offerings are Cuvée Blanc, a
blend of Riesling and Seyval, and a Pinot Noir.
Picnic tables on the terrace afford a beautiful view
of the lake.

*Scott Osborne, co-owner, and Peter Bell, winemaker, of
Fox Run Vineyards.*

Marguerite Thomas

FOX RUN VINEYARDS
315-536-4616; 800-636-9786.
www.foxrunvineyards.com.
E-mail: foxrun@fltg.net.
670 Rte. 14, Penn Yan, NY
  14527.
Directions: From I-90 take
  exit 42 to Rte. 14 south.
  The winery is on Rte. 14
  between Geneva and
  Dresden.
Owner: Scott Osborne.
Open: Mon.–Sat.
  10am–6pm, Sun.
  11am–6pm.
Price Range of Wines: $4.99
  for Arctic Fox; $8.99 for

Fox Run owner Scott Osborne and winemaker
Peter Bell have played an important role in setting the standards for contemporary Finger Lakes
wines. Scott is soft-spoken and modest. He is also
hardworking, smart, and ambitious, and he's recognized as a leader who is working to propel the
Finger Lakes into the national spotlight as a premium wine-producing region. He has absolute
confidence in his cause.

Shortly after purchasing Fox Run in 1993, Scott
hired Peter Bell, a talented Canadian winemaker
with a degree in enology from Australia. In the
past couple of years, Peter's skills already have cat-
apulted the wines into a new and exciting dimen-

Riesling; $13.99 for Blanc de Blancs; $19.99 for Pinot Noir; $25 for Meritage.

- Chardonnay
- Riesling
- Sparkling Wine
- Pinot Noir
- Merlot
- Meritage

sion. Peter is a firm believer in the influence of climate and soil on Finger Lakes wine. "For example, wine made from Riesling grapes grown on Keuka Lake tastes different than wine made from grapes grown on Seneca Lake. Both are excellent; they're just different," he says. "Both are aromatic and steely, but those from Seneca have more apricot and tropical fruit flavor elements. The wines from Keuka have more apple blossom, lime peel, and slate. I have really gotten into Riesling since I came here." He is scarcely less enthusiastic about the potential of Fox Run's Pinot Noir, even though he describes this grape as his "biggest challenge." Nevertheless, Peter is convinced that, in the long run, Pinot Noir will be one of his signature wines. "We're in this for the long haul," he insists. In addition to Riesling and Pinot Noir, the winery makes Arctic Fox, a light, off-dry Chardonnay-based wine with the aroma of a juicy melon; Blanc de Blancs, an excellent, crisp sparkling wine; and a flavorful Merlot. The best vintages of Meritage, a Bordeaux-style blend of Cabernet Sauvignon, Cabernet Franc, and Merlot, are rich and powerful ("It cries out for rare roast beef," exclaims Peter). The Pinot Noir is, quite possibly, the best Pinot in the region.

A bottle of Fox Run wine would be a terrific addition to a picnic on the winery's deck. The pretty setting includes a sweep of vines down the hill behind the building and a view of the lake stretching out in front.

The winery maintains 50 acres of vines and produces 14,000 cases of wine annually.

GLENORA WINE CELLARS

607-243-5511, 800-243-5513; fax 607-243-5514.
www.glenora.com.
E-mail: wine@glenora.com.
5435 Rte. 14, Dundee, NY 14837.
Directions: From I-90 take exit 42 to Rte. 14 south. The winery is east of Dundee.
Owners: Gene Pierce, Ed Dalrymple, and Scott Welliver.
Open: Jul.–Aug.: daily 10am–8pm; Sept.–Oct.: daily 10am–6pm; Nov.–Apr.: Mon.–Sat. 10am–5pm, Sun. 12noon–5pm; May–June: daily 10am–6pm.

Surrounded by vineyards sweeping down to the lake, Glenora Wine Cellars has one of the best views in the region. The winery was founded in 1976, right after the passage of the New York Farm Winery Act.

The owners were quick to recognize that the climate and soil of the region were ideal for Chardonnay and Pinot Noir, the classic Champagne grapes. Glenora has carved out a distinctive niche for itself by focusing on sparkling wine made from the same grapes and produced in the same manner as classic French Champagne. The winery owns 215 acres of vines; some of its grapes are purchased from local growers and a small percentage (especially the red wine grapes) come from Long Island.

The winery averages 40,000 cases of wine a year. Glenora's very fine sparkling wines tend to be light and delicate in style rather than rich and complex.

Price Range of Wines: $7.99 to $11 for vinifera selections including Chardonnay, Cabernet, and Riesling; $24.99 for Sparkling Anniversary Cuvée.

Special Features: Café, restaurant & inn.

Special Events: Summer Jazz Concert Series, Leaves and Lobsters (autumn festival), and much more.

• Sparkling Wines

HAZLITT 1852 VINEYARDS

607-546-9463; fax 607-546-5712. www.hazlitt1852.com. E-mail: hazlitt@lightlink. com.

5712 Rte. 414, P.O. Box 53, Hector, NY 14841.

Directions: From Rte. 17 take exit 32 to Rte. 14 north. In Watkins Glen take Rte. 414 north. The winery is north of Hector.

Owners: The Hazlitt family.

Open: Daily 10am–5pm, Sun. 12noon–5pm.

Price Range of Wines: $6 for Vidal Blanc; $11 for Chardonnay; $14 for reds, including Cabernet Sauvignon, Merlot, and Cabernet Franc.

Special Feature: Schooner for charter on Lake Seneca.

• Pinot Noir Rosé
• "Schooner White"

Among them are a Brut, made from a blend of Pinot Noir, Pinot Blanc, and Chardonnay; a creamy Blanc de Blancs, made with Chardonnay and Pinot Blanc; and an elegant Brut Rosé. Glenora also makes a semi-dry sparkler that would be a good match for a wedding cake, as well as several non-sparkling wines, including classic Chardonnay and Riesling. The popular "Jazz" — 96 percent Chardonnay blended with 4 percent Riesling — comes in a blue bottle with a cheerful, vibrantly colored label.

Visitors can enjoy a light snack or meal in Glenora's Wine Garden Café or in the new restaurant.

The Hazlitt family has been growing grapes in this region since 1852, which makes theirs one of the oldest vineyards still held by its original family. Elaine and Jerry Hazlitt opened a winery in 1985 when the grape market declined. "But making wine was nothing new to us," says Elaine. "We'd always made our own wine at home." Today, they produce 15,000 cases, and Mike Sutterby is the winemaker.

The Hazlitt family presents a classic example of how tastes in wine are changing. "We like the older-style sweeter wines," says Elaine. "Our sons and daughters, however, prefer the dry, red table wines." The 55-acre Hazlitt Vineyards reflect this shift in taste. They previously grew primarily Cayuga and Catawba grapes, but recently planted Merlot, Cabernet, and Gewürztraminer.

The Hazlitt tasting room is located in a barn that resembles a hunting lodge, with animal and fish trophies decorating the walls. The wines, which have evolved impressively over the past couple of years, include an oaky but nicely balanced Chardonnay and a classic, dry Pinot Noir Rosé. Schooner White, a Chardonnay, Riesling, and Seyval blend, is a reminder that Doug Hazlitt is also the Captain of Chantey, a Seneca Lake schooner that is available for charter. Hazlitt reds include Cabernet, Merlot, and Pinot Noir, as well as Red Cat, a blend of Catawba and Baco Noir. According to the Hazlitts, Red Cat inspires hot tubs in the moonlight. If it's daylight when you're visiting, you might have to settle for something more modest, such as a cruise on Chantey, or even a simple picnic at the winery.

LAKEWOOD VINEYARDS

607-535-9252;
ax 607-535-6656.
E-mail: lwoodwine@
aol.com.
4024 Rte. 14, Watkins Glen,
NY 14891.
Directions: From I-90 take
exit 42 to Rte. 14 south.
Winery is between
Dundee and Watkins
Glen.
Owners: The Stamp family.
Open: May–Dec.: Mon.–Sat.
10am–5pm, Sun.
12noon–6pm; Jan.–Apr.:
Fri.–Sat. 10am-5:30pm,
Sun. 12noon–5pm,
weekdays by
appointment.
Price Range of Wines: $5.49
for Delaware, Niagara,
and White Catawba to
$13.99 for "Brut," a
sparkling wine.
Special Features: Children's
indoor play area, swings
outdoors.
Special Events: Steak and
wine dinners, other food
and wine pairings.

• Niagara

Lakewood is a family-operated winery, and it's family-friendly as well. Visitors bring their kids, who dive happily into the toys piled on the floor while their parents taste wine.

Four generations of the Stamp family have farmed the sloping hillside vineyards at Lakewood. Monty and Beverly Stamp now run the place. Their son David manages the vineyards, and Christopher, the oldest son, is the winemaker. Christopher graduated from Cornell with a degree in food sciences, and trained at Glenora Wine Cellars and at Cayuga Ridge.

Lakewood has 60 acres under cultivation, and production is 15,000 cases annually. The winery produces several American native labrusca wines such as Delaware, Niagara, and White Catawba. They make labrusca because "a lot of people don't sell this anymore," says Beverly, explaining that many customers request it. The winery's Chardonnay spends only a brief time in American oak barrels before it's transferred back to stainless steel tanks, "so you don't get splinters in your tongue," jokes Beverly. Long Stem Red is a dry blend of the hybrids Baco Noir and Leon Millot.

The whole family will enjoy a picnic here, and the kids can play on the swings if they get bored.

LAMOREAUX LANDING WINE CELLARS

607-582-6011;
fax 607-582-6010.
www.fingerlakes.net/lamo
reaux.
E-mail: llwc@epix.net.
9224 Rte. 414, Lodi, NY
14860.
Directions: From Rte. 17
take exit 32 to Rte. 14
north. In Watkins Glen
take Rte. 414 north. The
winery is south of Lodi.

Lamoreaux Landing produces a variety of wines that keep earning high praise from critics and top prizes in competitions. While the wines don't seem quite as dazzling as they did when the winery first opened, Lamoreux remains one of the most exciting young wineries in the region.

"People don't think of Chardonnay growing here, but we're finding that with proper canopy management you can get some really good flavors," says Lamoreaux Landing owner, Mark Wagner. Mark, whose family has been growing grapes in the Finger Lakes region since the 19th

The tasting room and winery facility at Lamoreaux Landing.

Marguerite Thomas

Owner: Mark Wagner.
Open: Mon.–Sat.
10am–5pm, Sun.
12noon–5pm.
Price Range of Wines: $7 for Estate White; $9 for Dry Riesling; $10 for Pinot Noir; $11 for Chardonnay; $16 for Merlot.

- Chardonnay
- Gewürztraminer
- Riesling
- Merlot
- Cabernet Franc

century, raises both vinifera and French-American varietals on his 130-acre vineyard. He sells the hybrids to other wineries; his own wines are made exclusively from vinifera grapes. Mark, incidentally, is only distantly related to Bill Wagner, owner of neighboring Wagner Vineyards.

In 1990, Mark founded his own winery, and in 1992, the striking Lamoreaux Landing tasting room and winemaking facility was built. Designed by architect Bruce Corson, who has offices in Ithaca and California, the building resembles a Greek temple — an appropriate reference to Bacchus. "I always liked the Greek Revival architecture that is so prevalent in this area," says Mark. In the earliest planning stages, he and the architect had talked about renovating an old barn on the property, Mark explains. "Then one day Bruce threw this drawing up on the wall and said we could use the barn for the winery, and put a Greek Temple on top of it for tasting."

Today, gazing out through the tall windows of the tasting room, one can look 20 miles north over the lake toward Geneva. High-quality rotating art

Mark Wagner

Mark Wagner has spent his entire life working with grapes. "My father was growing labrusca when I was born," he says. "Then he switched to French-American varietals. Now I've added vinifera to the property."

Mark's interest in grapes expanded to include wine at about the time he reached legal drinking age. "I had grown up with grapes and I had learned a lot about winemaking by association with the wineries we were growing for," he says. "At some point, I decided I'd like to have my own name on the bottle. It bothered me that other people were taking my grapes and doing who knows what with them."

Mark knew he wanted to concentrate on vinifera almost from the beginning. "I didn't want to do it halfway. I wanted to keep the quality up. Since I knew I didn't need to be the biggest winery in the world," he explains, "I set my eye on where I wanted to go — to make quality wine and to expand only as I'm able." He seeks a 25 percent annual growth in production. One way he ensures quality, says Mark, is by having control over the grapes. He supervises the vines' every aspect, from the day they're planted until the fruit is turned into wine.

The glacial till in the Finger Lakes, Mark explains, makes a superb environment for vineyards. "Deposits left in the Ice Age are of mixed-up soils," he says. "There is pure sand in one spot, gravel right next to it, then clay and loam. You can have all of these in a single vineyard." This is an unusual situation, says Mark, and he likes it very much. "Every soil gives the grapes a different character." He explains. "We're still experimenting here by mixing up the vines in different soil types and watching carefully. We're experimenting with different clones to discover which do best here."

The rigorous canopy management Mark has been practicing is proving to be particularly effective. Vines, he maintains, are like most plant life in the East. "Winter is so bleak. Then, suddenly, everything opens up and it's amazingly lush and then it dies. The same thing happens in a vineyard, and if you don't control it properly you end up with problems."

In addition to Chardonnay, Mark has been having excellent results with Riesling, Cabernet Franc, and Pinot Noir. This last, he says, is the trickiest to grow and to make into wine. "It's so finicky. It plays with your mind. One day you go down to the cellar and taste it and think, 'Wow!' The next week you wonder what you can do with it. Just driving Pinot Noir home in your car can interfere with it."

Actually, there is only one major vinifera grape that strikes Mark as truly problematic. "Cabernet Sauvignon is the one I feel most uneasy about in this climate," he confesses. "One year in every five or ten might be a great year. The other years we'll use the grapes in our Red Table Wine. It really hasn't been planted here long enough for us to learn much about it, though."

Does the challenge of making premium wine in the East bother him? Not much, it seems. "The strategy is just to develop an idea of where you want to be, and then make it happen," he says with equanimity. And what's the first step for getting where you want to be? "Recognize that you can't make good wine from bad grapes," says Mark firmly.

Mark Wagner is optimistic about the future. "Fifteen years ago," he says, "there wasn't much to write about. Now we're an up-and-coming region with the ability to do great things. We're making wines that can compete anywhere."

exhibits grace the walls, making this one of the most attractive spots in which to taste wine.

There are 8,500 cases of wine produced annually by winemaker Craig Mitrakul. They include a tart and bright Chardonnay, a pleasant and straightforward Riesling, and a good white blend called, simply, Estate White. The winery also makes an excellent Pinot Noir.

Picnic benches and tables overlooking the lake provide an inviting spot for lunch.

Nancy Newland, owner of New Land Winery.

Marguerite Thomas

NEW LAND VINEYARD
315-585-4432, 315-585-9844.
577 Lerch Rd., Geneva, NY
  14456.
Directions: From Rte. 17
  take exit 32 to Rte. 14
  north. In Watkins Glen
  take Rte. 414 north to Rte.
  96A in Ovid. Travel
  north on 96A to Lerch
  Road. Turn left. The
  winery is 1 mile past the
  junction with Rte. 336.
Owner: Nancy Newland.
Open: May–Nov. 15:
  Mon.–Fri. 12noon–5pm,
  Sat. 11am–6pm, Sun.
  11am–5pm; Nov.
  15–Dec.: Sat.–Sun,
  12noon–5pm, or by
  appointment.

Owner/winemaker Nancy Newland was the last of Dr. Konstantin Frank's students, and the master's touch is clearly tasted in New Land's exceptional wines. The winery's production of about one-third red wine is unusual for this region that specializes in whites. Perhaps the vineyard's unique location is particularly hospitable to red-wine vines.

The 10-acre vineyard is well situated on a protected bluff east of Seneca Lake. The site, Nancy insists, is one of the reasons her wine is so good. Certainly the setting is lovely. At any time of year the tiny tasting room affords a dramatic view of the open countryside and the sparkling lake. But to be there in the midst of a summer storm is particularly thrilling — like riding out a tempest in a trim little boat. On a recent visit, thunder crashed, lightning flashed, and a curtain of rain-drenched clouds

Price Range of Wines: $7 for Pinot Noir Blanc to $18 for Merlot and Cabernet Sauvignon.

- Chardonnay
- Sauvignon Blanc
- Merlot/Cabernet Blend

PREJEAN WINERY
315-536-7524, 800-548-2216; fax 315-536-7635.
www.prejeanwinery.com.
E-mail: wine@prejean winery.com.
2634 State Rte. 14, Penn Yan, NY 14527.
Directions: From I-90 take exit 42 to Rte. 14 south. The winery is south of Dresden.
Owner: Elizabeth Prejean and Tom Prejean.
Open: Mon.–Sat. 10am–5pm, Sun. 11am–5pm.
Price Range of Wines: $5.99 for Cayuga White to $18.99 for Merlot.
Special Events: Regular winemakers' dinners.

- Gewürztraminer
- Merlot
- Maréchal Foch

descended over the lake. We sat it all out snugly, tasting the Chardonnay (Nancy calls it American Meursault), the Sauvignon Blanc (perhaps the only one in the Finger Lakes), the Pinot Noir, the Merlot ("It goes very quickly," warns Nancy about this understandably popular wine), and the rich and complex Cabernet Sauvignon. New Land currently turns out only 2,000 cases of wine a year. Both red and white wines age very well. New Land is a little off the beaten track, but well worth the extra miles.

Elizabeth Prejean and her late husband, Jim, started producing estate-grown wines when they came to the Finger Lakes in 1986, producing Merlot, Chardonnay, Riesling, Maréchal Foch, Gewürztraminer, Cayuga, and Vignoles. Today Prejean turns out 6,000 cases of wine from its 33.5-acre vineyard.

The wines are among the region's best, but raising vines for making good wine is by no means a given here, as Libby Prejean is quick to point out. Take Gewürztraminer, for example, a fussy vine that many other Finger Lakes vintners have given up trying to grow. Prejean has devised a method of protecting the vines from winter damage by putting an extra wire on the trellis for the Gewürz. When the vines have hardened off at the approach of winter, the wire is dropped to the ground and buried; in spring, workers stationed at both ends of the wire give it a sharp tug, causing wire and vine to pop up. "We've never lost a vine, even during the very cold winters of 1992, 1993, and 1994," says Libby. But why go to this labor-intensive trouble in the first place? "Prejean is a Cajun name," Libby explains, "and Gewürztraminer is the best wine to drink with Cajun food."

The fact is most vinifera grapes in the Finger Lakes region require a certain amount of coddling. "Merlot is another one of our problem children," says Libby, "but we feel the rewards are worth it." Even the hybrid Seyval has to be cluster-thinned every year. If it's allowed to over-produce, the wine suffers and the vines weaken. "On the other hand, almost everyone can produce good Riesling here," Libby adds.

The hybrid Maréchal Foch is a winter-hardy hybrid that yields a deep purple, inexpensive, big-flavored wine that many folks adore. Prejean's Gewürztraminer gives off a haunting aroma of rose petals; the unusually powerful scent may arise because the grapes, once crushed, rest on their skins overnight before the juice is drained off (most of the aromas reside in a grape's skin). In good years, Prejean Merlot is among the top three or four in the Finger Lakes.

Buy a bottle of Prejean Riesling or Merlot and enjoy it on the deck overlooking the lake. Or, bring a picnic of Cajun-style chicken breasts to the winery, and drink a bottle of Gewürztraminer.

RED NEWT CELLARS
607-546-4100;
  fax 607-546-4101.
E-mail: dwhiting@
  baka.com.
3675 Tichenor Rd., Hector,
  NY 14841.
Owners: David and Debra
  Whiting.
Open: Fri.–Sun.
  12noon–6pm.
Price Range of Wines: $6
  for Vidal Cayuga Blend
  to $16 for Merlot.
Special Feature: The Bistro.

Scheduled to open in the summer of 1999, Red Newt's wines were not yet available for tasting when research for this book was underway. The fact that the owner/winemaker is David Whiting, however, leaves little room for doubt about the potential of the winery. As consulting winemaker for many of the region's top wineries, Dave has a mild manner and shy smile that belie an unwavering talent and passionate dedication to winemaking. When an empty winery facility (the former Wickham Winery, which opened in 1981 and went bankrupt five years later) unexpectedly became available in 1998, Dave seized the opportunity to fulfill his dream of having a winery of his own. His plan is to acquire vineyards gradually; for the moment, Dave will carefully select choice grapes from the best local vineyards to produce Chardonnay, Riesling, a blush-style Cayuga/Vidal blend, Merlot, and Cabernets Franc and Sauvignon. Deb Whiting, who owns Seneca Savory, a successful catering company, will operate the Red Newt Bistro. The winery's name, incidentally, comes from the Whitings' fondness for the indigenous Red Spotted Newt — "One of nature's most beautiful but often overlooked creatures," says Dave.

SHALESTONE
  VINEYARDS LLC
607-582-6600.
E-mail: shalestone
  vineyards@yahoo.com.
9681 Rte. 414, Lodi, NY
  14860.
Directions: From Rte 17
  take exit 32 to Rte 14
  north. In Watkins Glen
  take Rte. 414 north to the
  winery.
Owners: Rob and Kate
  Thomas.

Open only since Labor Day 1998, Shalestone is already hailed as one of the most exciting wineries in the region. Skilled winemaker Rob Thomas made his name at Lamoreaux Landing. One of the distinctive things about Rob's own winery is that he makes only red wines. "Why red wine in what's widely perceived as a white wine region? That's the most often asked question," says Rob's wife, Kate. The answer is simple: Rob has a passion for red wine and a belief that it's important to focus entirely on just one thing. All of the grapes come from the Thomas' own five-acre vineyard; all

Open: Apr.–Nov.: Fri.–Sun.
12noon–5pm.
Price Range of Wines: $8
for Rosé to $16 for
Merlot.

• Merlot
• Cabernet Sauvignon
• Legend
• Dry Rosé

of the wines (including Legend, a Bordeaux-style blend of Merlot, Cabernet Sauvignon, and Cabernet Franc) are delicious.

Martha Macinski of Standing Stone Vineyards.

Marguerite Thomas

STANDING STONE VINEYARDS

607-582-6051, 800-803-7135;
fax 607-582-6312.
E-mail: ssvny@aol.com.
9934 Rte. 414, Hector, NY
14841.
Directions: From Rte. 17
take exit 32 to Rte. 14
north. In Watkins Glen
take Rte. 414 north. The
winery is north of Valois.
Owners: Martha and Tom
Macinski.
Open: Fri. 11am–5pm, Sat.
10am–6pm, Sun.
12noon–5pm.
Price Range of Wines: $6.99
for dry Vidal; $12.99 for
Gewürztraminer; $15.50
for Chardonnay Pinnacle;
$16.50 for Bordeaux blend.

Standing Stone shot out of the starting gate with the clear indications of a winner a few years ago and has never slowed down. The winery's success is partly due to the talented David Whiting, who was the original winemaker. Another reason, according to owners Martha (Marti) and Tom Macinski, is that their soil is particularly well suited to grapes. Marti claims the wine is already half made when the grapes are harvested.

Even so, the winery has expanded at a faster rate than the Macinskis had anticipated. "We certainly never dreamed we would sell all our wines 12 weeks after we opened," says Marti. Despite this initial success, both Macinskis continue to pursue other full-time jobs. She is a lawyer and he works for IBM. "We could keep the winery going without having other jobs, but expansion would be much slower," says Marti.

Special Events: Barrel
   tastings by reservation.

- Chardonnay
- Gewürztraminer
- Riesling
- Cabernet Franc
- Merlot
- Pinnacle

Standing Stone has been garnering awards as far away as California for its exceptional Gewürztraminer and Riesling. The winery makes one of the best dry Vidals in the East. The red wines, including Pinnacle, a Bordeaux-type blend of Cabernet Sauvignon, Cabernet Franc, and Merlot, are also beginning to move into the spotlight. The winery has 35 acres of vines, producing around 6,000 cases of wine a year. Dave Whiting left as winemaker in 1998 to start his own winery, Red Newt.

The tasting room is in a handsomely restored chicken coop, embellished with a large wooden terrace with picnic tables overlooking the vineyards and lake.

WAGNER VINEYARDS
607-582-6450;
   fax 607-582-6446.
E-mail: wagwine@ptd.net.
9322 Rte. 414, Lodi, NY
   14860.
Directions: From Rte. 17
   take exit 32 to Rte. 14
   north. In Watkins Glen
   take Rte. 414 north. The
   winery is between Valois
   and Lodi.
Owner: Bill Wagner.
Open: Daily 10am–5pm.;
   last tour and tasting ends
   at 4:15pm. Closed
   Thanksgiving,
   Christmas, New Year's
   Day.
Price Range of Wines: $4.99
   for Reserve Red and
   Reserve White; $5.99 for
   Melody; $12.99 for
   Merlot and Reserve
   Chardonnay.
Special Features: Gift shop,
   café, brewery.
Special Events: Live music
   Fri. nights in summer,
   Harvest Dinner,
   Valentine's Day Dinner.

Wagner Vineyards is BIG. It produces 40,000 cases of wine a year, it maintains 240 acres of vines, and it is enormously popular. The tasting room is perennially crowded with visitors sampling the vast selection of Wagner wines and, more recently, a wide selection of beers produced by the on-site brewery. Not surprisingly, the Wagner gift shop is larger than most.

Bill Wagner first got into agriculture in the Finger Lakes region in 1947, when he started a vegetable and dairy farm. He also raised grapes that he sold to various wineries, and he continues to sell about half his fruit. In the 1960s, he eliminated his other crops to concentrate on grapes, and in 1978 he released his first vintage.

Wagner wines are made from native American, French-American hybrid, and European (vinifera) grapes. The assortment includes three different Chardonnays, four or more Rieslings, a bunch of blushes, and Pinot Noir in various guises. Several wines are produced from grapes unique to the Finger Lakes region. Wagner's Melody, for example, is made from the Melody grape, a cross between Seyval and Geneva White, which, itself, is a cross between Pinot Blanc and Ontario. The Melody grape was developed in the late 1960s by the New York State Experiment Station in Geneva. Wagner winemaker Ann Rafetto describes the white, intensely fruity Melody as "fruit salad in a glass, a perfect summertime wine."

HERMANN J. WIEMER VINEYARD, INC.

607-243-7971, 800-371-7971; fax 607-243-7983.
www.wiemer.com.
E-mail: wiemer@linkny.com.
Rte.14, P.O. Box 38, Dundee, NY 14837.
Directions: From I-90 take exit 42 to Rte. 14 south. Winery is halfway between Geneva and Watkins Glen.
Owner: Hermann Wiemer.
Open: Apr.–Nov.: Mon.–Sat. 10am–5pm, Sun. 11am–5pm; Dec.–Mar.: Mon.–Fri. 10am–5pm.
Price Range of Wines: $7.50 for Estate White or Dry Rosé; $9 for dry Riesling; $13 for Pinot Noir; $16.50 for sparkling wines.

- Chardonnay
- Gewürztraminer
- Riesling
- Sparkling Wine
- Individual Bunch Select Late Harvest Riesling

After a couple of stellar recent vintages, Wiemer wines are achieving their true potential. The winery produces 12,000 cases annually, including a Riesling that could be the paragon of the region, a wonderful Alsace-style Gerwüztraminer, and a very special Individual Bunch Select Late Harvest Riesling. This is made in the German Trockenbeerenauslese (TBA) tradition from hand-selected grapes that have been affected by the noble botrytis mold.

One reason Hermann Wiemer started his own winery was because of a dispute with Walter S. Taylor, his boss at Bully Hill Vineyards. Taylor, like most Finger Lakes winemakers in the mid-1970s, was adamantly committed to hybrid grapes, which he believed were the only grapes that could survive the region's cold winters. Hermann, who came from the cool Moselle region of northern Germany, was convinced that vinifera could grow in the Finger Lakes, where the hills slope gently to the water as they do in the Moselle, and the slatey glacial soils are also comparable. He was profoundly influenced by Konstantin Frank's success with European vinifera grapes.

In 1979, he bought an abandoned 145-acre soybean farm on the shores of Seneca Lake, and he began planting Riesling, Pinot Noir, and other vinifera grapes. As the vineyard grew, it first became successful because of the young vines it supplied to other vineyards. In this endeavor he was following in the footsteps of his father, who had run Germany's largest nursery and supervised the replanting of that country's vineyards after World War II. Today, Hermann Wiemer has some 65 acres under vines. The vineyard supplies some 200,000 vines a year to vineyards in Latin America and the United States, including such notable California wineries as Buena Vista, Caymus, and Kendall Jackson. Wiemer's handsome winery, designed by Simon Ungers of UZK Architects of Ithaca, is actually built inside an old dairy barn. The grounds provide a nice backdrop for a picnic.

KEUKA LAKE

Patio restaurant at Bully Hill Vineyards.

Marguerite Thomas

BULLY HILL VINEYARDS

607-868-3610, 607-868-3210; fax 607-868-3205.

www.bullyhill.com.

E-mail: bullyhill@ptd.net.

8843 Greyton H. Taylor Memorial Dr., Hammondsport, NY 14840.

Directions: from Rte. 17 take exit 38 to Rte. 54. In Hammondsport, take Rte. 54A along west side of lake to County Rte. 76. Follow Rte. 76 for 1.5 miles to Greyton H. Taylor Memorial Dr. and winery.

Owner: Walter S. Taylor.

Open: Mon.–Sat. 9am–5pm, Sun. 12noon–5pm.

Price Range of Wines: $6.95 for Love My Goat to $9 for Chardonnay Elise.

Special Features: Café, gift shop, museum.

The saga of Walter S. Taylor and his quirky winery, with its colorful, fun-filled labels, is the stuff of American legend. Taylor's chronicle began in the late 19th century when his grandfather, also named Walter Taylor, arrived in Hammondsport. The elder Taylor purchased a vineyard and established a winery. Taylor's wine was shipped 22 miles up Keuka Lake by steamboat to Penn Yan, then transported across to Seneca Lake and over to the Erie Canal. From there, it made its way to the large markets in New York City.

The Taylor winery expanded rapidly in the 1920s, and it began purchasing grapes from local growers. The original site atop Bully Hill was sold, and the operation was moved to larger quarters. The firm rode out Prohibition by switching to grape juice, which was also shipped down the river in barrels. The elder Taylor audaciously wrote on them: "Please do not add sugar or keep in a warm place or contents will ferment."

By the 1950s, Taylor Wine had become a leader in the New York wine industry, but success was somewhat tarnished for grandson Walter S. Taylor by disputes with the rest of the Taylor clan over the quality of the wine. Walter argued that they should switch from native American labrusca grapes to the more universally appealing hybrid grapes. Furthermore, he believed they should stop adulterating the wine with additives such as sugar and water. "It's easy to tell when the Taylor Company is making wine," he used to joke, "because the level of Keuka Lake drops several feet." His relatives were not amused.

The Taylor Wine Company, by now made up of numerous relatives who had had enough of Walter's zeal for reform, invited him to leave the firm in 1970. So, Walter and his father, Greyton, bought back the original Taylor site on Bully Hill and began their own winery. Little did Walter know his troubles were just beginning.

When the Coca-Cola Corporation purchased the Taylor Wine Company, they immediately filed, and eventually won, a lawsuit forbidding Walter to use the Taylor name on his wine. So Walter threw a party. He provided his guests with marking pens and plenty of wine to drink, and they spent the night inking out the word "Taylor" on thousands of bottles of wine. Unable to use the family name, Walter proceeded to design labels using portraits of his ancestors instead of their name. When Coca-Cola got a court order forbidding him to do that, he put masks on their faces, but — you guessed it — he was hauled back to court for another losing battle.

The denouement of the drama came when Walter was ordered to turn over everything he owned that related to the Taylor family. He led a motorcade hauling paintings, documents, and a host of other objects down the road to the Taylor Wine Company, where he dumped everything in a large pile on the front steps of the winery. Then he persuaded his goat, named Guilt Free, to pose on top of the heap. "They got my name and heritage, but they didn't get my goat," was Walter's now legendary quip.

Of course all of these legal wrangles cost Walter a bundle, but did any of it hurt Bully Hill sales? Absolutely not. Walter may have lost the battles, but he won the war. The Taylor Wine Company, which changed hands several more times, has now disappeared. Bully Hill, however, produces an enormous assortment of very popular wines.

Bully Hill wines are all made from French-American hybrid grapes, grown on 150 acres. Harbor Lights is a semi-sweet white blend of Vidal, Cayuga, and Verdelet, and Red Wine is made from Baco Noir, Chancellor, and Chelois. Writer John Baxavanis said of this particular wine, "For those with a taste for French-American, this wine may be as important as a religious experience."

Walter S. Taylor, while confined to a wheelchair as the result of an automobile accident a few years ago, is still involved in running the winery. Bully Hill, which is part theme park and part winery, is enormously popular, receiving thousands of visitors each year. It offers unusually entertaining tours and it has an abundantly stocked gift shop and a museum. There's a café that serves pizza and other informal meals, as well as a picnic area with a view of the lake.

Marguerite Thomas

Willy Frank, owner of Dr. Frank's Vinifera Wine Cellars/Chateau Frank, and son of legendary vintner Konstantin Frank.

DR. FRANK'S VINIFERA WINE CELLARS/ CHATEAU FRANK
Phone & fax: 607-868-4884; 800-320-0735.
www.drfrankwines.com.
E-mail: frankwines@ aol.com.
9749 Middle Rd., Hammondsport, NY 14840.
Directions: From Rte. 17 take exit 38 to Rte. 54 north. Travel north for 6 miles to Hammondsport. Take Rte. 54A north for 6 more miles, take the first left past the Hammondsport Motel onto County Rte. 76 (Middle Rd.).
Owner: Willy Frank.
Open: Mon.–Sat. 9am–5pm, Sun. 12noon–5pm.
Price Range of Wines: $5.95 for Premiere Blush to $22 for Cabernet Sauvignon.

- Sparkling Wine
- Gewürztraminer
- Riesling
- Chardonnay
- Pinot Noir
- Rkatsiteli

Vinifera Wine Cellars is where the Eastern American wine industry was really born, and Dr. Frank himself exemplifies the story of the American dream come true. An immigrant from the Soviet Union, Dr. Frank arrived in New York with his family in 1951. Although he was a professor of plant sciences in the U.S.S.R., the only job Konstantin Frank could find in America at first was hoeing blueberries at the New York State Agricultural Experiment Station in Geneva. This is where Charles Fournier, of Gold Seal Vineyards, discovered him.

Recognizing Frank's talents, Fournier hired him to plant and manage vinifera grapes at Gold Seal. By 1962, Konstantin Frank had purchased his own land, where he proved to a skeptical world that European vinifera grapes could be successfully cultivated in the Finger Lakes region.

Next he went on to produce critically acclaimed wine from his grapes, including a Chardonnay and a Riesling, as well as almost 60 other varieties. Soon other prospective Eastern vintners sought Dr. Frank's advice and encouragement. Untold numbers of wineries today owe their success, directly or indirectly, to Konstantin Frank's visionary work. Vinifera Wine Cellars is now run by Willy Frank. Willy assumed control ten years ago when his father died at the age of 86. Approximately 20,000 cases of wine are produced here, from grapes grown on the property's 79 acres. The wines include a Riesling (Konstantin Frank;s favorite wine) and Gewürztraminer. "Gewürztraminer is the favorite grape of wild turkeys, but our sweet revenge is to serve Gewürz with Thanksgiving turkey," Willy chuckles. Pinot Noir, made from the oldest Pinot Noir vineyard in the Finger Lakes region, is excellent. "The mature vine roots go down 15 to 20 feet to find minerals and other elements," says Willy. "A young vine can't possibly give you the color, body, or complexity of older vines."

Other winners include Salmon Run Riesling, a personal favorite of mine, Chardonnay, and Cabernet Sauvignon. ("Growing Cabernet here is almost self flagellation," says Willy.) And don't miss the Rkatsiteli, made from a Russian grape that is almost unknown in this country, or the Late Harvest Sereksia and Muscat Ottonel, made only in exceptional years. Chateau Frank, another winery under the same management but not open to the public, makes sparkling wines that are also superior.

The wines of Heron Hill.

Marguerite Thomas

HERON HILL WINERY
607-868-4241, 800-441-4241; fax 607-868-3435.
www.heronhill.com.
E-mail: info@heronhill.com.
9249 County Rte. 76, Hammondsport, NY 14840.
Directions: From Rte. 17 take exit 38 to Rte. 54 north. Travel north 6 miles to Hammondsport. Take Rte. 54A north for 6 more miles, take the first

Heron Hill has recently undergone an exciting turnaround. A lavish expansion adds 2,500 square feet of new space and 1,000 feet of remodeled space, plus extensive terraces and open-air pavilions. (Charles Warren, a New York architect originally from the Finger Lakes, designed the new building.) Impressive though the new structure is, however, the real news here is the much-improved wine. Phil Hazlitt, the winemaker until early 1999, raised the quality of Heron Hill to an attention-grabbing level. The Chardonnays (especially the one made in stainless steel tanks without barrel

left past the Hammonds-
port Motel onto County
Rte. 76 (Middle Rd.).
Follow winery signs.
Owners: John and
Josephine Ingle.
Open: Mon.–Sat. 10am–5pm,
Sun. 12noon–5pm.
Price Range of Wines:
$7.99 for semi-dry
Riesling to $17.99 for
Barrel Fermented
Chardonnay.
Special Features:Box
lunches, gift shop.
Special Events: Year-round;
call for schedule.

- Chardonnay
- Johannisberg Riesling

fermentation) are fruity and very drinkable. The
so-called Johannisberg Riesling is aromatic and,
with a residual sugar level of 2 percent, relatively
sweet. (The term "Johannisberg," borrowed from
California, is relatively meaningless; Heron Hill
uses it to indicate sweetness.) The handsomely
packaged Game Bird series has distinct appeal, and
each bottle comes with an original recipe, created
by the Ingles, for preparing game birds. The winery currently has 19 acres of vines, producing
12,000 cases annually.

Art Hunt, owner, Hunt Country Vineyard.

Marguerite Thomas

HUNT COUNTRY VINEYARD
315-595-2812, 800-946-3289;
fax 315-595-2835.
www.fingerlakes.net/keuka
wines/keuhunt.html.
E-mail: huntwine@
eznet.net.
4021 Italy Hill Rd.,
Branchport, NY 14418.
Directions: From Rte. 17
take exit 38 to Rte. 54. In

Art Hunt is the sixth generation of his family to
live on this farm above Keuka Lake. Art's
father was raised here, but during the Depression
he left the farm to work at the Corning Glass
Works. Art grew up in Corning, but spent summers on the farm, which he ultimately inherited
from his uncle.

While not a farmer himself, Art had a keen
attachment to the land. In the 1960s, when local
wineries were looking for premium grapes, he

The entrance to Hunt Country Vineyard.

Marguerite Thomas

Hammondsport, take Rte. 54A along west side of Lake Keuka to Branchport. Turn onto Italy Hill Rd. and continue straight up the hill to the winery.Owners: Art and Joyce Hunt.

Open: Jul.–Oct.: Mon.–Sat. 10am–6pm, Sun. 12noon–6pm; Jan.–Jun. & Nov.–Dec.: Mon.–Sat. 10am–5pm, Sun. 12noon–5pm; Jan.–Mar.: call for weekend appointment.

Price Range of Wines: $5.99 for Foxy Lady; $8.99 for Riesling; $9.99 for Chardonnay; $24 for Vidal Ice Wine.

Special Feature: Gift shop.

Special Event: Panorama Horse Sanctuary Benefit, a fundraiser to benefit a sanctuary for abused and unwanted horses.

- "Foxy Lady"
- Vidal Ice Wine

decided that his sloping acreage of deep, well-drained soil was ideally suited for grapes. With borrowed money, he started planting vines and learning about viticulture. Then, in the 1970s, everything changed. Popular taste shifted from red to white wine. The Taylor Wine Company, which had purchased crops from local growers, was acquired by Coca-Cola.

The Finger Lakes area, like most of the rest of the country, was being swept from a regional economy into global economics. "Banks didn't even want to hear you knock on their door. In the early 1970s the cost of everything tripled," says Art. "Most growers had to start their own winery or get out of the grape business."

In 1981, the Hunts opened a winery. "The growers who survived had to learn to be more efficient, though in our case, it was more groping than brilliant management," Art says. "But we did learn how to do it. We learned how to hedge the vines, for example, and reduce the acreage of grapes that don't have a long-time future, such as Delaware."

While the Hunt vineyard still features native and hybrid species on its 55 acres, experimentation is being conducted with other grapes. Art Hunt, one of the few Finger Lakes vintners to tackle the thorny problem of how to sell wine in an already crowded market, travels every week to the Union Square Farmers' Market in New York City to sell his wines.

Despite the difficulty of adjusting to the changes, Art remains essentially upbeat. "When you stand back and look at things from a distance, you realize this whole premium wine thing couldn't have happened any other way." He says. "We could still be growing the same grapes for Taylor."

The future looks good, he says. Hunt Country produces around 10,000 cases of commendable country wine annually, which, as Art points out, gets better all the time. "And look at that tasting room," he nods towards the refurbished farm outbuilding that now houses a well-stocked gift shop and tasting bar. "I've never seen it as busy as this year." Among the wines to be sampled are Foxy Lady (blush), Riesling, Barrel Reserve Chardonnay, and Vidal Ice Wine.

There is a lovely spot for a picnic on the deck, or visitors might like to set out from the vineyards for a bike ride or a hike.

KEUKA SPRING VINEYARDS

315-536-3147;
fax 716-621-4850.
www.frontier.net/
~ksvwine.
E-mail: ksvwine@
frontier.net.
273 East Lake Rd. (Rte. 54),
Penn Yan, NY 14527.
Mail: 50 Sugar Maple Dr.,
Rochester, NY 14615.
Directions: From Rte. 17
take exit 38 to Rte. 54
north. Travel north 6
miles to Hammondsport.
Continue on Rte. 54 to
the winery, 3 miles south
of Penn Yan.
Owners: Judy and Len
Wiltberger.
Open: June–Aug.:
Mon.–Sat. 10am–5pm,
Sun. 12noon–5pm;
Sept.–Oct. & May: Sat.
10:30am–5pm, Sun.12
noon– 5pm; closed
Nov.–Apr.
Price Range of Wines: $6
for Blush to $14 for
Merlot.

Keuka Spring's winery and tasting room are located in an old barn overlooking the lake. Owners Judy and Len Wiltberger commute between their home in Rochester and the winery. Len is another of the Finger Lakes vintners who work at Eastman Kodak.

"We concentrate on what we feel is a good cross section of wine for the variety of folks who come in the door," says Judy. The range of styles includes a selection of whites such as classic Chardonnay and Riesling, and some reds, including Crooked Lake Red, a fruity red blend that, in Judy's words, "is the wine people want to take home to serve with their pasta." Like many Eastern vintners, the Wiltbergers say that visitors to the winery often claim they don't like sweet wine. "But then they walk out with Vignoles," laughs Judy, referring to a semi-sweet wine with a fruity flavor reminiscent of apricots.

Keuka Spring owns a 10-acre vineyard, and it purchases about 30 percent of its grapes from local growers. The winery produces 1,500 cases annually. Picnic tables in front of the winery look out over the lake.

McGREGOR VINEYARDS & WINERY

800-272-0192;
fax 607-292-6929.

McGregor Winery has the unusual distinction of raising hardy Russian vinifera varietals, as well as European vinifera grapes. "They seem to tol-

www.linkny.com/~msg.
E-mail: mcg@linkny.com.
5503 Dutch St., Dundee, NY
14837.
Directions: From Rte. 17
take exit 38 to Rte. 54
north. Travel north 6
miles to Hammondsport.
Continue on Rte. 54 to
Hyatt Hill Rd. Turn up
Hyatt Hill Rd. to Dutch
St. Turn left. The winery
is 1 mile further.
Owner: Robert McGregor.
Open: Apr.–Dec.: Mon.–Sat.
10am–6pm; Jul.–Aug.:
Fri. 10am–8pm, Sun.
11am–6pm; Jan.–Mar.:
daily, 11am–5pm.
Price Range of Wines: $6.99
for table wines to $12.99
for Vintner's Reserve
Chardonnay.
Special Events: Harvest
Brunch Series, December
Gourmet Dinner, regular
food & wine pairings;
call for additional events.

• Muscat Ottonel
• Late Harvest Vignoles

erate the winters here," observes Robert McGregor,"
and they produce unusually deep red wine.

Robert, who retired early from Kodak in 1986,
had planted vines on this slope of land in 1971.
Today, from its 35-acre vineyard, McGregor produces about 7,000 cases of very good wine. Don't
miss the Muscat Ottonel, a luscious sweet wine
made in limited amounts. Late Harvest Vignoles is
another fine dessert wine made here. Also available are limited amounts of Black Russian Red
from a blend of Russian Grapes — Black Sereksia
and Saperavia.

Visitors may picnic outside on the terrace or, if
the weather is cool, sit at tables inside the cozy tasting room overlooking the lake.

CAYUGA LAKE

**CAYUGA RIDGE
ESTATE WINERY**
607-869-5158, 800-598-
WINE; fax 607-869-3412.
E-mail: crew@epix.net.
6800 Rte. 89, Elm Beach,
Ovid, NY 14521.
Directions: From Ithaca
take Rte. 89 north for 22.5
miles to the winery.
Owners: Tom and Susie
Challen.
Open: Mid-May–mid-Nov.:
daily 12noon–5pm; mid-
Nov.–mid-May: Sat. &

Tom Challen had almost 20 years of wine background and vineyard management experience
in Canada, when he and his wife, Susie, purchased
Cayuga Ridge in 1991. The winery and vineyards
had been established in 1980 by Bob and Mary
Plane.

Tom's judgement is that the Finger Lakes is one
of the best regions for producing fine wines. Rather
than make sweeping changes, the Challens have
elected to carry on the traditions started by the
Planes. Their labels still sport a quatrefoil, an
ancient symbol for quality. They carry on the win-

Sun. 12noon–4pm, or by appointment.

Price Range of Wines: $6.25 for Duet; $9.95 for Chardonnay; $14.95 for Pinot Noir.

Special Events: Monthly food & wine events, fall harvest events.

ery's vigneron tradition, a program that allows participants to lease vines and harvest their own grapes, which the winery will then vinify if the owners wish.

The Challens also are continuing to produce the same respectable, if not dazzling, wines as the Planes, including Riesling, Vignoles, a buttery Chardonnay, and several red wines such as Pinot Noir and Cabernet Franc. Duet is a semi-sweet Cayuga/ Vignoles blend that the Challens recommend serving with barbecue. They have a 38-acre vineyard and bottle 4,500 cases of wine a year.

Cayuga Ridge's tasting room is in an enormous old barn, which has a deck with picnic tables and overlooks the lake.

The distinctive doors of Hosmer's tasting room.

Marguerite Thomas

HOSMER
607-869-3393,
    888-HOSWINE;
    fax 607-869-9409.
6999 Rte. 89, Ovid, NY 14521.
Directions: From Ithaca take Rte. 89 north for 22 miles to the winery.
Owners: Cameron and Maren Hosmer.
Open: Apr.–Dec.: Mon.–Sat. 10am–5pm, Sun. 12noon–5pm; closed Jan.–Mar. and Easter, Thanksgiving, and Christmas.

This lakeside farm was purchased by the Chicago-based Hosmer family in the 1930s as a vacation retreat. Cameron Hosmer, who studied fruit sciences (pomology) at Cornell, began his current career as a home winemaker. He made wine for friends and family from grapes his father planted in 1972. In 1985, Cameron and his wife, Maren, opened their winery. They now produce 6,000 cases a year from their 40-acre vineyard, and they also supply grapes to other local wineries.

Hosmer wines include a Riesling with a pretty, floral aroma and a Cayuga that would be a good match for spicy Asian or Mexican dishes. Hosmer's

Price Range of Wines: $6 for Cayuga White to $16 for Pinot Noir.

Special Features: Gift shop, gourmet foods.

Special Event: Asparagus Day in May.

KNAPP VINEYARDS WINERY AND RESTAURANT

607-869-9271, 800-869-9271; fax 607-869-3212.

www.knappwine.com.

E-mail: knappwine@aol.com.

2770 County Rte.128, Romulus, NY 14541.

Directions: From I-90 take exit 41 to Rte. 414, follow Rte. 414 south to Rte. 20/5, go east on 20/5 to Rte. 414 south, go south to County Rte. 128, turn east onto Rte. 128 (Ernsberger Rd.) to the winery.

Owners: Doug and Suzie Knapp.

Open: Apr.–Dec.: Mon.–Sat. 10am–5pm, Sun. 11:30am–5pm; closed Jan.–Mar.

Price Range of Wines: $6.95 for Pasta Red to $23.95 for Late Harvest Vignoles.

Special Features: Restaurant, distillery.

Special Events: Harvest festival, winemaker's dinners.

- Chardonnay
- Sangiovese

young Cabernet Franc has bold tannins that will probably mellow with time.

The tasting room, which is entered through a carved door that displays Hosmer's signature grape-leaf pattern, includes a large gift shop where prospective picnickers can stock up on cheese, chips, and snack food to enjoy with a bottle of wine at the tables outside.

Doug and Suzie Knapp met in Panama while he was working for an electronics firm. They got married and eventually, in 1971, decided to buy a chicken farm in the Finger Lakes region, which they converted to vineyards. They now have 99 acres of grapes.

"Like most growers around here, we were supplying grapes to the Taylor Wine Company," recalls Suzie. "And, like most growers in the region, we were growing native American grapes. These grapes had been the backbone of the American wine industry for 150 years. Besides, most people felt that since we didn't have a Mediterranean climate, we couldn't grow anything else."

By the mid-1970s, everything had changed. The Taylor family was no longer involved in the business. Under the ownership of Coca-Cola, and then Seagrams, the company was no longer responsive to local growers. As Suzie explains, the large corporation started allocating grapes and dropping prices. "Grapes aren't like corn," she says. "You can't just change your crop from year to year according to the whims of the market. By 1976, a lot of people could see the writing on the wall."

Once the New York Farm Winery Act was passed, a lot of growers started their own wineries. Those growers who changed — the ones who ripped out their vineyards of American grapes, replanted with more currently popular varieties, and opened their own winery — have mostly survived. "Of the others, few stayed in business," Suzie says.

Suzie is quick to point out that while the wine industry has reinvented itself in the Finger Lakes region, the wineries are not owned by wealthy investors. Unlike other areas of the country, she says, "We don't have Wall Street types and advertising executives buying up the vineyards. Here, land remains cheap and we're still mostly just farmers." Although this may be true, these "farmers" have become increasingly savvy. Many now produce wines that are fine enough to please the most discriminating palate.

Knapp's excellent wines include a Chardonnay that balances fruit and the flavor from oak barrels nicely. Dutchman's Breeches, a combination of Vidal and Vignoles, has a handsome label and is understandably popular. Knapp is virtually the only Finger Lakes winery (so far) to produce Sangiovese. The grapes come from local grower Jim Hazlitt, and while the wine may not taste like it originated in Tuscany (Sangiovese's home), it is fruity and pleasing. Knapp distills brandy and grappa in a beautiful still with a hand-hammered copper onion-dome roof made in Portugal. It also produces a Ruby Port that visitors snap up.

One other imperative reason to visit Knapp is its fine restaurant, nestled in an enchanting garden setting.

LUCAS VINEYARDS

607-532-4825,
800-682-WINE (NY only);
fax 607-532-8580.
E-mail: lucaswyn@epix.net.
3862 County Rd. 150,
Interlaken, NY 14847.
Directions: From Ithaca
take Rte. 89 north to
County Rd. 150, travel
west to the winery.
Owners: Bill and Ruth
Lucas.
Open: May–Dec.: Mon.–Sat.
10:30am–5:30pm, Sun.
12noon–5:30pm;
Jan.–Apr.: Sat.
10:30am–5:30pm, Sun.
12noon–5:30pm.
Price Range of Wines: $5.50
for Captain's Belle;
$13.99 for Brut and Pinot
Noir.
Special Event: Summer
Anniversary Party.

Lucas Vineyards is the oldest winery on Cayuga Lake, founded by the Lucas family in 1974. They moved to the 68-acre site from New York City and planted grapes that they sold to the Taylor Wine Company. In 1980 the Lucases opened their own winery.

Lucas Vineyards currently has 29 acres planted in vines, from which it has produced 15,000 cases of wine annually. While the wines have generally been very pleasant in the past, the establishment has lately been undergoing personal problems; if and when the dust settles, the wines will have to be reevaluated.

SWEDISH HILL
VINEYARD & WINERY

315-549-8326,
888-549-WINE;
fax 315-549-8477.
www.fingerlakes.net/
swedishhill.

Dick and Cindy Peterson planted their first vines on this site in 1969, while she was still working for a bank and he had a job with the Seneca Falls school system. Their first vintage, produced in 1985, was so successful that the Petersons quit their other jobs to devote themselves full-time

E-mail: swedhill@flare.net.
4565 Rte. 414, Romulus, NY
14541.
Directions: From I-90 take
exit 41 to Rte. 414, follow
Rte. 414 south. Winery is
8 miles south of Seneca
Falls.
Owners: Dick and Cindy
Peterson.
Open: Daily 9am–6pm.
Price Range of Wines: $6.99
for Cayuga to $16.99 for
Vintage Port.
Special Feature: Gift shop.
Special Events: Horse-
drawn wagon tours
May–Oct.

- Riesling
- Svenska White
- Svenska Red
- Late Harvest Vignoles

to the winery. The wines have been winning awards and garnering praise ever since.

Today the Petersons produce 34,000 cases of wine annually in their high-tech winery; they have 35 acres of vines that provide them with about 40 percent of the fruit they need (the rest is purchased locally). Swedish Hill has a large tasting room with three separate tasting bars, a well-stocked gift shop, and a selection of home-winemaking equipment for sale.

One key to the Petersons' success is that they have staked out a niche market that they fill better than anyone else: Swedish Hill produces excellent wines from labrusca and hybrid grapes. Svenska White, made from Catawba, Golden Muscat, and Cayuga White, is grapey, sweet, and flavorful, with little of the aggressive labrusca flavors that often characterize wines made from hybrid grapes. Svenska Red (Concord, Ives, Rougeon, Catawba, and Vincent grapes) is equally appealing. If you're curious about traditional Eastern American wines, you'll find no better examples than Swedish Hill's.

**KING FERRY WINERY/
TRELEAVEN WINES**
315-364-5100, 800-439-5271;
fax 315-364-8078.
www.treleavenwines.com.
E-mail: treleaven@aol.com.
658 Lake Rd., King Ferry,
NY 13081.
Directions: From the north
follow Rte. 90, on the east
side of Cayuga Lake, to
Lake Rd. From the south
take Rte. 90 to 34B. Turn
left onto Lake Rd.
Owners: Peter and Tacie
Saltonstall.
Open: Mon.–Sat.
10am–5pm, Sun.
12noon–5pm.
Price Range of Wines: $8.99
for Semi-dry Riesling to
$29.95 for Vintner's
Reserve Chardonnay.
Special Events: Harvest
Fest, Pheasants Forever,

Located about mid-point on the east side of Cayuga Lake, Treleaven may be out of the way, but the wines are absolutely worth the long, scenic drive. The Saltonstalls, who have been producing wine here for just over a decade, clearly know what they're doing as virtually everything they make is outstanding (total production is about 6,000 cases, from 17 acres of vines). The barrel-fermented Chardonnay is a textbook example of how the delicacy of cool-climate fruit can be enriched with just a touch — not a wallop — of oak. The main Chardonnay, which does not come in contact with oak barrels, has clean, bracing fresh fruit aromas. The Pinot Noir is light but flavorful, the Gewürztraminer aromatic and full-bodied, and the Dry Riesling delicate yet not wimpy. "Saumon" is a somewhat sweet rosé-style wine that's simple without being stupid — Treleaven's answer to blush. Noble Chardonnay is a superb sweet wine made from grapes that were attacked by botrytis cynerea — the so-called "noble rot" that produces

Winemaker's dinners, and other events.

- Chardonnay
- Merlot
- Pinot Noir
- Gewürztraminer
- Riesling
- Noble Chardonnay

the world's greatest dessert wines. Don't get attached to it, however: so far, only one vintage has been made (1996), and there won't be another until the right conditions prevail again.

CANANDAIGUA LAKE

WIDMER'S WINE CELLARS
716-374-6311, 800-836-5253; fax 716-374-2028.
1 Lake Niagara Lane, Naples, NY 14512.
Directions: From I-390 take exit 2 to Rte. 371 north. In North Cohocton, take Rte. 21 north. Watch for winery signs before the town of Naples.
Owners: Canandaigua Wine Company.
Open: June–Oct.: Mon.–Sat. 10am–4pm, Sun. 11:30am–4:30pm; Nov.–May: daily 1pm–4pm.
Price Range of Wines: $4.99 to $29.95 (for 30-year-old blend sherry).
Special Features: Museum, gift and wine shop.
Special Events: Grape Festival, wagon rides.

Perhaps Swiss immigrants are attracted to the Finger Lakes because the landscape, punctuated by green hills sweeping down to idyllic lakes, reminds them of their own country. While we don't know for certain why John Jacob Widmer moved here in 1882, he certainly made a success of it once he settled on this site.

Widmer planned to plant table grapes on his property. But since refrigeration was not sophisticated enough in those days to assure safe passage of such a fragile product to the markets in Manhattan and Philadelphia, he decided to raise wine grapes instead, and to open his own winery. As it turned out, Widmer's shale-based soil proved a boon for vines, allowing their roots to penetrate deep into the earth.

Widmer was innovative. Rather than making only table wine, he established a solera system for making sherry that is still in use today. Based on traditional Spanish techniques, the sherry is placed in seven-year-old Tennessee and Kentucky bourbon barrels. These are stored on the winery's roof, where the wine ages in the sun from four to six years. Visitors to the winery will see about 1,000 barrels, each holding 50 gallons, basking in the sun on the roof of the main building. The winery makes a full range of sherries, from pale dry versions to rich, sweet cream sherries. While this wine will certainly not put the fine sherries of Spain out of business, Canandaigua's sherries, particularly the sweeter ones, can be very pleasant sippers. Widmer also produces an enormous range of sparkling and still wines, many of them based on Niagara, Elvira, and other native grapes that were the backbone of the original wine industry here. Winemaker Bonnie Abrams also is expanding a line of classic premium wines. In addition to her winemaking expertise, Bonnie is a popular songwriter and local TV and radio performer who sings her own creations, such as "Winemaker's Blues."

Widmer produces 250,000 cases a year, and it owns 250 acres of vines that are planted with 24 different grape varieties. It also procures fruit from about 750 additional acres of leased land. The winery, now owned by the huge Canandaigua Company, is well equipped to receive the great number of visitors that flock to its doors. It offers very knowledgeable tour and tasting guides, and has a museum of early winemaking tools. The well-stocked gift and wine shop includes a large selection of kosher wines.

OTHER FINGER LAKES WINERIES

AMERICANA VINEYARDS AND WINERY (607-387-6801; fax 607-387-3852; e-mail: wineinny@aol.com; 4367 East Covert Rd., Interlaken, NY 14847) This is a small, family-operated winery that produces pleasant wines from native American and hybrid grapes.

FRONTENAC POINT VINEYARD (607-387-9619; e-mail: cdj4@cornell.edu; 9501 Rte. 89, Trumansburg, NY 14886) Owners Jim and Carol Doolittle produce Chardonnay, Riesling, Chambourcin, and a Late Harvest Vignoles, plus a handful of other good, dry table wines. The Doolittles have also played an active role in promoting the region's wines. Jim was a major force in getting the Farm Winery Bill of 1976 passed, and the couple continues to educate the public about the benefits of moderate wine consumption. They have 22 acres under cultivation and produce 2,000–4,000 cases annually.

SIX MILE CREEK VINEYARD (607-273-6219 or 607-273-1551; www.spinners.com/sixmileacre; e-mail: smc@lightlink; Slaterville Rd., Rte. 79 East, Ithaca, NY 14850) is the first winery one passes when driving to the Finger Lakes from Binghampton. An attractive introduction to the region, this small, family-run winery is housed in a restored Dutch-reform barn. There's a large deck overlooking the vineyard. A variety of wines, from Chardonnay to Chancellor, is produced here.

PART THREE

The Mountains

The Virginia Highlands

Central Pennsylvania

PART THREE
The Mountains

This statue greets visitors to Château Morrisette, on the Blue Ridge Parkway.

Marguerite Thomas

Except for a few isolated areas, the weather in the mountainous regions of the East is too extreme for grapes to grow. In certain places, however, specific microclimates offer a more hospitable environment. Small viticultural regions in the mountains of Pennsylvania and Virginia, for example, may be at relatively high altitudes, but the right combination of proper soil and degrees of sunlight, coupled with warm days and cool nights, provide conditions in which grapes thrive.

Furthermore, the mountain air tends to be drier than in the muggier Uplands and Benchlands, which discourages fungus and molds from proliferating in the vineyards. Because the growing season in the mountains is long and relatively cool, grapes ripen slowly and develop intense color and flavors that are imparted to the wine.

From the traveler's perspective, these mountains still convey the sense of isolation and wild beauty for which this nation is noted. There are hundreds of lakes, thousands of forested acres, and miles and miles of hiking trails that charm sportsmen and nature lovers from all over the world.

THE VIRGINIA HIGHLANDS

The bell at Rockbridge Vineyards.

Marguerite Thomas

The Blue Ridge, Shenandoah, Allegheny, and Cumberland Mountains frame Virginia's western border. And the 105-mile Blue Ridge Parkway (and its continuation as Skyline Drive) offer some of the finest scenery in America. These two-way roads are devoid of buildings, billboards, villages, restaurants, or motels, allowing travelers to savor uninterrupted natural splendor.

Late spring is a fine time to travel here, when the white dogwoods, the orange- and lemon-colored rhododendron, and the delicate pink wild azalea bloom. The clouds cast shadows that look like pancakes on the foothills and the Shenandoah Valley below. But every season presents its own charms along this ribbon of road. To enhance any visit, it's also possible to segue over to some of the best wineries in Virginia.

As in the rest of Virginia, history plays a strong role in this region. A common thread links the entire Monticello appellation, which includes wineries in both the Uplands and the Mountains. As Tom Corpora of Virginia's Afton Mountain Vinters points out: "At some point, Jefferson traversed it all on horseback."

Another Virginia winemaker, Bob Harper, owner of Naked Mountain Vineyard and Winery in Markham, is a walking encyclopedia of geological, culinary, and historical facts about the area, which he'll share in an inspired moment. Here are some of the things I learned from Bob in a single afternoon: Route 688, where his winery is located, is the same road Robert E. Lee took on his way to Gettysburg. Lee caught influenza along the way and had to spend a few days recuperating in Markham. Sweet Georgia Brown is buried in the local cemetery. Revolutionary War hero Daniel Morgan was painted only in profile because one of his ears was bitten off in a barroom brawl. The town of Pumpkinville, where George Washington lived, changed its name to Paris after Lafayette came to visit in the 1790s. The Shenandoah Valley is one of the largest lamb-producing regions in the U.S. Flint Hill, Virginia, still has the original white post set by George Washington when he surveyed the area.

Tom and Shinko Corpora, owners of Afton Mountain Vineyards.

Marguerite Thomas

AFTON MOUNTAIN VINEYARDS
540-456-8667;
    fax 540-456-8002.
234 Vineyard Lane (Rte.
    631), Afton, VA 22920.
Directions: From I-64 take
    exit 107 and go west on
    Rte. 250 for 6 miles to
    Rte. 151, then go south
    for 3 miles on Rte. 151 to
    Rte. 6; go west on Rte. 6
    for 1.8 miles to Rte. 631,
    go south 1.2 miles to
    winery entrance on left.
Owners Tom and Shinko
    Corpora.
Open: Mar.–Dec.:
    Wed.–Mon. 10am–6pm;
    Jan.–Feb.: Fri.–Mon.
    11am–5pm, or by
    appointment.
Price Range of Wines: $8
    for Festiva Red and
    White; $14 for
    Gewürztraminer; $15 for
    Pinot Noir.

Tom Corpora had a distinguished career as a journalist. He was with UPI for 10 years and with NBC News for 18. During this time he covered six presidential campaigns and four wars on five different continents. Throughout it all, he entertained a vague fantasy about living on a farm.

When the "golden handshake" came from NBC, Tom seized the moment and began searching for his idyllic spot. As parents, Tom and his wife, Shinko, were particularly attracted to Virginia because of its publicly supported upper education system. They knew they didn't want to raise animals or start a new farm from scratch, but otherwise they hadn't any particular notion of what they *did* want to do.

Then, one day in 1988, a real-estate broker drove Tom down a gravel road that cut through a gap in the eastern slope of the Blue Ridge Mountains, where the scenery is, as Tom describes it, "almost sublime in its beauty." There was a six-acre vineyard, verdant in its early summer growth, and a 20-acre lake, large enough to have a moderating effect on the vineyard's microclimate. Tom's fate was

- Chardonnay
- Gewürztraminer
- Chenin Blanc

sealed. "But we don't know anything about grow-ing grapes or making wine," protested Shinko, when Tom broke the news to her. "We can learn," he said.

Almost a decade later, Tom looks back at that moment and points out that the world consists of two kinds of people: those who grew up on a farm and those who didn't. "A corollary of that might be that those who grew up on farms are too smart to want to have anything more to do with them," he sighs. "I was in the second category, and though I knew people in the first, and had been warned by them about the hard work of farm-ing, I still wasn't prepared for the reality."

In addition to the usual labor involved in farming, the Corporas were faced with a vineyard that had been sadly neglected and needed a massive amount of trimming and replanting. Gabriele Rausse, Virginia's preeminent vintner, became their vineyard advisor and, ultimately, their close friend. Gabriele taught Shinko how to make wine. The state enologist and viticulturist also pro-vided invaluable advice.

The Corporas planted more vineyards, raising their total vineyard acreage to 11 acres, and they opened a winery. They now produce 2,000 cases of wine annually, which they hope to steadily increase. Clearly it has been a struggle, emotionally as well as economically. "It's not as lucrative as NBC News," says Tom dryly.

This isn't to say that Tom and Shinko have stopped dreaming. "People say you can't make Gewürztraminer in Virginia. I'm hoping to prove them wrong," says Shinko, and after tasting her recent Gewürz, one can believe she'll do just that. "I tell people who like our dry, Chablis-style Chardonnay to just say no to oak and get the grape back into Chardonnay," Shinko adds. Among the other very good wines at Afton are a delicate Pinot Noir and a Vouvray-style Chenin Blanc.

The tasting room overlooks the scenery that first caught Corpora's eye. And visitors can enjoy a snack and the view at café tables there.

CHÂTEAU MORRISETTE
540-593-2865;
    fax 540-593-2868.
www.chateaumorrisette.
    com.
E-mail: chmorrisette@
    aol.com.
287 Winery Rd. SW, Floyd,
    VA 24091.
Mail: P.O. Box 766,
    Meadows of Dan, VA
    24120.
Directions: From the Blue
    Ridge Pkwy. turn west at

This fine winery grows and grows. Most recently, it has expanded into spectacular new winemaking and tasting room facilities. Built in 1998 from massive beams recycled from the St. Lawrence Seaways, the 2,400-square-foot building houses a tasting room inside a 83-foot tall tower, and a winery that is surely one of the most impressive winemak-ing facilities in the East—or anywhere, for that mat-ter. The excellent restaurant has now expanded to occupy all the space in the original stone building.

The two vineyards (32 acres in all) owned by this property tell a story of mountain grape growing. The

mile post 171.5, onto Black Ridge Rd.(Rte. 726), take an immediate left on Winery Rd. to the winery on the right.

Owners: The Morrisette family.

Open: Mon.–Sat. 10am–5pm, Sun. 11am–5pm.

Price Range of Wines: $7.50 for Sweet Mountain Laurel to $14 for Chardonnay.

Special Feature: Restaurant.

Special Events: Winemakers' Dinners, Black Dog Jazz Concerts,

- Cabernet Franc
- Chardonnay
- Merlot
- Black Dog Wines
- Sweet Mountain Laurel

smaller of the two, visible from the winery, is gradually being replanted with Niagara grapes to replace the original Vidal grapes, which were having difficulty surviving at 3,450 feet above sea level. The larger vineyard, only 10 miles away and at an elevation of 1,800 feet, seems to be a fine place to grow red grapes — Merlot, Cabernet Sauvignon, Pinot Noir, and Chambourcin — as well as Chardonnay and Seyval. All the wines made from these grapes tend to be rich, full-bodied, and satisfying.

Wine director Bob Burgin is a believer in the advantages of blending grapes from different climates, as well as different vineyards. The Chardonnay, for example, is usually made by mixing several wines that have been fermented and aged separately. Grapes from different vineyards go into the blend: austere, high-acid mountain grapes are blended with fatter, flabbier fruit from central Virginia.

Black Dog is an unassuming blend of red grapes that's a good bet for people who haven't developed a taste for heavy, tannic reds, while Black Dog Blanc is the simple white equivalent. Black Dog Blush is, of course, a sweetish pink wine, and Our Dog Blue is a fruity red in a blue bottle. Sweet Mountain Laurel is a very sweet wine made from Niagara.

LANDWIRT VINEYARD
Phone & fax: 540-833-6000.
www.valleyva.com/
   landwirt.html.
E-mail: landwirt@
   shentel.net.
8223 Simmers Valley Rd.,
   Harrisonburg, VA 22802.
Directions: From I-81 take
   exit 257. Go south on Rte.
   11 for 2 miles; turn right
   on Rte. 806 for 2.5 miles.
   Go straight at
   intersection of Rtes 806 &
   619, 0.8 mile to the
   winery on the right.
Owners: Gary and Teresa
   Simmers.
Open: Sat. & Sun.
   1pm–5pm, or by
   appointment.
Price Range of Wines: $9
   for Riesling to $12 for
   Cabernet Sauvignon.

- Cabernet Sauvignon
- Chardonnay
- "Gewchardignon"
- Pinot Noir
- Riesling

Landwirt is one of those surprising wineries that makes a big splash the moment it jumps into the competition.

While Gary and Teresa Simmers have been raising grapes on their farm since 1982, the tasting room opened only in June of 1996. It quickly became a popular destination for Washingtonians who are becoming adept at spotting a promising source of outstanding wines. The tasting room and the winery are housed in a former chicken coop that stood here for many decades. "I've been farming all my life," says Gary, adding that this farm has been in his family for several generations. The chickens are gone now, as are the dairy cows — replaced exclusively by wine. "When I took into account how many gold medals Shenandoah and other wineries were winning from our grapes, I finally decided to pursue the winery end of the business," Gary says.

The vintner goes on to explain that the region is admirably well suited to growing grapes with unusually fruity flavors. "We have lots of variation of climate here in the Shenandoah. The mountains play games with our local weather. But one thing in our favor is that grapes are not so susceptible to spring frosts, and we have less of a problem with humidity here at 1,200–1,300 feet above sea level." Sitting on a little volcanic ridge, the soil, says Gary, is typically rock with shale and limestone mixed in.

How did Gary learn to make such fine wines? By attending seminars, reading, learning from winemaker friends, and "mostly by hard knocks." Gary, who could handily win a John Updike look-alike contest, also gives the state government due credit for its varied support. The wines are a knockout. The Chardonnays tend to have the richness of tropical fruit, while the Riesling has evocative, smoky aromas. "Gewchardignon," Landwirt's blend of Chardonnay, Sauvignon Blanc, and Gewürztraminer, has a hint of sweetness with a fruity backbone. In good years the Cab Sauvignon is intense and full-bodied, the Cab Franc is softer and less tannic. The Pinot Noir is just great — when you can get it (not surprisingly, it sells out quickly).

There are 14 acres of vines, and the winery produces about 2,500 cases of wine a year.

LINDEN VINEYARDS
540-364-1997;
   fax 540-364-3894.

Jim Law's science and agricultural background helped him determine what conditions to look for when he decided to plant a vineyard in

Linden Vineyards.

Marguerite Thomas

www.lindenvineyards.
com.
E-mail: linden@
crosslink.net.
3708 Harrels Corner Rd.,
Linden, VA 22642.
Directions: From
Washington, D.C., take I-
66 to exit 13 in Linden, go
1 mile east on Rte. 55,
then turn right onto Rte.
638 and go 2 miles to the
winery.
Owner: Jim Law.
Open: Apr.–Nov.:
Wed.–Sun. 11am–5pm;
Dec.–Mar.: Sat. & Sun.
11am–5pm.
Price Range of Wines: $12
for Seyval to $16 for
Cabernet Sauvignon.
Special Events: Vintners'
dinners with guest chefs

Virginia. "We knew we wanted a mountain site," Jim said, explaining that the cooler air in the mountains helps delay the ripening of the grapes, which promotes more intense flavors. "When grapes grow in hot and humid climates, they ripen in August and don't have a lot of finesse. In our area, the sunny days and cool nights allow the grapes to ripen over a longer period of time. We feel that this adds elegance and harmony to the wine."

Jim chose a spot at a 1,300-foot elevation in the Blue Ridge Mountains for his vineyard in 1985. "It's ideal for grapes," he says. "They ripen late in October, when the fruit has great intensity." The winery produces 6,000 cases of wine annually from its 16 acres of vines, and it continues to grow. An important new development at Linden is that three staff members, who got bitten by the wine bug, have planted their own vineyards (13 acres in all) and are selling their grapes to the winery. "We've from local fine restaurants, winter soup weekends, barrel tasting in April.

- Chardonnay
- Cabernet Franc
- Late Harvest Vidal
- Cabernet Sauvignon
- Sauvignon Blanc
- Seyval

found such an incredible difference in each vineyard that, as of 1997, we've started making vineyard-designated wines," says Jim, adding, "We felt this was the way to make the best wines we could."

The first Sauvignon Blanc was released in 1998; the first reds are due in '99, the Chardonnays in 2000. Every Linden wine is highly recommendable; the top-of-the-line wines are among the best in the East — they could compete in quality with wines from anywhere in the world. Try the Sauvignon Blanc (the staff favorite), the intensely aromatic Seyval, the harmonious Chardonnays including the powerhouse Reserve Chardonnay, the Cabernet Franc (less tannic than Cab Sauvignon, therefore a flexible food wine), and the best-selling Riesling/Vidal blend. The Cabernet Sauvignon (rounded out with small amounts of Cabernet Franc and Petit Verdot) is rich, intense, and well balanced, a terrific wine indeed. The Late Harvest Vidal is a dessert wine with medium body and sweetness — a wine more for fruit tarts than for chocolate mousse.

Bob Harper and the Naked Mountain truck.

Marguerite Thomas

NAKED MOUNTAIN VINEYARD AND WINERY
540-364-1609;
  fax 540-364-4870.
www.nakedmtn.com.
2747 Leeds Manor Rd.,
  Markham, VA 22643.
Directions: From
  Washington, D.C., take
  I-66 to exit 18 in
  Markham, go 1.5 miles

The name provokes a lot of speculation. "More than a few people get carried away by the name Naked Mountain," admits winery owner Bob Harper, flashing a wicked grin. In fact, the name, which is found in the original 1765 deed to the property, aptly describes the mountain, whose soil composition is mostly schist and decomposed rock.

Because of a thermal inversion, the eastern slope of the Blue Ridge Mountains is relatively sheltered from winds and enjoys milder winter temperatures north on Rte. 688 to the winery.

Owner: Robert and Phoebe Harper.

Open: Mar.–Dec.: Wed.–Sun. including holidays 11am–5pm; Jan.–Feb.: Sat. & Sun. 11am–5pm.

Price Range of Wines: $12 for Cabernet Franc to $17 for barrel-fermented Chardonnay.

Special Feature: light snacks.

Special Events: Chef's dinners, Lasagne Lunch weekends Jan.–Mar., New Orleans Jazz Festival first weekend in Oct., Bluegrass Bar-B-Que in June.

- Chardonnay
- Cabernet Franc
- Cabernet Sauvignon
- Riesling

and cooler summers than many other areas in the state. "It is the best place in Virginia for grapes," says Bob. Of course, there are certain problems, such as the Clipper, a wind-borne cold front that sometimes whips through here. Bob seems unfazed when such topics are mentioned. "This is agriculture," he shrugs. "There are no freebies."

Naked Mountain Winery produces 6,500 cases of vinifera wine annually from its 20-acre vineyard plus some additional grapes from local growers. Altogether the winery has three white and two red wines, all of them clean, pleasing, and well made.

Bob is a former lubricants engineer with Texaco. "I'm just working with another kind of lubricant now," he jokes. The winery is less than an hour from Washington, D.C., and Bob is proud to point out that Naked Mountain wine has been served in the Clinton White House.

NORTH MOUNTAIN
540-436-9463.
www.valleylife.net/north
   mountain.
E-mail: vineyard@rma.edu.
4374 Swartz Rd.,
   Maurertown, VA 22644.
Directions: From
   Washington, D.C., take I-
   66 west to I-81, 10 miles
   to exit 291 (Tom's Brook).
   Go west 1 mile on Rte
   651 to Mt. Olive; turn left
   on Rte 623 for 2 miles,
   then left on Rte. 655, 5
   miles to winery.
Owners: Brad Foster, Krista
   Jackson-Foster, John
   Jackson.
Open: Daily 10am–5pm.
Price Range of Wines: $9
   for Vidal to $10 for
   Chambourcin.

I n October 1998, this winery acquired new owners, who appear to be revamping the entire operation, from building a new tasting room to expanding the vineyard. The site is beautiful, and the
small, new winery is tucked in among the vines.

Courtesy Oakencroft Vineyard & Winery

The picturesque buildings at Oakencroft, near Charlottesville, Virginia.

**OAKENCROFT
 VINEYARD & WINERY**
804-296-4188 (ext. 25
 on weekends);
 fax 804-293-6631.
www.oakencroft.com.
E-mail: mail@oakencroft.
 com.
1486 Oakencroft Lane,
 Charlottesville, VA
 22901.
Directions: From Rte. 29
 go 3.5 miles west on
 Barracks Rd. (Rte. 654)
 to Garth Rd. Winery
 entrance is on the left.
Owner: Felicia Warburg
 Rogan.
Open: Apr.–Dec.: daily
 11am–5pm; Jan.–Feb.: by
 appointment; Mar.:
 weekends only
 11am–5pm.
Price Range of Wines: $9.50
 for Countryside White;
 $16.50 for Chardonnay
 Reserve and Merlot.
Special Events: Rites of
 Spring Open House,
 Spring Fiesta, Holiday
 Open House, Christmas
 Open House and
 Candlelight Tour.

• Chardonnay
• Riesling
• Merlot

**ROCKBRIDGE
 VINEYARD**
540-377-6204,
 888-511-WINE;
 fax 540-377-6204.
E-mail: rockwine@cfw.com.
30 Hill View Lane,
 Raphine, VA 24472.
Directions: From I-81/I-64
 take exit 205 and go west
 on Rte. 606 for 1 mile to
 winery.
Owners: Shepherd and Jane
 Rause.

In the past couple of years, Oakencroft has earned gold medals and rave reviews. Felicia Warburg Rogan and her late husband, John, were owners of Charlottesville's famous Boar's Head Inn when they first became interested in making their own wine. They planted an experimental vineyard and made Seyval Blanc, Chardonnay, and Merlot with amateur equipment in a converted tool shed.

In 1982, Felicia Warburg Rogan got serious. She hired a vineyard manager, planted a 17-acre vineyard, and began producing a variety of wines from hybrid and vinifera grapes. One of her smartest recent moves was to engage the services of Shepherd Rouse (owner of Rockbridge Vineyard). The wines, reflecting his skillful touch, just keep getting better and better. Current production is 6,500 cases annually.

Oakencroft wines have traveled far in their relatively brief history. In 1988 they went to Moscow with President Reagan, who presented Mikhail Gorbachev with a gift of Oakencroft Seyval Blanc. Oakencroft wine has also been poured at diplomatic events in Taipei, in Hawaii, and at the American Embassy in Paris.

At 2,000 feet above sea level, Rockbridge grapes tend to ripen later than the fruit in other regions. Chardonnay, for example, is about two weeks behind most Virginia Chardonnay. The extra ripening time gives ample opportunity to develop full, rich flavors, which is one of the reasons that Shepherd and Jane Rause share a quiet optimism about the future of their winery.

Shep, who previously worked at wineries in Germany and in California's Napa Valley (where he specialized in sparkling wines), is one of the state's leading vintners. His name is inevitably at

Open: May–Oct.:
  Wed.–Sun. 12noon–5pm;
  Apr. & Nov.–mid-Dec.:
  Sat. & Sun. 12noon–5pm;
  closed mid-Dec.–Mar.
Price Range of Wines: $8
  for Vidal Blanc to $18 for
  Merlot.
Special Events: Summer
  Breeze Fête, End of
  Summer Solace, Fall
  Harvest Fest, Holiday
  Open House.

* Chardonnay
* Cabernet Sauvignon
* Merlot
* Tuscarora Red and White
* Vidal Blanc
* V'd'Or (Vidal dessert
  wine)

SHENANDOAH VINEYARDS

540-984-8699;
  fax 540-984-9463.
www.shentel.net/shenvine.
E-mail: shenvine@
  shentel.net.
3659 South Ox Rd.,
  Edinburg, VA 22824.
Directions: From I-81 take
  exit 279, go west at the
  bottom of ramp onto
  Stony Creek Rd. Take the
  first right onto South Ox
  Rd., go 1.5 miles to
  winery on left.
Owner: Emma Randel.
Open: Mar.–Nov.: daily
  10am–6pm; Dec.–Feb.:
  daily 10am–5pm.
Price Range of Wines: $7.95
  for Shenandoah Blanc to
  $14.95 for Merlot.
Special Events: Valentine's
  Day Dinner, April Bread
  and Wine Festival, July
  Pig Roast, Harvest
  Festival (first weekend

the top of the list whenever Virginia winemakers are discussed.

Visitors to the Rauses' big, restored dairy barn and 13-acre vineyard can discover Rockbridge's classy, award-winning wines for themselves. There's an intensely aromatic Moselle-style Riesling, for example, and a flavorful and harmonious Chardonnay. Tuscarora White, a Riesling/Vidal blend with a touch of sweetness, is named after the Tuscarora White sandstone deposits that are prevalent in the region. Tuscarora was also the name of the Iroquois tribe that migrated south from New York to hunt in the Blue Ridge Mountains. The Meritage, Merlot, and Cabernet are delicious, full-bodied reds. Don't overlook Rockbridge's popular St. Mary's Blanc, a dry, spicy wine made from Vidal that has been fermented in French oak. It's named after the nearby St. Mary's Wilderness Area, which is a beautiful place to go hiking. Rockbridge currently produces about 6,500 cases of wine annually.

Nestled at the base of the Blue Ridge Mountains of the Shenandoah Valley, this winery opened its doors about a quarter of a century ago. It was the first commercial winery in the Shenandoah Valley, and one of the first in Virginia. Today, Shenandoah Vineyards makes about 8,000 cases of vinifera and hybrid wines, mostly from grapes raised in the winery's own 40-acre vineyard. Shenandoah Blanc, a medium-dry white blend based on Vidal and Riesling, is a mouth-filling wine, and Blushing Belle, named after the owner's mother, is a new, already popular, dark pink wine. In our era of Merlot mania, this variety sells out quickly, and Shenandoah's Chambourcin also has legions of devoted followers "Oooh, it's so delicious," sighed an enraptured tourist in the tasting room. "Your boss really clipped me — she sold me one of those devices for resealing the corks to keep leftover wine," grumbled another visitor. "Was there a problem with it?" inquired the anxious young woman behind the counter. "Yes. The problem is that there's never any wine we buy here left over!"

after Labor Day),
Christmas Open House.

- Chambourcin
- Chardonnay
- Riesling
- Shenandoah Blanc
- Merlot

WHITE HALL VINEYARDS

804-823-8615;
  fax 804-823-4366.
www.whitehallvineyards.
  com.
5184 Sugar Ridge Rd.,
  White Hall, VA 22987.
Directions: From Rte. 29 in
  Charlottesville: Go west
  on Barracks Rd. to White
  Hall. From I-64: Take
  Crozet exit, then Rte. 250
  east, and left on Rte. 240;
  take Rte. 810 to White
  Hall. In White Hall: Take
  Rte. 810 north (Brown's
  Gap Turnpike); turn left
  on Break Heart Rd. (Rte.
  674), and continue to
  Sugar Ridge Rd. Winery
  is 1.5 miles on right.
Open: Wed.–Sun.:
  11am–5pm; closed Dec.
  15–Mar. 1.
Owners: Antony and Edith
  Champ.
Price Range of Wines: $8.99
  for Sugar Ridge White
  (off-dry Vidal Blanc) to
  $18.99 for Reserve
  Chardonnay.
Special Events: Art Festival
  in the Vineyards
  (October), Feast Day of
  St. Vincent Ferrer, patron
  saint of winemakers.

- Chardonnay
- Cabernet Franc
- Cabernet Sauvignon
- Merlot
- Gewürztraminer

Shenandoah's tasting room and gift shop are housed in a converted red barn surrounded by vineyards, with great views out over the Blue Ridge Mountains.

Considering that the vineyard was planted in 1991 and the winery just opened in 1996, White Hall is already producing some astonishingly good wines. When Tony Champ took early retirement from the corporate world, he and his wife, Edie, spent a year looking for an appropriate place where they could fulfill their longtime dream of growing grapes and producing wine. They finally settled on a site at an 800-foot elevation at the foot of the Blue Ridge Mountains, where they now have 20 acres planted exclusively in vinifera grapes. "We get a breeze blowing almost constantly through a gap in the mountains, so we've had nice clean fruit and little problem with frost or humidity," says Edie. Wines produced by White Hall — 4,000 cases annually — include Chardonnay, Cabernet Sauvignon, Merlot, and Cabernet Franc. The winery is beautifully situated, with spectacular views of the Blue Ridge Mountains.

Mike Riddick of Wintergreen Vineyards.

Marguerite Thomas

**WINTERGREEN
VINEYARDS
& WINERY**
804-361-2519; fax 804-361-
  1510.
Rte. 664, P.O. Box 702,
  Nellysford, VA 22956.
Directions: From
  Charlottesville: Go south
  on Rte. 151 for 14 miles to
  Rte. 664; turn west and
  go 0.5 mile to the winery.
  From the Blue Ridge
  Parkway: Exit onto Rte.
  664 at mile-post 13. The
  winery is 5 miles on the
  left.
Owners: Mike and Kathy
  Riddick.
Open: Apr.–Dec.: Daily
  10am–6pm; Jan.–Mar.
  10am–5pm.
Price Range of Wines: $7.99
  for Blush to $14.97 for
  Black Rock Chardonnay
  or Merlot.
Special Events: Open house
  Fri. & Sat. after
  Thanksgiving.

• Chardonnay

Mike and Kathy Riddick bought a 400-acre farm in the Blue Ridge Mountains in 1988. "Before long," says Mike, "we were tired of watching cows eat grass." In 1989 they planted vines, knowing that by 1992, when it was time for the first harvest, they would have to decide whether to hire a winemaker or learn winemaking themselves.

The Riddicks spent the intervening years reading everything they could about wine. They traveled to wineries in California, the Finger Lakes, and Long Island. "Even then, of course, we didn't know what we were doing," acknowledges Mike cheerfully.

Mike is an upbeat kind of guy who clearly enjoys life. "It's fun making wine," he says. "It's especially fun now that we're getting some recognition, and it's fun hearing the cash register ring." Every year the cash register rings twice as often as it did the year before.

Mike makes only the kind of wine he likes to drink. "I like a big, buttery California-style Chardonnay," he says, "so that's what I strive for here." He likes a semi-dry (slightly sweet) Riesling. "I can't think of a wine I'd rather have with Maryland crab cake."

Mike gives full credit for the success of the wines to his vineyard. Planted in an old apple orchard with rocky, clay loam, it is, he says, a great place to grow vines. "The old-timers recognized that it was a frost-free microclimate, without really understanding the implications. No matter how we make the wine, we constantly win awards." Wintergreen produces over 5,500 cases a year.

The winery is next to Wintergreen Resort, where summer hiking and golf and winter skiing attract tourists year-round.

OTHER VIRGINIA HIGHLANDS VINEYARDS

VALHALLA VINEYARDS (540-774-2610, fax 540-772-7858; e-mail: valhallava@aol.com; 5371 Silver Fox Rd., Roanoke, VA 24014) This is a brand-new winery owned by Jim and Debra Vascik. I'm looking forward to seeing how it progresses.

Marguerite Thomas

BROOKMERE FARM VINEYARDS
717-935-5380;
   fax 717-935-5349.
www.villagehost.com/
   brookmere.
Rte. 655, Belleville, PA
   17004.
Directions: From Rte. 322
   take Rte 655 southwest
   for 5 miles to winery.
Owners: Don and Susan
   Chapman
Open: Mon.–Sat.
   10am–5pm,
   Sun.1pm–4pm, winter
   hours subject to change.
Price Range of Wines: $5.50
   for Autumn Gold to $12
   for Cabernet Sauvignon.

• "Tears of the Goose"

Brookmere is located in the Kishaquillas Valley, more commonly known as "Big Valley." The valley is only three miles wide by 35 miles long, but it's framed by seven mountains. It is quietly lovely, fertile, and verdant, with farmhouses standing guard over fields and an occasional Amish family clip-clopping along the road in a horse and buggy.

Don Chapman is clearly at home here in Big Valley. He and his wife, Susan, are relative newcomers, having purchased this farm 25 years ago. The farm itself is part of a 700-acre land grant dating back to William Penn. Before they moved here, the Chapmans lived in Connecticut, where Don, who has a background in engineering, owned a company that manufactured various metal objects, ranging from hatchets to fans.

A home-winemaker whose hobby got out of control, Don took courses in enology at Cornell, U.C./Davis, and Pennsylvania State College while easing into the business professionally with, as he puts it, "more guts than brains." He describes the art of making wine in simple terms: "You're just solving chemistry problems, shooting for a balance between the acidity and the sugar content." The local land, he adds, is full of limestone caves and thus is ideal for grapes, since it is rich in potassium and calcium.

Brookmere produces 3,500 cases of wine from grapes grown on its own five-acre vineyard, plus additional grapes purchased from other Pennsylvania growers. About 2,500 people visit the winery each season. The Chapmans' goal has been to produce a wide range of wines, from dry to semi-sweet to sweet (about 18 selections in all), so that people can try different styles in order to find out what they like.

What visitors mostly like now is sweet, so that's what Brookmere's wines tend to be. Happily, the wines are crafted well enough to appeal to experienced wine drinkers as well as to those less experienced. Autumn Gold is a fairly sweet white, but Chardonnay is drier. Valley Mist is a pleasant blend of Seyval, Vidal, and Chardonel. Brookmere Riesling usually exhibits a good balance between sweetness and acidity. Tears of the Goose, a blush wine that is more interesting than many blushes offered by well-known producers, is made in honor of Goose Day, a favorite local holiday related to the British Michaelmas feast. As this September holiday is supposed to honor debtors, people who are invited out to dinner traditionally bring money and a goose to the host.

Bring your own picnic fare (a goose might be messy), buy a bottle of wine after tasting the selections, and enjoy an afternoon of picnicking in Brookmere's vineyard. Save some time for visiting the gift shop, which has unusually appealing selections made by local artists and craftspeople.

OAK SPRINGS WINERY
814-946-3799;
   fax 814-943-4245.
Old Rte. 220, Altoona, PA
   16001.
Directions: From Altoona
   take I-99 north for 3 miles
   to the Pine Croft exit.
   Turn right at the light
   and continue to winery,
   0.5 mile on right.
Owners: John and Sylvia
   Schraff.
Open: Daily 11am–6pm.
Price Range of Wines: $6.50
   for Steuben to $12.50 for
   Chardonnay.

This family-operated winery, owned by John and Sylvia Schraff, makes about 8,500 cases of wine annually from grapes grown in its own four-acre vineyard, plus those purchased from other Pennsylvania growers. The vineyard, at a 1,200-foot elevation, is planted on a hillside that maximizes sunlight and takes advantage of the morning breeze.

"This is a good growing area," says winemaker Scott Schraff, John's son. "Yes, the weather is sometimes extreme — we got over 100 inches of snow during two recent consecutive winters. But even then we only lost a couple of vines, and that was from the wind."

The advantages of the area include thousands of reservoirs, which means that there has never been a drought. There is also less humidity here than in many other Eastern regions, thanks to the altitude and the breezes. In fact the prevailing winds are so reliable that the annual world hang-gliding championships are held here. Folks theorize that it would be possible to take a glider from here to Kentucky and back on the same current.

"Actually, conditions may be good enough here that we could grow vinifera," says Scott, "but Chambourcin is probably the best red-wine grape for the region. You can get your Bordeaux-style wines from California, but Chambourcin is the recognizable Pennsylvania wine."

Scott was a successful young photo-journalist in New York when he decided to become a vintner in the Pennsylvania mountains. He did so partly out of a desire to move his young family from the city to a congenial rural area, and partly because his stepmother, Sylvia Schraff, had started the winery. It captured his interest. "We learned to make wine by doing it," he says. "My stepmother and I work together on it."

Scott was also drawn to this area because his grandfather had come to Altoona to help build the railroad. "In those days immigrants put down roots," said Scott, describing how the German, Italian, and Polish men who built the railroad settled here when the job was finished.

There are no picnic grounds at the winery, but the surrounding region is full of sylvan spots for an al fresco meal. What the winery lacks in quaintness it makes up for in convenience, as it is located on a major road.

OREGON HILL WINERY
717-353-2711.
840 Oregon Hill Rd.,
Morris, PA 16938.
Directions: From Wellsboro follow Rte. 287 south for 17 miles. When you reach the log-cabin restaurant "Inn 287," turn right onto the paved road. Go 1 mile to winery.
Owner: Eric Swendrowski.
Open: Daily 10am–5:30pm.
Price Range of Wines: $5.95 for Mountain White and Mountain Red to $14.95 for Cabernet Sauvignon.

Eric Swendrowski was a child prodigy in the world of wine. At the age of 12, he made his first wine. (His Belgian-born father had always made wine at the family farm in Pennsylvania while Eric was growing up.) At the age of 18, he formed a corporation, and at 19, he opened his winery.

Now in his early 30s, Eric purchases his grapes from local farmers. Oregon Hill's own vinifera vineyard was phased out after six years of struggling to maintain it in this inhospitable spot. "We get June frosts up here," said Eric. "We're basically at the top of a crater, with poor soil and poor drainage. But, as one of our neighbors, who's a farmer, said, 'Just because I don't have my own chickens doesn't mean I can't make an excellent omelette.'"

Eric produces about 2,000 cases of wine a year in 17 different varieties, and all are for sale at the winery. They range from a dry, oak-aged Cabernet to Niagara. Mountain White and Mountain Red, both Niagara-based wines, are popular.

Located near the Pennsylvania Grand Canyon, in one of the state's remotest areas, Oregon Hill attracts hikers, hunters, and nature lovers. There are no picnic facilities at the winery, but it is surrounded by hundreds of acres of idyllic picnic sites.

OTHER CENTRAL PENNSYLVANIA WINERIES

Travelers to the Pittsburgh region can swing by **LAPIC WINERY** (724-846-2031; 902 Tulip Dr., New Brighton, PA 15066), where a variety of dry to semi-sweet wines has been produced for the past two decades. When the steel mills in this area shut down years ago, young people left in droves to seek work elsewhere. Today, when they return to visit families in the region, they are apt to stock up on Lapic Wine to carry back to their new homes in Texas, Arizona, or even Australia.

Appendixes

How Wine Is Made

When Is a Wine Ready to Drink?

Tasting Wine in a Winery

Where to Buy Eastern Wines

Touring the Eastern States Wineries

Wineries Listed by State

Top Twenty Wines of the East: Selected Favorites

Bibliography

HOW WINE IS MADE

The best way for consumers to learn about winemaking is to visit a few wineries. A first-hand glimpse at the various winemaking steps — from vineyard practices through the bottling operation — leads to a better understanding of the process. While the precise methods of making wine may vary from winery to winery, the fundamental techniques are the same everywhere.

Although the equipment used in winemaking is now high tech, and winemakers have become better at controlling the forces of nature, the basics of winemaking have not changed significantly since the dawn of civilization. When it was first discovered that fermented fruit juice tasted good and could have a pleasant effect on anyone who drank enough of it, wine became a magic potion; it still is today. The various steps, then and now, for converting grapes into the alcoholic beverage we call wine can be easily understood.

Harvesting the grapes: Grapes are picked either by hand or by machine. Ideally, the fruit has reached a maximum degree of ripeness by the time it is harvested. Vintners can tell how ripe the grapes are and what the sugar content is through a refractometer, which measures fruit on the vine in "degrees Brix." Underripe fruit yields thin-flavored, overly acidic juice; overripe fruit lacks the touch of acidity that gives a wine backbone, and it may even have acquired off-flavors because of mold or rotting.

Crushing: The harvested fruit is transferred to the winery, where weight is applied via some device — originally human feet, today most likely mechanical crushers. Crushing splits the grape skins, thereby releasing the juice.

Pressing: In the case of white wines a press is used to gently squeeze the juice away from the skins and seeds before beginning fermentation. Red wines are generally fermented for a time along with their skins, which lends both flavor and color to the wine. Most grapes, even those with red skins, are white inside.

Fermenting: After pressing, the juice, which is called "must" at this point, is transferred for fermentation to large, open, wood vats, concrete vats or, more commonly today, large cylindrical stainless steel tanks. Certain premium wines, both red and white, may be fermented in small oak barrels. Barrel fermentation is trickier than fermenting in stainless steel tanks and it requires more attention from the winemaker, but complex and pleasing flavors picked up from the wood can be transmitted to the wine.

Yeasts (either manmade or natural yeasts clinging to the fruit) feed on the sugars in grape juice. As the sugar is consumed, it is converted to alcohol and carbon dioxide. One of the most significant advances in modern winemaking is the vintner's ability to control the temperature of fermenting must. For white wines, particularly, going through a longer, cooler fermentation has resulted in fruitier, fresher wines.

The skins are left in the tank with fermenting red wine until the desired color has been extracted from them, then the must is "racked," or transferred away from the skins into another tank.

Good rosé wine, incidentally, is usually made by leaving the skins in the fermentation tank just long enough to create a rosy color. Some rosés are a mixture of red and white wine, though the end result is usually less interesting and appealing.

Wine sometimes undergoes a second fermentation, called "malolactic fermentation." This procedure converts harsh and astringent malic acid (the kind found in apples) into supple, softer lactic acid (the kind found in milk). Wines that have gone through "malo" generally have a creamier texture.

After fermentation: Fermentation stops when all of the sugar molecules have been converted to alcohol. The resulting alcoholic content of the wine varies from an average of 7 to 9 percent (especially when grapes are grown in very cool regions such as Germany) to 10 to 14 percent (most of the table wines we drink fall in this latter range). When all the sugar in the wine has been used up, we say it is a "dry" wine as opposed to "sweet."

In actuality, it is almost impossible for all of the different types of sugar in grape juice to be converted to alcohol. The few remaining sugar cells are called "residual sugar," or RS. The amount of RS in wine can vary from one gram per liter to 2.5 grams or more, but most wine that contains less than two grams of residual sugar will be perceived as dry. Obviously, the higher the amount of residual sugar, the sweeter the wine will taste.

Aging: Wine that has just finished fermenting may look cloudy and smell gassy or yeasty. Red wine usually leaves a rough, abrasive feel in the mouth from the tannins that have been extracted from the skins and seeds. All wine needs a period of "aging" to allow these unpleasant side-effects of fermentation to dissipate or at least to have their rough edges smoothed over.

White wine is frequently aged for a few months in stainless steel tanks before it is bottled. The resulting wine will, ideally, taste as crisp and bright as a fresh apple or pear. Some premium white wines, especially those made from Chardonnay and, increasingly, Seyval grapes, are matured in small oak barrels. The oak can add complex and appealing nuances, often likened to the flavor of vanilla. When aged in oak, wine is usually left "*sur lie*." This means it is left on the lees, the sediments left behind by the yeasts. Aging on the lees also adds richness and depth of taste to the wine.

Red wine may be aged from a few weeks to three years or more before bottling. Longer maturing usually takes place in oak barrels, also called "*barriques*." The *barriques* favored by the majority of winemakers today hold about 225 liters, or 60 gallons. This follows the example set in Burgundy and Bordeaux.

Aging in oak helps to soften and round out the harsh tannins in red wine. The oak also imparts certain desirable flavors to wine that remind people of vanilla, various spices, or toasted bread. Since contact with oak barrels also improves a wine's ability to age, most of the fine wines that may be kept in a cellar for several years to mellow and mature have usually spent some time in oak barrels.

Some winemakers like to use new oak barrels, which impart a stronger "oaky" flavor. After three or four years, they may sell their barrels to other vintners, who prefer the subtler flavors imparted by older, seasoned oak.

Classic *barriques* are usually made from French oak, but many American winemakers are turning to less expensive American oak. There are various arguments on each side of the issue, ranging from "American oak is better for American wine" to "American oak is too tannic" or "too sappy." American oak, incidentally, is widely used in the viticultural regions of South America, Australia, and Spain, where its more aggressive flavor is counteracted by the potent wines from these warm countries. One of the principal virtues of American oak is that it is much less expensive than French barrels, costing half as much on average. In the past few years, the quality of the best American barrels has improved thanks to several factors such as air versus kiln drying.

An alternative to expensive oak barrels is the use of oak chips — little nuggets of wood that are usually added to wine during fermentation to impart some of the desirable characteristics provided by oak barrels. While oak chips are obviously a lot less expensive than barrels, they will never give wine the same subtlety and complexity.

Clarifying the wine: Wine is left with a certain amount of sediment after maturing, and various methods have been employed over the ages to remove it. This is known as "clarifying" or "fining" the wine. One of the oldest techniques, and one still commonly used, is the application of beaten egg whites to attract particles suspended in the wine. Other methods for fining wine include the addition of gelatin or various kinds of clay, such as bentonite.

Filtering: Before bottling, most wines are passed through a filter to remove any remaining particles. But many winemakers, and consumers as well, object to rigorous clarification and filtration of wine, claiming that these procedures rob wine of some of its character and complexity. The American public, particularly, has been accused of demanding a squeaky-clean product — a beautifully transparent wine, but one perhaps lacking some of its personality. The trend today, at least in certain wineries, is away from obsessive fining and filtration.

Adding sulfites: Preservatives have been used in winemaking since antiquity. Sulfite, which includes various compounds of sulfur, notably sulfur dioxide (SO_2), is the chemical used for this purpose. It is a sterilizing agent, usually added during bottling, to protect wine against harmful bacteria and spoilage. Although regulations permit adding up to 220 parts per million of sulfite to wine, most wineries today bottle with only 40 to 60 parts per million. It is virtually impossible to make drinkable wine on a commercial scale without adding sulfites. For that matter, since SO_2 is one of the natural by-products of fermenting grapes, wine, like bread dough, contains certain sulfites inherently.

Aging in the bottle: Unless it has been pasteurized, wine continues to evolve even after it has been bottled, as tannins, pigments, alcohols, and certain microscopic elements act, react, combine, and interact with the wine.

WHEN IS A WINE READY TO DRINK?

Numerous factors determine when a wine is ready to drink: the type of wine, the year the grapes were grown, the vintner's skills, and even the storage conditions. Most white wines and rosés are ready to drink as soon as they are purchased. A year or two after they have been released they may become oxidized, acquiring a brownish tint and a tired flavor resembling unpleasant sherry. A few of the most well-made, oak-aged white wines may gain richness and intensity of flavor over a period of a few years. Some of the greatest whites are still good after ten years or more, but these are exceptions.

Red wines vary even more in their ability to improve with age. Most Eastern American reds are best consumed right away or within a couple of years of their release, for they are unlikely to improve significantly, if at all, over the years. A few wines, like certain people, get better as they get older, improving in complexity and depth of character after 10 or even 20 years.

In the Eastern states more than in temperate California, the climate of any given year will affect the outcome of the wine to a greater or lesser degree. Frost-kill during bud development can significantly decrease grape production, while cool, rainy days around harvest time can limit the fruit's sugar production. Long stretches of warm summer days and cool evenings promote grapes with a good sugar/acid ratio, while too much rain at the wrong time can lead to flabby flavors.

In the Northeastern viticultural regions particularly, summers are sometimes too cool and short for many grape varieties to ripen properly. Pinot Noir, for example, may perform beautifully in good years, but fail to ripen when conditions are unfavorable. This is where winemaking skills are important. Vintners must decide whether to produce the wine, perhaps under a second, less expensive label; to sell the crop to another, less demanding, winery; or simply to write it off as a loss. "Vintage conditions put the house to the test," observes Chaddsford Winery's Eric Miller. "In trying times, a house should never relinquish responsibility to excellence."

TASTING WINE IN A WINERY

Most wineries have a tasting room, where visitors are invited to sample the wines. There is usually no fee for tasting, although a few wineries have begun to charge a modest amount, usually a couple of dollars, for this age-old custom. This is usually done for two reasons: to cut the winery's losses and to discourage visitors from drinking too much before getting back in their cars. Even with nominal winery fees, tasting enables consumers to try the wines of a given region without making a heavy capital investment.

While every vintner entertains the fond hope that tasters will become buyers, there is little pressure to buy in the tasting room. After all, it is in a winery owner's best interests to acquaint as many people as possible with the product he is selling. In actuality, most visitors do end up buying at least a bottle or two if they like what they've sampled.

It makes good business sense for a winery to introduce people, especially those who are unfamiliar with wine, to the pleasures of drinking it. Sampling a variety of selections at different wineries is one way for consumers to learn more about wine, while at the same time the vintner discovers the kinds of wine they like best.

Tasting at a winery used to involve standing around a chilly wine cellar that was undecorated except for the barrels of wine, a dim light bulb, and the winemaker himself, who would dribble wine into glasses that might or might not have been washed. Many wineries in France and Italy are still like this, but in America, owners sometimes invest in their tasting rooms as soon as they plant their vines.

American tasting rooms range from a simple counter in a corner of the winery to vast rooms where the customer can indulge in gift-shopping as well as tasting. In addition to wine, there may be corkscrews and other wine-related products, posters, food, glassware, or books for sale.

There will probably be a bar in the tasting room, and behind the bar, a person who knows something about the wines being poured. The best thing that can happen is that the winemaker himself or herself will be on duty pouring. In some of the bigger wineries there may be a young "intern" who can rattle off a series of memorized facts, but who won't necessarily be able to help much with detailed questions. But never mind — you're here to taste the wine. Here's how to do it.

Selecting the wines to taste: Tasting wine and drinking wine are two different activities — the former a somewhat unnatural imitation of the latter. One thing that differentiates the two is that in most wine-drinking situations, such as a dinner party, one generally consumes only a few different wines. In an average tasting room, the selection may range from 6 to 12, or even more.

For those interested in sampling an entire range of wines, the general rule of thumb is to start dry and finish sweet. In other words, begin with the simplest, driest white wine, moving on to more complex whites that have, perhaps, been aged in oak. Then it's on to light and medium-bodied reds, finishing with the fullest, most complex red wines. If the winery makes dessert wines, try these at the very end of the tasting.

Another difference between tasting and drinking is that wine is meant to go with food. In a tasting room, there is rarely any food except perhaps a dish of bread chunks or crackers. These are not really meant as hors d'oeuvres — they're for cleansing the palate between wines.

Looking at the wine: Several character traits can be revealed by studying the wine in the glass for a moment. For example, one of the first things people may notice is a film of clear liquid on the glass just above the wine, forming droplets that trickle down the sides of the glass back into the wine. This occurrence, known as "tears," or "legs," is not related to viscosity or to glycerol, as is commonly assumed; it is a complicated phenomenon having to do with tensions between liquid and glass, and with the evaporation of alcohol from water. One thing it tells us is that the wine has a fairly high level of alcohol — at least 12 percent.

To see the wine's color precisely, it helps to look at it against a white or light-colored surface. Tipping the glass at a slight angle reveals a concentration of color around the edge. Certain grape varieties produce lighter- or darker-colored wines.

Color also indicates something about a wine's age. Young white wines, for example, are usually pale yellow, often deepening in color as they age. Full-bodied whites, especially those that have been aged in oak, tend to take on a rich, golden color. A brownish tinge is a warning sign. Just as oxidation turns a cut apple brown, it will also cause white wine to discolor, indicating it is too old.

Unlike white wines, reds *lose* color intensity as they age. A young red wine is usually drenched in deep purplish colors, evolving into translucent ruby or garnet hues over time. With further aging, the density of color fades; older wines are often a clear brick-red. They may have brownish tones around the edges, which isn't necessarily a sign of trouble, but may indicate instead that the wine has matured into a fine, mellow vintage ready to be savored.

Smelling the wine: The way experienced wine tasters swirl their glass and sniff, swirl again and sniff, sniff and swirl, may seem like obsessive concentration on this aspect of the wine, but in fact aroma can reveal far more than taste alone. Swirling air through the wine by rotating the glass in gentle circles fans the perfumes up toward the top of the glass (to prevent wine from sloshing over the side, glasses should never be more than half filled). After swirling the wine, some tasters plunge their entire nose over the rim of the glass to inhale the released scents; others dip one nostril at a time over the glass or pass the glass back and forth under their nose.

Most of what we call "taste" is really smell, which is why food tastes so bland when we have a cold. Taste buds can actually perceive only four different sensations: sweet, bitter, salty, and sour, while the nose is capable of detecting at least 10,000 different aromas. One of the body's most important recipients of pleasurable sensations, the nose can tell us whether the wine is young or old: young wines tend to have a simple fruity smell, while older wines can develop complex aromas.

Experienced wine drinkers recognize and describe these nuances in terms of similar odors. White wines, for example, may exude aromas that resemble pineapple, mango, melon, and other tropical fruits, or even butterscotch and caramel. The typical odor of Sauvignon Blanc is said to be "herbaceous" or "grassy." Some white wines, particularly Riesling, may smell like flowers, and a fine Riesling sometimes has a distinctive, oily odor described as "petrol." When a wine gives off only a very faint aroma, or none at all, it is said to be "closed," or going through a "dumb" phase. If it is a good wine, it may develop an aroma after a few moments, or further bottle aging may be required before that particular wine develops a bouquet.

The aroma of red wine may resemble any number of red fruits, including cherries and various berries. It may smell like roses, or violets, or like certain trees, such as cedar or eucalyptus. An earthy odor resembling mushrooms or wet leaves might also be detected. A whiff of black pepper can often be picked up, or of licorice, mint, smoke, or tobacco. Certain vegetable smells are often associated with red wine — green peppers or beets, for example. Many fine red wines give off hints of cheese rinds, or "wet dog," or the oft-encountered "barnyard smell." While many of these descriptions may not sound appealing — and overbearing doses of any one of them would be considered a flaw — they are part of the subtle, evocative appeal of wine.

A myriad of aromas are found in the best wines, to be released by a swirl of the glass, the way a gust of wind sends forth the full fragrance of an apple tree in blossom. The better the wine, the more layers of half-hidden perfume are there awaiting discovery. Beginning tasters usually wonder what the fuss is all about, but those who persist soon discover that it takes both experience and concentration before one begins to recognize and identify a variety of aromas in wine. This is part of the fun and the challenge of wine tasting.

Of course, sometimes one encounters an unpleasant or "off" smell in the wine glass. Two of the most easily recognizable of these are "corkiness," an odor like wet cardboard that indicates a cork has gone bad, and the presence of sulfur, which smells like hard-boiled eggs. Hints of sulfur often dissipate after a few moments, while a "corked" wine never fully recovers.

Tasting: Having gained an impression of the wine through its aroma, the time has finally come to taste it. The standard procedure is to take a sip, allowing the wine to sit for a few moments on the tongue while the taste buds do their job of sorting out sweetness, acidity, astringency, bitterness, and tannin. The mouth registers spritziness, an indication of carbon dioxide, and it evaluates whether the wine feels thin, or if it has viscosity or "body." The sum of these impressions is known as "mouth feel."

At this point some tasters swish the wine around in their mouth. They may "chew" the wine, or aerate it by carefully (sometimes noisily) inhaling air through their mouth. These activities send aromas to the brain via the olfactory receivers, and perceptions from both the mouth and nose are synthesized into the sensation we call "taste."

Most experienced wine tasters spit each wine out after "mouthing" it. While novices find this a bizarre and unappetizing practice, its advantage for the professional wine taster, or for anyone else who plans to taste many different wines in one day, is obvious. And remember, especially if you're driving, all those little sips *do* add up.

What are some of the impressions one might expect to get from all the swirling and sipping? While each winery produces wines with its own distinctive characteristics, certain generalizations might be made in identifying wines from the Eastern states.

First, it's important to remember that this is mostly a cool-weather growing region. The wines, therefore, will be typically crisp and lively rather than rich and opulent except, perhaps, when they come from some of the warmer regions, such as Virginia, or from an unusually warm-weather vintage.

Eastern wine tends to be delicate and subtle, rather than bold and overbearing. It may not be as intensely colored as wine made from warm-weather grapes. Because of the cool weather and shorter growing season, Eastern wines may be relatively high in acidity, which, when balanced with other flavor components such as fruitiness or tannins, makes them a good match for food. Thanks to this hint of acidity, many of the slightly sweeter wines are clean-tasting rather than cloying, which also makes for an appealing accompaniment to food.

The best Eastern late-harvest wines and eiswein-style wines — those made from grapes that have a high concentration of sugar either because they have been picked after fully ripening or because they have been frozen — can be nice after-dinner sipping wines. These are excellent whether on their own or with dessert.

The attentive consumer will soon discover that wine from the Eastern states, like all good wine, can be as mysterious, elusive, and multifaceted as fine poetry.

WHERE TO BUY EASTERN WINES

Most of the wine produced in the East is purchased right at the individual winery. As I travel around the various wine regions in the East, I am often reminded of France, where Parisian, Italian, German, and English customers make annual pilgrimages to Bordeaux or Burgundy to buy wine. Some of these customers visit a variety of wineries every year to taste and compare the new vintages, while others head straight for their favorite winery, whether it is a renowned chateau or an obscure country wine cellar. The goal, for all, is the same: to load up the back of the car with enough cases of wine to last until they return again the following year.

In the Eastern United States, similar rituals occur. Some loyal consumers come to stock up at their local winery because they like driving out into the countryside, tasting a variety of wines right where they were made, and chatting with the winemaker about that particular vintage. In short, they like the personal contact.

Many folks travel to wineries simply because a particular wine that has captured their fancy is only available at the winery. Indeed, the majority of wines produced in the Eastern states are available only from the winery itself. Those relatively few vintners who make enough wine to sell outside the winery may also distribute their products in local wine shops. A few of the largest producers may reach markets outside their own region, particularly in large urban centers such as New York, Boston, Washington, D.C., or even, in a handful of rare cases, in California and Europe.

Nevertheless, the usual and most dependable way to buy wines made in the Eastern states is to pick it up in person at the individual winery, or to have the winery ship it to you (a telephone call will generally reveal the shipping policy).

TOURING THE EASTERN STATES WINERIES

Many dedicated wine buffs like to focus an entire weekend, or even a week-long holiday, exclusively on wineries. Most vacationers, however, prefer to intersperse winery visits with other activities. Following are a variety of suggested wine country tours — from one-day visits to week-long outings — that can be tailored to meet almost everyone's idea of a great visit to the wine regions of the Eastern states.

DAY TRIPS

I. From Washington, D.C.: One way to break up a visit to the capital's historic monuments and political shrines is to escape for an entire day to the idyllic countryside of northern Virginia. Heading directly west from the capital, one can comfortably take in Tarara, Loudoun, and Willowcroft wineries. Combine a trip to historic Harpers Ferry with a visit to Loudoun and Breaux. Alternatively, head south on the Beltway toward Swedenburg, Piedmont, and Meredyth wineries.

II. From the Connecticut shore or from New York City: A quick ferry ride across Long Island Sound or a short drive east from New York City brings one to the wine country of the North Fork. Because the North Fork's wineries are spaced closely together along two main roads, it is possible to make a quick stop at almost all of them in a single day. On the other hand, visitors who wish to adopt a more leisurely pace can concentrate on four or five wineries during a one-day outing, with plenty of time to savor each one.

III. From Buffalo/Niagara Falls: Honeymooners and other visitors to this region will enjoy a pleasant day trip driving along Lake Erie, with stops at Woodbury Winery and Johnson Estate Wines.

IV. From Cleveland: A day's outing to the Lake Erie wineries near Cleveland should lay to rest any doubts about whether good wine can be made in this area. Start at Firelands Winery in Sandusky, then hop a ferry to Put-In-Bay for a visit to Heineman Winery.

V. From Atlantic City or Philadelphia: After spending too many hours playing the slot machines in Atlantic City, a breath of fresh air is called for. From either Atlantic City or Philadelphia, one can easily fit in visits to Tomasello, Amalthea, and Sylvin Farms wineries. Alternatively, from Philadelphia, one can head northwest to Smithbridge, Chaddsford, and Twin Brook wineries for an easy day's outing. A visit to Cape May Winery is a good excuse to explore this charming seaside community.

WEEKEND TRIPS

I. From New York: The Delaware River region has long been a popular weekend getaway for New Yorkers who are attracted by the superb scenery and good restaurants. A winery tour can add yet another dimension to the enjoyment of this area that stretches along the New Jersey–Pennsylvania border. Stop at Unionville winery in New Jersey, and then head across the river to Sand Castle and Buckingham Valley Vineyards in Pennsylvania. Or work your way down the Delaware River from Franklin Hill Vineyards to Peace Valley, both in Pennsylvania.

II. In New England: Fall, which is the peak season for sightseeing in New England, is also an ideal time to visit the region's wineries. Visit Westport Vineyards in Massachusetts, and Greenvale, Newport, and Sakonnet in Rhode Island. The next day, drive to Connecticut, stopping in at Stonington Vineyards and Chamard Vineyards. There will be plenty of fall foliage to take in along the way. Or head head west, to the charming town of Litchfield, for more leaf-peeping plus visits to Haight, Sandy Hook Vineyards, and Hopkins Winery.

III. The Hudson River Region: A wealth of scenic and cultural sights have attracted weekend visitors to the magnificent Hudson River for hundreds of years. Winery touring is yet another reason to travel to this area. Highlights include visits to Benmarl, set in one of the world's most spectacular landscapes, and to Millbrook's impressive winery. Cascade and Clinton Vineyards are both set in idyllic country landscapes.

TRIPS OF A WEEK OR LONGER

I. The Mountains: While it is entirely possible to zip through all the Blue Ridge wineries in a couple of days, there are few trips quite as rewarding as a slow-paced, leisurely drive through this region, with Blue Ridge stops at

Château Morrisette and Villa Appalaccia. From Naked Mountain, head south to Linden, Oasis, and Farfelu. When visiting Monticello, be sure and swing by Jefferson Vineyards.

II. The Finger Lakes: So many fine wineries have emerged in the past few years in the Finger Lakes region that a week-long visit, interspersed with activities such as boating, fishing, and antiquing, is the best way to do justice to all of them. Alternatively, spend a few days concentrating on Lake Seneca's wineries, starting at Fox Run and driving completely around the lake to New Land.

III. Pennsylvania's Appalachian Trail: The mountainous country of Pennsylvania is a paradise for nature lovers who can travel up to the high altitude of Altoona, where Oak Spring Winery, one of the East's highest wineries, is located. It's possible to drive from there to Brookmere in a couple of hours, but why not stop along the way to explore the landscape, hike, swim, sail, or fish.

WINERIES LISTED BY STATE

CONNECTICUT
CONNECTICUT COAST (BENCHLANDS)
Chamard Vineyards
Heritage Trail Vineyards
Sharpe Hill Vineyard
Stonington Vineyards

WESTERN CONNECTICUT (UPLANDS)
DiGrazia Vineyards and Winery
Haight Vineyards
Hopkins Vineyard
McLaughlin Vineyards

MARYLAND (UPLANDS)
Basignani Winery
Boordy Vineyards
Catoctin Vineyards
Cygnus Wine Cellars
Elk Run Vineyards & Winery
Fiore Winery and La Felicetta Vineyard
Woodhall Vineyards & Wine Cellars

MASSACHUSETTS (BENCHLANDS)
Cape Cod Winery
Mellea Vineyard
Nantucket Vineyard
Truro Vineyards of Cape Cod
Westport Rivers Vineyard & Winery

NEW JERSEY

SOUTHEASTERN NEW JERSEY (BENCHLANDS)
Amalthea Cellars
Balic Winery
Cape May Winery & Vineyard
Renault Winery
Sylvin Farms
Tomasello Winery

THE DELAWARE RIVER REGION (UPLANDS)
Alba Vineyard
Amwell Valley Vineyard
Cream Ridge Winery
Four Sisters Winery
King's Road Vineyards and Winery
LaFollette Vineyard and Winery
Poor Richard's Winery
Unionville Vineyards

NEW YORK

LONG ISLAND (BENCHLANDS)
Bedell Cellars
Bidwell Vineyards
Channing Daughters
Corey Creek Vineyards
Duck Walk Vineyards
Gristina Vineyards
Hargrave Vineyard
Jamesport Vineyards
Laurel Lake Vineyards
Lenz Winery
Macari Vineyards
Osprey's Dominion

Palmer Vineyards
Paumanok Vineyards
Peconic Bay Vineyards
Pellegrini Vineyards
Pindar Vineyards
Pugliese Vineyards
Sagpond Vineyards/Wolffer Estate
Schneider Vineyards
Ternhaven Cellars

HUDSON RIVER VALLEY (UPLANDS)
Adair Vineyards
Applewood Winery
Baldwin Vineyards
Benmarl Wine Company
Brimstone Hill Vineyard
Brotherhood Winery
Cascade Mountain Winery
Clinton Vineyards
Millbrook Vineyards & Winery
Rivendell
Riverview
Royal Kedem Winery
Warwick Valley Winery
White Cliff

THE FINGER LAKES (UPLANDS)
Americana Vineyards and Winery
Anthony Road Wine Company
Arcadian Estate Vineyards
Bully Hill Vineyards
Castel Grisch Estate Winery
Cayuga Ridge Estate Winery
Chateau LaFayette Reneau
Dr. Frank's Vinfera Wine Cellars/Chateau Frank
Fox Run Vineyards
Frontenac Point Vineyard
Glenora Wine Cellars
Hazlitt 1852 Vineyards
Heron Hill Winery
Hosmer
Hunt Country Vineyard
Keuka Spring Vineyards
King Ferry Winery/Treleaven Wines

Knapp Vineyards Winery
Lakewood Vineyards
Lamoreaux Landing Wine Cellars
Lucas Vineyards
McGregor Vineyards & Winery
New Land Vineyard
Prejean Winery
Red Newt Cellars
Shalestone Vineyards LLC
Six Mile Creek Vineyard
Standing Stone Vineyards
Swedish Hill Vineyard & Winery
Wagner Vineyards
Widmer's Wine Cellars
Hermann J. Wiemer Vineyard, Inc.

LAKE ERIE REGION (BENCHLANDS)
Johnson Estate Wines
Woodbury Winery & Vineyards

OHIO

LAKE ERIE (BENCHLANDS)
Buccia Vineyards
Chalet Debonne Vineyards
Claire's Grand River Wine Company
Firelands Winery
Harpersfield Vineyard
Heineman Winery
Klingshirn Winery
Lonz Winery
Markko Vineyard

PENNSYLVANIA

DELAWARE RIVER REGION (UPLANDS)
Big Creek Vineyard
Blue Mountain Vineyards
Buckingham Valley Vineyards
Clover Hill Vineyards & Winery
Franklin Hill Vineyards
Hunters Valley Winery

Peace Valley Winery
Pinnacle Ridge Winery
Rushland Ridge Vineyards & Winery
Sand Castle Winery
Slate Quarry Winery
Vynecrest Winery

SOUTHERN PENNSYLVANIA (UPLANDS)
Adams County Winery
Allegro Vineyards
Calvaresi Winery
Chaddsford Winery
French Creek Ridge Vineyards
Naylor Vineyards & Wine Cellar
Nissley Vineyards and Winery Estate
Seven Valleys Vineyard and Winery
Smithbridge Cellars
Twin Brook Winery

CENTRAL AND WESTERN PENNSYLVANIA (MOUNTAINS)
Brookmere Farm Vineyards
Oak Springs Winery
Oregon Hill Winery
Lapic Winery

LAKE ERIE REGION (BENCHLANDS)
Conneaut Cellars Winery
Mazza Vineyards & Winery
Penn Shore Winery & Vineyards
Presque Isle Wine Cellars

RHODE ISLAND (BENCHLANDS)
Diamond Hill Vineyards
Greenvale Vineyards
Newport Vineyards
Sakonnet Vineyards

VIRGINIA

COASTAL VIRGINIA (BENCHLANDS)
Hartwood Winery
Ingleside Plantation Vineyards

Lake Anna Winery
Williamsburg Winery
Windy River Winery

NORTHERN AND CENTRAL VIRGINA (UPLANDS)
Barboursville Vineyards
Breaux Vineyards
Burnley Vineyards
Dominion Wine Cellars
Farfelu Vineyard
Gray Ghost Vineyards
Horton Vineyards
Jefferson Vineyards
Loudoun Valley Vineyards
Meredyth Vineyards
Oasis Vineyards
Piedmont Vineyards & Winery
Prince Michel and Rapidan River Vineyards
Swedenburg Estate Vineyard
Tarara Vineyard & Winery
Totier Creek Vineyard & Winery
Willowcroft Farm Vineyards

THE VIRGINIA HIGHLANDS (MOUNTAINS)
Afton Mountain Vineyards
Château Morrisette
Landwirt Vineyard
Linden Vineyards
Naked Mountain Vineyard and Winery
North Mountain
Oakencroft Vineyard & Winery
Rockbridge Vineyard
Shenandoah Vineyards
Valhalla Vineyards
White Hall Vineyards
Wintergreen Vineyards & Winery

TOP TWENTY WINES OF THE EAST: SELECTED FAVORITES

Bordeaux-style Blended Red "Merican" ....Chaddsford Winery
Chambourcin...Naylor Vineyards & Wine Cellar
Chardonnay...Piedmont "Native Yeast"
Chardonnay...Harpersfield Vineyard
Chardonnay...King Ferry Winery/
    Treleaven Wines
Cabernet Franc ....Pellegrini Vineyards
Cabernet Sauvignon ....Linden Vineyards
Cabernet Sauvignon "Cadenza"........................Allegro Vineyards
Dessert Wine "Philéo" ....Barboursville Vineyards
Gewürztraminer ....White Hall Vineyards
Pinot Noir...Fox Run Vineyards
Pinot Noir...Landwirt Vineyard
Merlot ....Bedell Cellars
Merlot ....Sagpond Vineyards/
    Wolffer Estate
Sparkling Wine..Sylvin Farms
Riesling..Dr. Frank's Vinifera Wine Cellars
Riesling..Hermann J. Wiemer Vineyards
Seyval ....Clinton Vineyards
Vidal Blanc (dry)..Sakonnet Vineyards
Viognier...Horton Vineyards

BIBLIOGRAPHY

Adams, Leon D. *The Wines of America*. New York: McGraw-Hill, 1985.

Beltrami, Edward J., and Palmedo, Philip F. *The Wines of Long Island — Birth of a Region*. Great Falls,VA: Waterline Books, 1993.

Borello, Joe. *Wineries of the Great Lakes*. Lapeer, MI: Raptor Press, 1995.

Brenner, Leslie. *Fear of Wine: An Introductory Guide to the Grape*. New York, Toronto, and London: Bantam Books, 1995.

Lee, Hilde Gabriel, and Lee, Allan E. *Virginia Wine Country Revisited*. Charlottesville, VA: Hildesigns Press, 1994.

Martell, Alan R., and Long, Alton. *The Wines and Wineries of the Hudson River Valley* . Woodstock, VT: Countryman Press, 1995.

McCarthy, Edward, and Mulligan, Mary Ewing. *Wine for Dummies*. Boston: IDG Books, Worldwide, Inc., 1995.

Wiener, Susan. *Finger Lakes Wineries*. Ithaca: McBooks Press, 1992.

Index

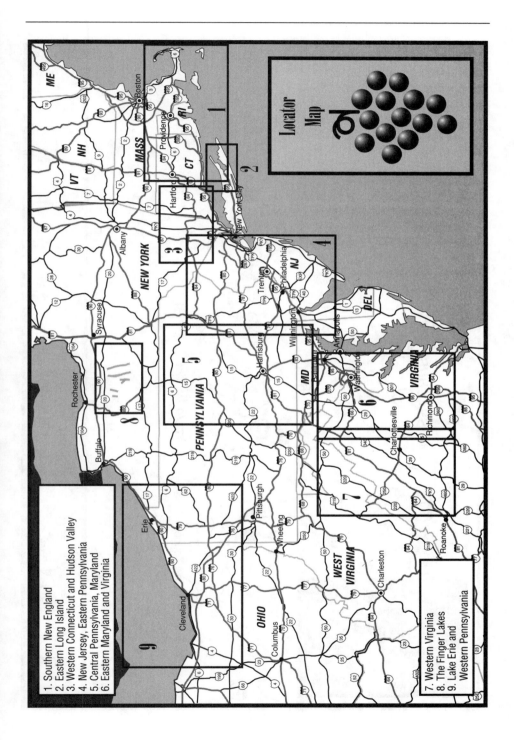

Locator Map

1. Southern New England
2. Eastern Long Island
3. Western Connecticut and Hudson Valley
4. New Jersey, Eastern Pennsylvania
5. Central Pennsylvania, Maryland
6. Eastern Maryland and Virginia
7. Western Virginia
8. The Finger Lakes
9. Lake Erie and Western Pennsylvania

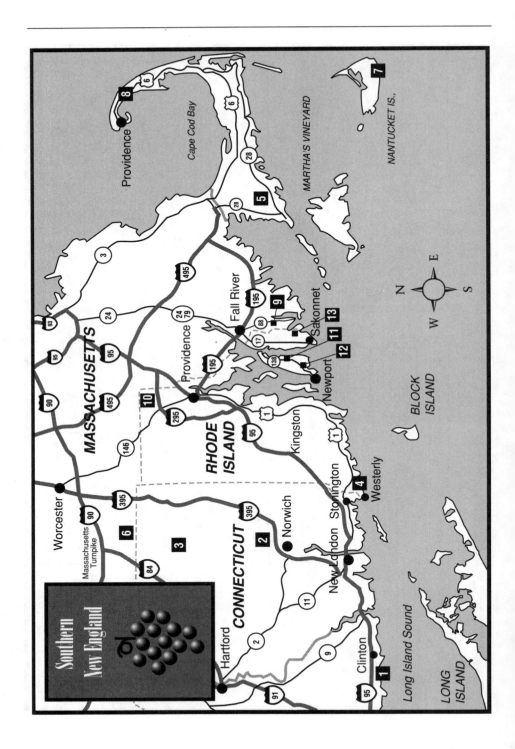

Map Legend — SOUTHERN NEW ENGLAND (BENCHLANDS)

Southern and Eastern Connecticut

1. Chamard Vineyards, 115 Cow Hill Rd., Clinton, CT 06413
2. Heritage Trail Vineyards, 291 North Burnham Hwy., Lisbon, CT 06351
3. Sharpe Hill Vineyards, 108 Wade Rd., Pomfret, CT 06285
4. Stonington Vineyards, 523 Taugwonk Rd., Stonington, CT 06378

Massachusetts

5. Cape Cod Winery, 681 Sandwich Rd., East Falmouth, MA 02536
6. Mella Winery, 108 Old Southbridge Rd., Dudley, MA 01571
7. Nantucket Vineyard, Bartlett Farm Rd., Nantucket, MA 02554
8. Truro Vineyards of Cape Cod, 11 Shore Rd., North Truro, MA 02652
9. Westport Rivers Vineyard & Winery, 417 Hixbridge Rd., Westport, MA 02790

Rhode Island

10. Diamond Hill Vineyards, 3145 Diamond Hill Rd., Cumberland, RI 02864
11. Greenvale Vineyards, 582 Wapping Rd., Portsmouth, RI 02871
12. Newport Vineyards, 909 East Main Rd. (Rte. 138), Middletown, RI 02842
13. Sakonnet Vineyards, 162 West Main Rd. (Rte. 77), Little Compton, RI 02837

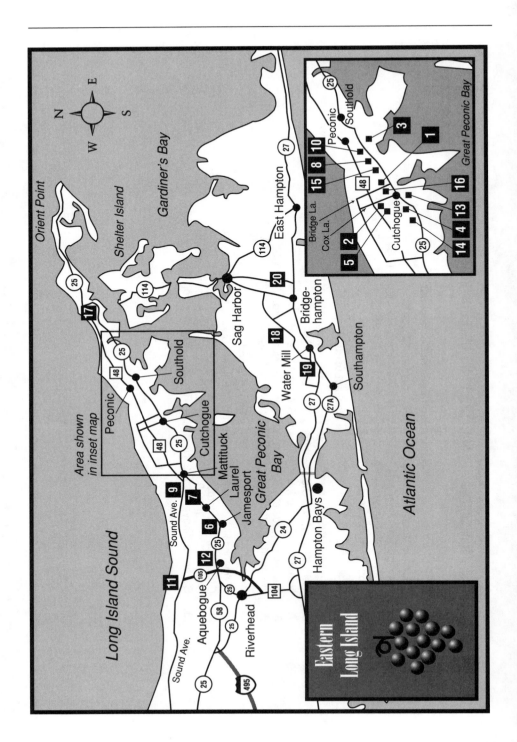

Map Legend — LONG ISLAND

(Benchlands)

North Fork

1. Bedell Cellars, Main Rd. (Rte. 25), Cutchogue, NY 11935
2. Bidwell Vineyards, North Rd. (Rte. 48), Cutchogue, NY 11935
3. Corey Creek Vineyards, Main Rd. (Rte. 25), Southold, NY 11971
4. Gristina Vineyards, Main Rd. (Rte. 25), Cutchogue, NY 11935
5. Hargrave Vineyard, North Rd. (Rte. 48), Cutchogue, NY 11935
6. Jamesport Vineyards, 842 Main Rd., Jamesport, NY 11947
7. Laurel Lake Vineyards, 3165 Main Rd. (Rte. 25), Laurel, NY 11948
8. Lenz Winery, Main Rd. (Rte. 25), Peconic, NY 11958
9. Macari Vineyards, 150 Bergen Ave., Mattituck, NY 11952
10. Osprey's Dominion, 44075 Main Rd. (Rte. 25), Peconic, NY 11958
11. Palmer Vineyards, Sound Ave. (Rte. 48), Aquebogue, NY 11931
12. Paumanok Vineyards, Main Rd. (Rte. 25), Aquebogue, NY 11931
13. Peconic Bay Vineyards, Main Rd. (Rte. 25,) Cutchogue, NY 11935
14. Pellegrini Vineyards, 23005 Main Rd. (Rte 25), Cutchogue, NY 11935
15. Pindar Vineyards, Main Rd. (Rte. 25), Peconic, NY 11958
16. Pugliese Vineyards, Main Rd. (Rte. 25), Cutchogue, NY 11935
17. Ternhaven Cellars, 331 Front St., Greenport, NY 11944

South Fork

18. Channing Daughters, 1927 Scuttlehole Rd.,, Bridgehampton, NY 11932
19. Duck Walk Vineyards, 231 Montauk Hwy,, Water Mill NY 11976
20. Sagpond Vineyards/Wolffer Estate, 139 Sagg Rd.,, Sagaponack, NY 11962

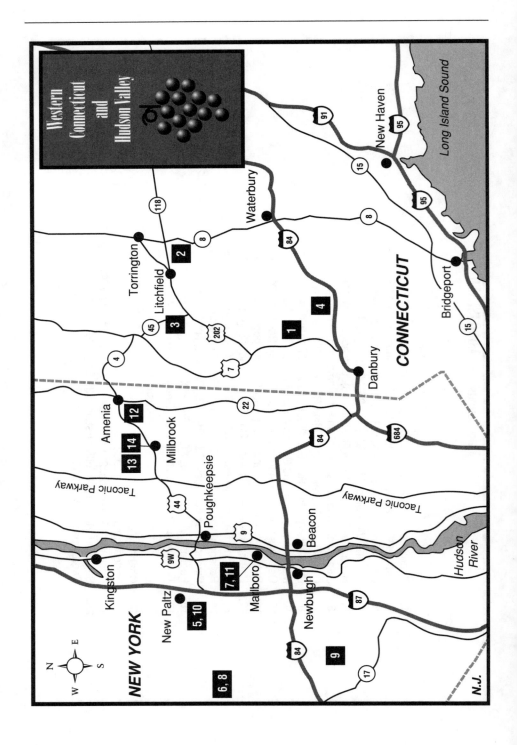

Map Legend — WESTERN CONNECTICUT AND THE HUDSON RIVER VALLEY

Western Connecticut (Uplands)

1. DiGrazia Vineyards and Winery, 131 Tower Rd., Brookfield, CT 06804
2. Haight Vineyards, 29 Chestnut Hill Rd., Litchfield, CT 06759
3. Hopkins Vineyard, 25 Hopkins Rd., New Preston, CT 06777
4. McLaughlin Vineyards, Albert Hill Rd., Sandy Hook, CT 06482

The Hudson River Valley (Uplands)

West Side of the Hudson River

5. Adair Vineyards, 52 Allhusen Rd., New Paltz, NY 12561
6. Baldwin Vineyards, 176 Hardenburgh Rd, Pine Bush, NY 12566
7. Benmarl Wine Company, 156 Highland Ave., Marlboro, NY 12542
8. Brimstone Hill Vineyard, 61 Brimstone Hill Rd., Pine Bush, NY 12566
9. Brotherhood Winery, 100 Brotherhood Plaza, Washingtonville, NY 10992
10. Rivendell, 714 Albany Post Rd., New Paltz, NY 12561
11. Royal Kedem Winery, 1519 Route 9W, Marlboro, NY 12542

East Side of the Hudson River

12. Cascade Mountain Winery, Flint Hill Rd., Amenia, NY 12501
13. Clinton Vineyards, Schultzville Rd., Clinton Corners, NY 12514
14. Millbrook Vineyards & Winery, Wing Rd., Millbrook, NY 12545

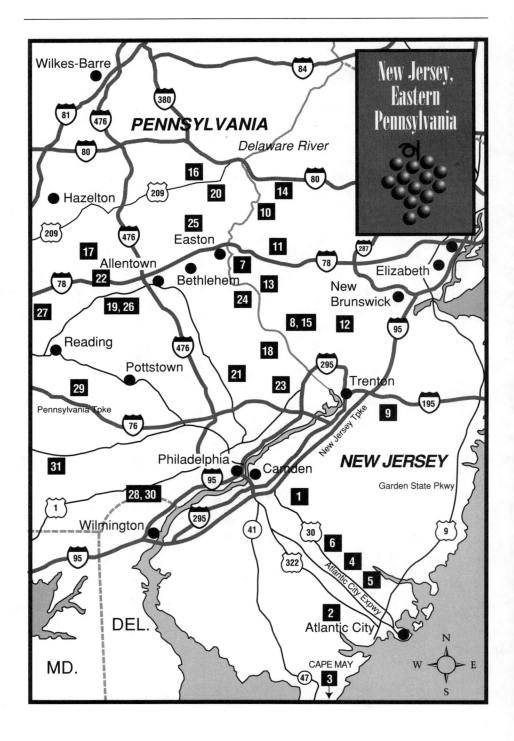

Map Legend —— NEW JERSEY, EASTERN PENNSYLVANIA

Southeastern New Jersey (Benchlands)

1. Amalthea Cellars,
   209 Vineyard Rd., Atco, NJ 08004
2. Balic Winery, Rte. 40,
   Mays Landing, NJ 08330
3. Cape May Winery & Vineyard,
   709 Townbank Rd., Cape May, NJ 08204
4. Renault Winery, 72 N. Bremen Ave.,
   Egg Harbor City, Galloway Township, NJ 08213
5. Sylvin Farms, 24 N. Vienna Avenue,
   Germania, NJ 08215
6. Tomasello Winery,
   225 White Horse Pike, Hammonton, NJ 08037

Northern New Jersey and the Delaware River Region (Uplands)

New Jersey Side of the Delaware River

7. Alba Vineyard, 269 Rte. 627,
   Village of Finesville, Milford, NJ 08848.
8. Amwell Valley Vineyard,
   80 Old York Rd., Ringoes, NJ 08551
9. Cream Ridge Winery, 145 Rte. 539,
   Cream Ridge, NJ; 08514
10. Four Sisters Winery,
    10 Doe Hollow Lane, Rte. 519, Belvidere, NJ 07823
11. King's Road Vineyards and Winery,
    360 Rte. 579, Asbury, NJ 08802
12. LaFollette Vineyard and Winery,
    64 Harlingen Rd., Belle Mead, NJ 08502
13. Poor Richard's Winery,
    220 Ridge Rd., Frenchtown, NJ 08825
14. Tamuzza Vineyards,
    111 Cemetery Rd., Hope, NJ 07844
15. Unionville Vineyards,
    9 Rocktown Rd., Ringoes, NJ 08551

Pennsylvania Side of the Delaware River

16. Big Creek Vineyard, Keller Rd.,
    Kresgeville, PA 18333

17. Blue Mountain Vineyards,
    7627 Grape Vine Dr., New Tripoli, PA 18066
18. Buckingham Valley Vineyards,
    1521 Rte. 413, Buckingham, PA 18912
19. Clover Hill Vineyards & Winery,
    9850 Newtown Rd., Breinigsville, PA, 18031
20. Franklin Hill Vineyards,
    7833 Franklin Hill Rd., Bangor, PA 18013
21. Peace Valley Winery,
    300 Old Limekiln Road, Chalfont, PA, 18914
22. Pinnacle Ridge Winery,
    407 Old Rte. 22, Kutztown, PA 19530
23. Rushland Ridge Vineyard & Winery,
    2665 Rushland Rd, Rushland, PA 18956
24. Sand Castle Winery, 755 River Rd.,
    Erwinna, PA 18920
25. Slate Quarry Winery,
    460 Gower Rd., Nazareth, PA 18064
26. Vynecrest Winery,
    172 Arrowhead Lane, Breinigsville, PA 18031

(See also map of Central Pennsylvania)

Southern Pennsylvania (Uplands)

27. Calvaresi Winery,
    107 Shartlesville Rd., Bernville, PA 19506
28. Chaddsford Winery,
    632 Baltimore Pike (Rte. 1), Chadds Ford, PA 19317
29. French Creek Ridge Vineyards,
    200 Grove Rd., Elverson, PA 19520
30. Smithbridge Cellars, 159 Beaver
    Valley Rd., Chadds Ford, PA, 19317
31. Twin Brook Winery, 5697 Strasburg
    Rd., Gap, PA 17527

(See also map of Central Pennsylvania)

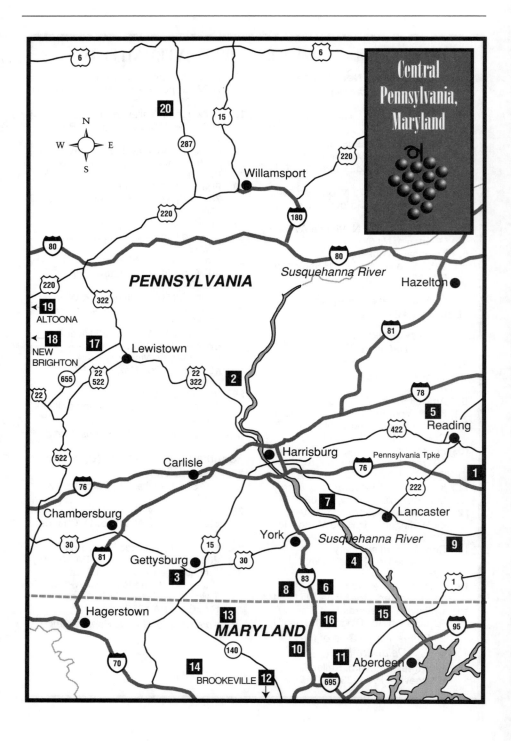

Map Legend —— CENTRAL PENNSYLVANIA, MARYLAND

Pennsylvania Side of the Delaware River (Uplands)

1. French Creek Ridge Vineyards, 200 Grove Rd., Elverson, PA 19520
2. Hunters Valley Winery, Rtes. 11 & 15, Liverpool, PA 17045

   (See also map of Eastern Pennsylvania)

Southern Pennsylvania (Uplands)

3. Adams County Winery, 251 Peach Tree Rd, Orrtanna, PA 17353
4. Allegro Vineyards, Sechrist Rd., Brogue, PA 17309
5. Calvaresi Winery, 107 Shartlesville Rd., Bernville, PA 19506
6. Naylor Vineyards & Wine Cellar, 4069 Vineyard Rd., Stewartstown, PA 17363
7. Nissley Vineyards and Winery Estate, 140 Vintage Dr., Bainbridge, PA 17502
8. Seven Valleys Vineyard and Winery, 885 Georges Ct., Glen Rock, PA 17327
9. Twin Brook Winery, 5697 Strasburg Rd., Gap, PA 17527

   (See also map of Eastern Pennsylvania)

Maryland (Uplands)

10. Basignani Winery, 15722 Falls Rd., Sparks, MD 21152
11. Boordy Vineyards, 12820 Long Green Pike, Hydes, MD 21082
12. Catoctin Vineyards, 805 Greenbridge Rd., Brookeville, MD 20833
13. Cygnus Wine Cellars, 3130 Long Lane, Manchester, MD 21102
14. Elk Run Vineyards & Winery, 15113 Liberty Rd., Mt. Airy, MD 21771
15. Fiore Winery and La Felicetta Vineyard, 3026 Whiteford Rd., Pylesville, MD 21132
16. Woodhall Vineyards and Wine Cellars, 17912 York Rd., Parkton, MD 21120

    (See also map of Eastern Pennsylvania)

Central and Western Pennsylvania (Mountains)

17. Brookmere Farm Vineyards, Rte. 655, Belleville, PA 17004
18. Lapic Winery, 902 Tulip Dr., New Brighton, PA 15066
19. Oak Springs Winery, Old Rte. 220, Altoona, PA 16001
20. Oregon Hill Winery, 840 Oregon Hill Rd., Morris, PA 16938

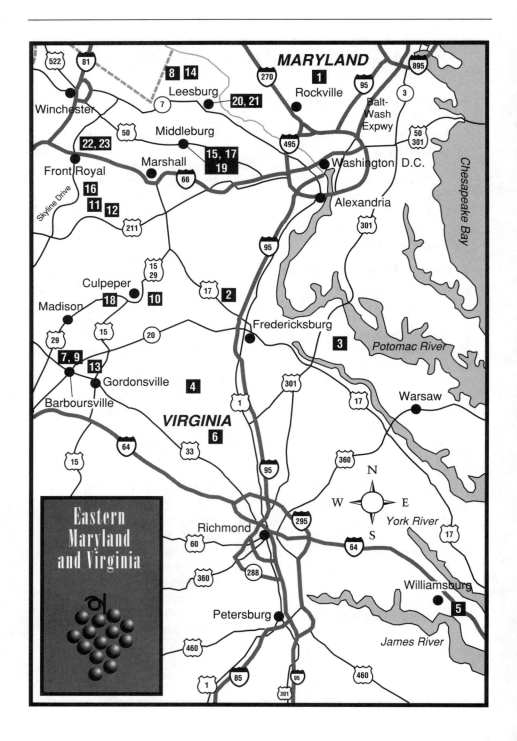

Map Legend — EASTERN MARYLAND AND VIRGINIA

Maryland (Uplands)

1. Catoctin Vineyards, 805 Greenbridge Rd., Brookeville, MD 20833

Coastal Virginia (Benchlands)

2. Hartwood Winery, 345 Hartwood Rd., Fredericksburg, VA 22406
3. Ingleside Plantation Vineyards, 5872 Leedstown Rd., Oak Grove, VA 22443
4. Lake Anna Winery, 5621 Courthouse Rd., Spotsylvania VA 22553
5. Williamsburg Winery, 5800 Wessex Hundred Rd., Williamsburg, VA 23183
6. Windy River Winery, 20268 Teman Rd., Beaverdam, VA 23015

(See also map of Western Virginia)

Northern and Central Virginia (Uplands)

7. Barboursville Vineyards, 17655 Winery Rd., Barboursville, VA 22923
8. Breaux Vineyards, 13860 Harpers Ferry Rd., Purcellville, VA 20132
9. Burnley Vineyards, 4500 Winery Lane, Barboursville, VA 22923
10. Dominion Wine Cellars, 1 Winery Ave., Culpeper, VA 22701
11. Farfelu Vineyard, 13058 Crest Hill Rd., Flint Hill, VA 22627
12. Gray Ghost Vineyards, 14706 Lee Hwy., Amissville, VA 20106
13. Horton Vineyards, 6399 Spottswood Tr. (Rte. 33), Gordonsville, VA 22942
14. Loudoun Valley Vineyards, 38638 Old Wheatland Rd., Waterford, VA 20197
15. Meredyth Vineyards, Rte. 628, Middleburg VA 20118
16. Oasis Vineyards, 14141 Hume Rd., Hume, VA 22639
17. Piedmont Vineyards & Winery, Rte. 626, Middleburg, VA 20118
18. Prince Michel and Rapidan River Vineyards, Rte. 29, Leon, VA 22725
19. Swedenburg Estate Vineyard, Rte. 50, Middleburg, VA 20117
20. Tarara Vineyard & Winery, 13648 Tarara Lane, Leesburg, VA 20176
21. Willowcroft Farm Vineyards, 38906 Mt. Gilead Rd., Leesburg, VA 20175

Virginia Highlands (Mountains)

22. Linden Vineyards, 3708 Harrels Corner Rd., Linden, VA 22642
23. Naked Mountain Vineyard and Winery, 2747 Leeds Manor Rd., Markham, VA 22643

(See also map of Western Virginia)

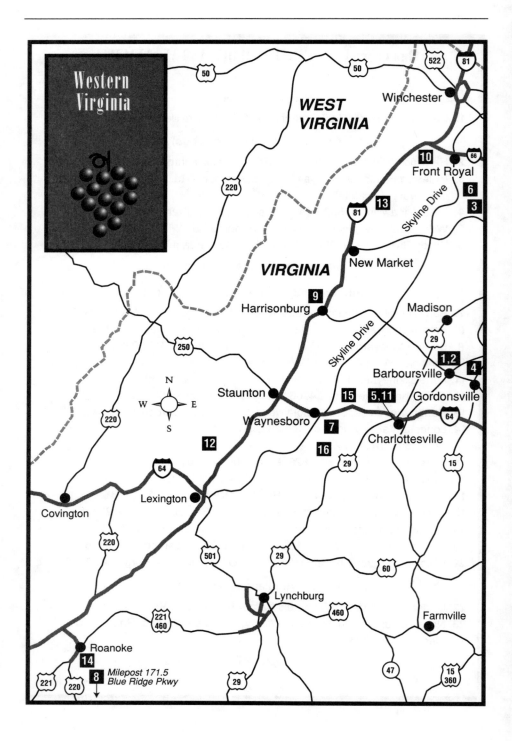

Map Legend —— WESTERN VIRGINIA

Northern and Central Virginia (Uplands)

1. Barboursville Vineyards, 17655 Winery Rd., Barboursville, VA 22923

2. Burnley Vineyards, 4500 Winery Lane, Barboursville, VA 22923

3. Farfelu Vineyard, 13058 Crest Hill Rd., Flint Hill, VA 22627
4. Horton Vineyards, 6399 Spottswood Tr. (Rte. 33), Gordonsville, VA 22942
5. Jefferson Vineyards, 1353 Thomas Jefferson Pkwy. (Rte. 9), Charlottesville, VA 22902

6. Oasis Vineyards, 14141 Hume Rd., Hume, VA 22639

(See also map of Eastern Virginia)

Virginia Highlands (Mountains)

7. Afton Mountain Vineyards, 234 Vineyard Lane (Rte. 631), Afton, VA 22920

8. Château Morrisette, 287 Winery Rd. SW, Floyd, VA 24091
9. Landwirt Vineyard, 8223 Simmers Valley Rd., Harrisonburg, VA 22802

10. North Mountain, 4374 Swartz Rd., Mauretown, VA 22644
11. Oakencroft Vineyard & Winery, 1486 Oakencroft Lane, Charlottesville, VA 22901

12. Rockbridge Vineyard, 30 Hill View Lane, Raphine, VA 24472

13. Shenandoah Vineyards, 3659 South Ox Rd., Edinburg, VA 22824

14. Valhalla Vineyards, 5371 Silver Fox Rd., Roanoke, VA 24014

15. White Hall Vineyards, 5184 Sugar Ridge Rd., White Hall, VA 22987

16. Wintergreen Vineyards & Winery, Rte. 664, Nellysford, VA 22956

(See also map of Eastern Virginia)

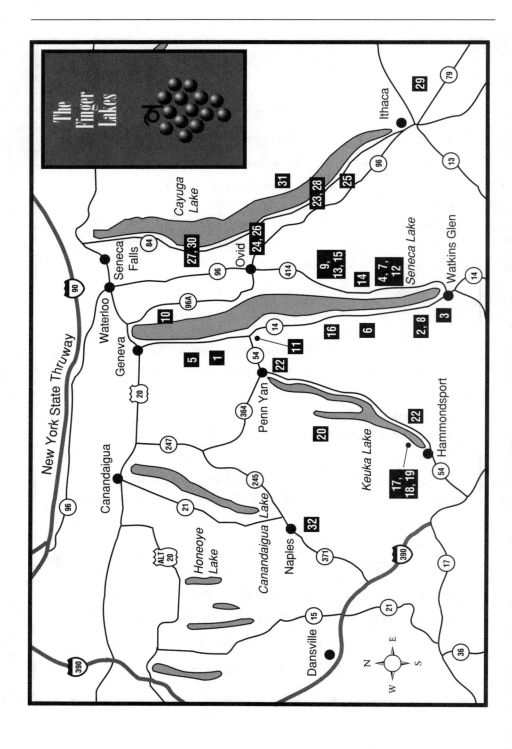

Map Legend — THE FINGER LAKES (UPLANDS)

Seneca Lake

1. Anthony Road Wine Company, 1225 Anthony Rd., Penn Yan, NY 14527
2. Arcadian Estate Vineyards, 4184 Rte. 14, Rock Stream, NY 14878
3. Castel Grisch Estate Winery,3380 County Rte. 28, Watkins Glen, NY 14891
4. Chateau LaFayette Reneau, 670 Rte. 414, Hector, NY 14841
5. Fox Run Vineyards, 670 Rte. 14, Penn Yan, NY 14527
6. Glenora Wine Cellars, 5435 Rte. 14, Dundee, NY 14837
7. Hazlitt 1852 Vineyards, 5712 Rte. 414, Hector, NY 14841
8. Lakewood Vineyards, 4024 Rte. 14, Watkins Glen, NY 14891
9. Lamoreaux Landing Wine Cellars, 9224 Rte. 414, Lodi, NY 14860
10. New Land Vineyard, 577 Lerch Rd., Geneva, NY 14456
11. Prejean Winery, 2634 State Rte. 14, Penn Yan, NY 14527
12. Red Newt Cellars, 3675 Tichenor Rd., Hector, NY 14841
13. Shalestone Vineyards LLC, 9681 Rte. 414, Lodi, NY 14860
14. Standing Stone Vineyards, 9934 Rte. 414, Hector, NY 14841
15. Wagner Vineyards, 9322 Rte. 414, Lodi, NY 14860
16. Herman J. Wiemer Vineyard, Inc., Rte. 14, Dundee, NY 14837

Keuka Lake

17. Bully Hill Vineyards, 8843 Greyton H. Taylor Memorial Dr., Hammondsport, NY 14840
18. Dr. Frank's Vinifera Wine Cellars/Chateau Frank, 9749 Middle Rd., Hammondsport, NY 14840
19. Heron Hill Winery, 9249 County Rte. 76, Hammondsport, NY 14840
20. Hunt Country Vineyard, 4021 Italy Hill Rd., Branchport, NY 14418
21. Keuka Spring Vineyards, 273 East Lake Rd. (Rte. 54), Penn Yan, NY 14527
22. McGregor Vineyards & Winery, 5503 Dutch St., Dundee, NY 14837

Cayuga Lake

23. Americana Vineyards and Winery, 4367 East Covert Rd., Interlaken, NY 14847
24. Cayuga Ridge Estate Winery, 6800 Rte. 89, Elm Beach, Ovid, NY 14521
25. Frontenac Point Vineyard, 9501 Rte. 89, Trumansburg, NY 14886
26. Hosmer, 6999 Rte. 89, Ovid, NY 14521
27. Knapp Vineyards Winery, 2770 County Rd.128, Romulus, NY 14541
28. Lucas Vineyards, 3862 County Rd. 150, Interlaken, NY 14847
29. Six Mile Creek Vineyard, Slaterville Rd., Rte. 79 East, Ithaca, NY 14850
30. Swedish Hill Vineyard & Winery, 4565 Rte. 414, Romulus, NY 14541
31. King Ferry Winery/Treleaven Wines, 658 Lake Rd., King Ferry, NY 13081

Canandaigua Lake

32. Widmer's Wine Cellars, 1 Lake Niagara Lane, Naples, NY 14512

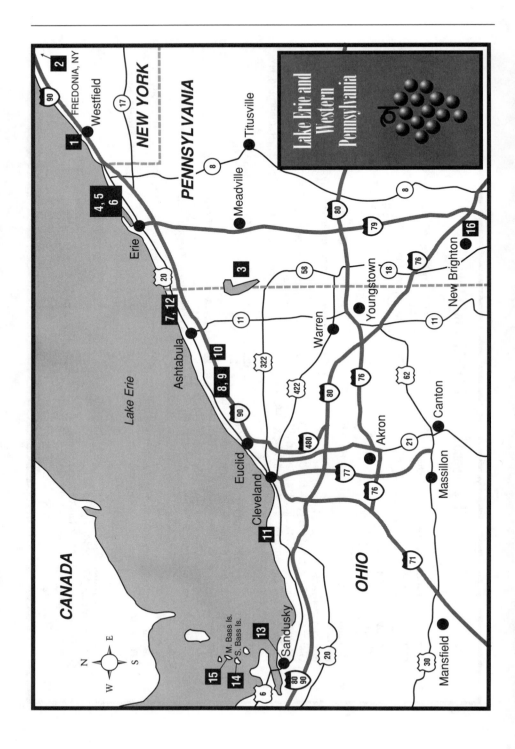

Map Legend — LAKE ERIE AND WESTERN PENNSYLVANIA

Lake Erie Region (Benchlands)

New York

1. Johnson Estate Wines, Rte. 20, Westfield, NY, 14787
2. Woodbury Winery & Vineyards, 3230 South Roberts Rd., Fredonia, NY 14063

Pennsylvania

3. Conneaut Cellars Winery, Rte. 322, Conneaut Lake, PA 16316
4. Mazza Vineyards, 11815 East Lake Rd. (Rte. 5), North East, PA16428
5. Penn Shore Winery & Vineyards, 10225 East Lake Rd. (Rte. 5), North East, PA 16428
6. Presque Isle Wine Cellars, 9440 Buffalo Rd., North East, PA 16428

Ohio

7. Buccia Vineyards, 518 Gore Rd., Conneaut, OH 44030
8. Chalet Debonne Vineyards, 7743 Doty Rd., Madison, OH 44057
9. Claire's Grand River Wine Company, 5750 South Madison Rd., Madison, OH 44041
10. Harpersfield Vineyard, 6387 State Rte. 307, Geneva, OH 44041
11. Klingshirn Winery, 33050 Webber Rd., Avon Lake, OH 44012
12. Markko Vineyard, 4500 South Ridge Rd., Conneaut, OH 44030

Island Wineries

13. Firelands Winery, 917 Bardshar Rd., Sandusky, OH 44870
14. Heineman Winery, Catawba St., Put-in-Bay, OH 43456
15. Lonz Winery, Middle Bass Island, OH 43446

Western Pennsylvania (Mountains)

16. Lapic Winery, 902 Tulip Dr., New Brighton, PA 15066

About the Author

Marsha Palanci

Born in California and raised in France, *Wine News* travel editor Marguerite Thomas began her research on Eastern Wines with great skepticism. *If this wine is so good, why haven't we heard of it before?* Thomas and Berkshire House skeptics were pleased enough with her research that we devoted an entire **Great Destinations**™ title to her findings! (And, we are pleased to report, Thomas's enthusiasm for these wines keeps growing. . . .)

In addition to her work with *Wine News*, Thomas regularly contributes to the Los Angeles Times Syndicate and *Saveur* magazine. She also writes about food, wine, travel, and people for a variety of publications, including *National Geographic Traveler* and *Travel Holiday*. She is the author of an acclaimed cookbook, *The Elegant Peasant*. She now makes her home in New York City.